ALL GLORY TO ŚRĪ GURU AND GAURĀṄGA

ŚRĪMAD BHĀGAVATAM

of

KṚṢṆA-DVAIPĀYANA VYĀSA

श्रीप्रह्लाद उवाच

श्रवणं कीर्तनं विष्णोः स्मरणं पादसेवनम् ।
अर्चनं वन्दनं दास्यं सख्यमात्मनिवेदनम् ॥
इति पुंसार्पिता विष्णौ भक्तिश्चेन्नवलक्षणा ।
क्रियेत भगवत्यद्धा तन्मन्येऽधीतमुत्तमम् ॥

śrī-prahrāda uvāca
śravaṇaṁ kīrtanaṁ viṣṇoḥ
smaraṇaṁ pāda-sevanam
arcanaṁ vandanaṁ dāsyaṁ
sakhyam ātma-nivedanam

iti puṁsārpitā viṣṇau
bhaktiś cen nava-lakṣaṇā
kriyeta bhagavaty addhā
tan manye 'dhītam uttamam (p. 246)

BOOKS by
His Divine Grace A. C. Bhaktivedanta Swami Prabhupāda

Bhagavad-gītā As It Is
Śrīmad-Bhāgavatam, Cantos 1-7 (21 Vols.)
Śrī Caitanya-caritāmṛta (17 Vols.)
Teachings of Lord Caitanya
The Nectar of Devotion
The Nectar of Instruction
Śrī Īśopaniṣad
Easy Journey to Other Planets
Kṛṣṇa Consciousness: The Topmost Yoga System
Kṛṣṇa, the Supreme Personality of Godhead (3 Vols.)
Perfect Questions, Perfect Answers
Transcendental Teachings of Prāhlad Mahārāja
Kṛṣṇa, the Reservoir of Pleasure
Life Comes from Life
The Perfection of Yoga
Beyond Birth and Death
On the Way to Kṛṣṇa
Rāja-vidyā: The King of Knowledge
Elevation to Kṛṣṇa Consciousness
Kṛṣṇa Consciousness: The Matchless Gift
Back to Godhead Magazine (Founder)

A complete catalogue is available upon request

The Bhaktivedanta Book Trust
3764 Watseka Avenue
Los Angeles, California 90034

ŚRĪMAD BHĀGAVATAM

Seventh Canto
"The Science of God"

(Part One—Chapters 1-5)

With the Original Sanskrit Text,
Its Roman Transliteration, Synonyms,
Translation and Elaborate Purports

by

His Divine Grace
A.C. Bhaktivedanta Swami Prabhupāda
Founder-*Ācārya* of the International Society for Krishna Consciousness

THE BHAKTIVEDANTA BOOK TRUST
New York · Los Angeles · London · Bombay

Readers interested in the subject matter of this book
are invited by the International Society for Krishna Consciousness
to correspond with its Secretary.

International Society for Krishna Consciousness
3764 Watseka Avenue
Los Angeles, California 90034

Library of Congress Catalogue Card Number: 73-169353
International Standard Book Number: 0-912776-86-2

First printing, 1976: 50,000 copies

Printed in the United States of America

Table of Contents

CHAPTER THREE
Hiraṇyakaśipu's Plan to Become Immortal

CHAPTER FOUR
Hiraṇyakaśipu Terrorizes the Universe

Preface

We must know the present need of human society. And what is that need? Human society is no longer bounded by geographical limits to particular countries or communities. Human society is broader than in the Middle Ages, and the world tendency is toward one state or one human society. The ideals of spiritual communism, according to *Śrīmad-Bhāgavatam,* are based more or less on the oneness of the entire human society, nay, on the entire energy of living beings. The need is felt by great thinkers to make this a successful ideology. *Śrīmad-Bhāgavatam* will fill this need in human society. It begins, therefore, with the aphorism of Vedānta philosophy (*janmādy asya yataḥ*) to establish the ideal of a common cause.

Human society, at the present moment, is not in the darkness of oblivion. It has made rapid progress in the field of material comforts, education and economic development throughout the entire world. But there is a pinprick somewhere in the social body at large, and therefore there are large-scale quarrels, even over less important issues. There is need of a clue as to how humanity can become one in peace, friendship and prosperity with a common cause. *Śrīmad-Bhāgavatam* will fill this need, for it is a cultural presentation for the re-spiritualization of the entire human society.

Śrīmad-Bhāgavatam should be introduced also in the schools and colleges, for it is recommended by the great student devotee Prahlāda Mahārāja in order to change the demonic face of society.

kaumāra ācaret prājño
dharmān bhāgavatān iha
durlabhaṁ mānuṣaṁ janma
tad apy adhruvam arthadam
(*Bhāg.* 7.6.1)

Disparity in human society is due to lack of principles in a godless civilization. There is God, or the Almighty One, from whom everything emanates, by whom everything is maintained and in whom everything is merged to rest. Material science has tried to find the ultimate source of creation very insufficiently, but it is a fact that there is one ultimate source of everything that be. This ultimate source is explained rationally and authoritatively in the beautiful *Bhāgavatam* or *Śrīmad-Bhāgavatam.*

Śrīmad-Bhāgavatam is the transcendental science not only for knowing the ultimate source of everything but also for knowing our relation with Him and our duty towards perfection of the human society on the basis of this perfect knowledge. It is powerful reading matter in the Sanskrit language, and it is now rendered into English elaborately so that simply by a careful reading one will know God perfectly well, so much so that the reader will be sufficiently educated to defend himself from the onslaught of atheists. Over and above this, the reader will be able to convert others to accept God as a concrete principle.

Śrīmad-Bhāgavatam begins with the definition of the ultimate source. It is a bona fide commentary on the *Vedānta-sūtra* by the same author, Śrīla Vyāsadeva, and gradually it develops into nine cantos up to the highest state of God realization. The only qualification one needs to study this great book of transcendental knowledge is to proceed step by step cautiously and not jump forward haphazardly as with an ordinary book. It should be gone through chapter by chapter, one after another. The reading matter is so arranged with its original Sanskrit text, its English transliteration, synonyms, translation and purports so that one is sure to become a God realized soul at the end of finishing the first nine cantos.

The Tenth Canto is distinct from the first nine cantos, because it deals directly with the transcendental activities of the Personality of Godhead Śrī Kṛṣṇa. One will be unable to capture the effects of the Tenth Canto without going through the first nine cantos. The book is complete in twelve cantos, each independent, but it is good for all to read them in small installments one after another.

I must admit my frailties in presenting *Śrīmad-Bhāgavatam,* but still I am hopeful of its good reception by the thinkers and leaders of society on the strength of the following statement of *Śrīmad-Bhāgavatam.*

tad-vāg-visargo janatāgha-viplavo
yasmin pratiślokam abaddhavaty api

nāmāny anantasya yaśo 'ṅkitāni yac
chṛṇvanti gāyanti gṛṇanti sādhavaḥ
(*Bhāg.* 1.5.11)

"On the other hand, that literature which is full with descriptions of the transcendental glories of the name, fame, form and pastimes of the unlimited Supreme Lord is a transcendental creation meant to bring about a revolution in the impious life of a misdirected civilization. Such transcendental literatures, even though irregularly composed, are heard, sung and accepted by purified men who are thoroughly honest."

Oṁ tat sat

A. C. Bhaktivedanta Swami

Introduction

"This *Bhāgavata Purāṇa* is as brilliant as the sun, and it has arisen just after the departure of Lord Kṛṣṇa to His own abode, accompanied by religion, knowledge, etc. Persons who have lost their vision due to the dense darkness of ignorance in the age of Kali shall get light from this *Purāṇa*." (*Śrīmad-Bhāgavatam* 1.3.43)

The timeless wisdom of India is expressed in the *Vedas*, ancient Sanskrit texts that touch upon all fields of human knowledge. Originally preserved through oral tradition, the *Vedas* were first put into writing five thousand years ago by Śrīla Vyāsadeva, the "literary incarnation of God." After compiling the *Vedas*, Vyāsadeva set forth their essence in the aphorisms known as *Vedānta-sūtras*. *Śrīmad-Bhāgavatam* is Vyāsadeva's commentary on his own *Vedānta-sūtras*. It was written in the maturity of his spiritual life under the direction of Nārada Muni, his spiritual master. Referred to as "the ripened fruit of the tree of Vedic literature," *Śrīmad-Bhāgavatam* is the most complete and authoritative exposition of Vedic knowledge.

After compiling the *Bhāgavatam*, Vyāsa impressed the synopsis of it upon his son, the sage Śukadeva Gosvāmī. Śukadeva Gosvāmī subsequently recited the entire *Bhāgavatam* to Mahārāja Parīkṣit in an assembly of learned saints on the bank of the Ganges at Hastināpura (now Delhi). Mahārāja Parīkṣit was the emperor of the world and was a great *rājarṣi* (saintly king). Having received a warning that he would die within a week, he renounced his entire kingdom and retired to the bank of the Ganges to fast until death and receive spiritual enlightenment. The *Bhāgavatam* begins with Emperor Parīkṣit's sober inquiry to Śukadeva Gosvāmī:

> "You are the spiritual master of great saints and devotees. I am therefore begging you to show the way of perfection for all persons, and especially for one who is about to die. Please let me know what a man should hear, chant, remember and worship, and also what he should not do. Please explain all this to me."

Śukadeva Gosvāmī's answer to this question, and numerous other questions posed by Mahārāja Parīkṣit, concerning everything from the nature of the self to the origin of the universe, held the assembled sages in rapt attention continuously for the seven days leading to the King's death. The sage Sūta Gosvāmī, who was present on the bank of the Ganges when Śukadeva Gosvāmī first recited *Śrīmad-Bhāgavatam*, later repeated the *Bhāgavatam* before a gathering of sages in the forest of Naimiṣāraṇya. Those sages, concerned about the spiritual welfare of the people in general, had gathered to perform a long, continuous chain of sacrifices to counteract the degrading influence of the incipient age of Kali. In response to the sages' request that he speak the essence of Vedic wisdom, Sūta Gosvāmī repeated from memory the entire eighteen thousand verses of *Śrīmad-Bhāgavatam*, as spoken by Śukadeva Gosvāmī to Mahārāja Parīkṣit.

The reader of *Śrīmad-Bhāgavatam* hears Sūta Gosvāmī relate the questions of Mahārāja Parīkṣit and the answers of Śukadeva Gosvāmī. Also, Sūta Gosvāmī sometimes responds directly to questions put by Śaunaka Ṛṣi, the spokesman for the sages gathered at Naimiṣāraṇya. One therefore simultaneously hears two dialogues: one between Mahārāja Parīkṣit and Śukadeva Gosvāmī on the bank of the Ganges, and another at Naimiṣāraṇya between Sūta Gosvāmī and the sages at Naimiṣāraṇya Forest, headed by Śaunaka Ṛṣi. Furthermore, while instructing King Parīkṣit, Śukadeva Gosvāmī often relates historical episodes and gives accounts of lengthy philosophical discussions between such great souls as the saint Maitreya and his disciple Vidura. With this understanding of the history of the *Bhāgavatam*, the reader will easily be able to follow its intermingling of dialogues and events from various sources. Since philosophical wisdom, not chronological order, is most important in the text, one need only be attentive to the subject matter of *Śrīmad-Bhāgavatam* to appreciate fully its profound message.

It should also be noted that the volumes of the *Bhāgavatam* need not be read consecutively, starting with the first and proceeding to the last. The translator of this edition compares the *Bhāgavatam* to sugar candy—wherever you taste it, you will find it equally sweet and relishable.

This edition of the *Bhāgavatam* is the first complete English translation of this important text with an elaborate commentary, and it is the first widely available to the English-speaking public. It is the product of the scholarly and devotional effort of His Divine Grace A. C. Bhaktivedanta Swami Prabhupāda, the world's most distinguished teacher of Indian religious and philosophical thought. His consummate Sanskrit scholarship and intimate familiarity with Vedic culture and thought as well as the modern way of life combine to reveal to the West a magnificent exposition of this important classic.

Readers will find this work of value for many reasons. For those interested in the classical roots of Indian civilization, it serves as a vast reservoir of detailed information on virtually every one of its aspects. For students of comparative philosophy and religion, the *Bhāgavatam* offers a penetrating view into the meaning of India's profound spiritual heritage. To sociologists and anthropologists, the *Bhāgavatam* reveals the practical workings of a peaceful and scientifically organized Vedic culture, whose institutions were integrated on the basis of a highly developed spiritual world view. Students of literature will discover the *Bhāgavatam* to be a masterpiece of majestic poetry. For students of psychology, the text provides important perspectives on the nature of consciousness, human behavior and the philosophical study of identity. Finally, to those seeking spiritual insight, the *Bhāgavatam* offers simple and practical guidance for attainment of the highest self-knowledge and realization of the Absolute Truth. The entire multivolume text, presented by the Bhaktivedanta Book Trust, promises to occupy a significant place in the intellectual, cultural and spiritual life of modern man for a long time to come.

—The Publishers

His Divine Grace
A. C. Bhaktivedanta Swami Prabhupāda
Founder-Ācārya of the International Society for Krishna Consciousness

PLATE ONE

The great Rājasūya sacrifice performed by Mahārāja Yudhiṣṭhira was attended by all the exalted demigods, the most expert *brāhmaṇas* and sages, and kings from different parts of the world. When all the respectable members of that assembly began worshiping Lord Kṛṣṇa as the most exalted personality, King Śiśupāla became very angry. From the very beginning of his childhood, when he could not even speak properly, Śiśupāla, the most sinful son of Damaghoṣa, began blaspheming the Lord. Thus, not being able to tolerate such honor to Kṛṣṇa and glorification of His qualities, he stood up suddenly and began speaking very strongly against Lord Kṛṣṇa. All the kings present in the assembly became very angry and immediately took up their swords and shields to kill Śiśupāla, but when Lord Kṛṣṇa saw that they were going to fight in the arena of the auspicious Rājasūya sacrifice, He personally pacified all of them. Out of His causeless mercy, He Himself decided to kill Śiśupāla. While Śiśupāla abused the kings who were about to attack him, Lord Kṛṣṇa took up His disc, which was as sharp as the blade of a razor, and immediately separated Śiśupāla's head from his body. In the presence of all the exalted persons in the assembly, Śiśupāla's spirit soul merged into the transcendental body of the Supreme Lord, Kṛṣṇa. *(pp. 21–26)*

PLATE TWO

Once, when the four sons of Lord Brahmā named Sanaka, Sanandana, Sanātana and Sanat-kumāra were wandering throughout the three worlds, by dint of mystic *yoga* they came to Viṣṇuloka. Although these four great sages were older than Brahmā's other sons, they appeared like small naked children only five or six years old. After passing through the six entrances of Vaikuṇṭha Purī, the Lord's residence, they saw at the seventh gate two shining beings, armed with maces and adorned with most valuable jewelry, earrings and diamonds. The two gatekeepers were garlanded with fresh flowers which attracted intoxicated bees and which were placed around their necks and between their four blue arms. When the gatekeepers, Jaya and Vijaya, saw the sages trying to enter Vaikuṇṭhaloka, they thought them ordinary children and forbade them to enter. Thus Sanandana and the other great sages, who were by far the fittest persons, having realized the truth of the self, very angrily cursed Jaya and Vijaya. "You two foolish doorkeepers," they said. "Being agitated by the material qualities of passion and ignorance, you are unfit to live at the shelter of the Lord's lotus feet, which are free from such modes. It would be better for you to go immediately to the material world and take birth in a family of most sinful *asuras*." *(pp. 45–52)*

PLATE THREE

The demoniac King Hiraṇyakaśipu wanted to be unconquerable and free from old age and dwindling of the body. He wanted to gain all the yogic perfections, to be deathless, and to be the only king of the entire universe, including Brahmaloka. In the valley of Mandara Hill, Hiraṇyakaśipu began performing his austerities by standing with his toes on the ground, keeping his arms upward and looking toward the sky. This position was extremely difficult, but he accepted it as a means to attain perfection. From the hair on Hiraṇyakaśipu's head there emanated an effulgent light as brilliant and intolerable as the rays of the sun at the time of dissolution. Because of Hiraṇyakaśipu's severe austerities, fire came from his head, and this fire and its smoke spread throughout the sky, encompassing the upper and lower planets, which all became extremely hot. Because of the power of his severe austerities, all the rivers and oceans were agitated, the surfaces of the globe, with its mountains and islands, began trembling, and the stars and planets fell. All directions were ablaze. *(pp.130–133)*

PLATE FOUR

Lord Brahmā, who is carried by a swan airplane, at first could not see where Hiraṇyakaśipu was, for Hiraṇyakaśipu's body was covered by an anthill and by grass and bamboo sticks. Because Hiraṇyakaśipu had been there for a long time, the ants had devoured his skin, fat, flesh and blood. Then Lord Brahmā spotted him, resembling a cloud-covered sun, heating all the world by his austerity. Struck with wonder, Lord Brahmā smiled and then addressed him as follows: "O son of Kaśyapa Muni, please get up! I have been very much astonished to see your endurance. In spite of being eaten and bitten by all kinds of worms and ants, you are keeping your life air circulating within your bones. Certainly this is wonderful. Who within these three worlds can sustain his life for one hundred celestial years without even drinking water? O best of the demons, I am now prepared to give you all benedictions, according to your desire." Lord Brahmā, the original being of this universe, who is extremely powerful, then sprinkled transcendental, infallible, spiritual water from his waterpot upon Hiraṇyakaśipu's body, which had been eaten away by ants and moths. Hiraṇyakaśipu arose, endowed with a full body with limbs so strong that they could bear the striking of a thunderbolt. With physical strength and a bodily luster resembling molten gold, he emerged from the anthill a completely young man. *(pp. 142–150)*

PLATE FIVE

After receiving benedictions from Lord Brahmā, Hiraṇyakaśipu conquered the rulers of all the planets in the three worlds, seizing their power and influence. He thus began residing in heaven in the most opulent palace of Indra, the celestial King. The palace was as beautifully made as if the goddess of fortune of the entire universe resided there. Being situated on Indra's throne, Hiraṇyakaśipu severely controlled the inhabitants of all the other planets.

Once Hiraṇyakaśipu affectionately seated his young son Prahlāda Mahārāja on his lap and inquired what he had learned from his teachers. Prahlāda replied with exalted Vaiṣṇava philosophy describing how one achieves the perfection of life by dedicating everything to the service of the Supreme Lord, Kṛṣṇa. After Prahlāda Mahārāja had spoken in this way, Hiraṇyakaśipu, blinded by anger and hatred for the Supreme Lord, threw the boy off his lap and onto the ground. Indignant and angry, his reddish eyes like molten copper, Hiraṇyakaśipu said to his servants, "O demons, take this boy away from me! He deserves to be killed. Kill him as soon as possible!" *(pp.174–178, 245–274)*

PLATE SIX

After being ordered by Hiraṇyakaśipu to kill Prahlāda Mahārāja, his servants, the demon Rākṣasas, began striking the tender parts of Prahlāda Mahārāja's body with their tridents. The demons all had fearful faces, sharp teeth and reddish, coppery beards and hair, and they appeared extremely threatening. Making a tumultuous sound, shouting, "Chop him up! Pierce him!" they began striking Prahlāda Mahārāja, who sat silently, meditating upon the Supreme Personality of Godhead. Prahlāda Mahārāja was a great devotee, undisturbed by material conditions and fully engaged in meditating upon and serving the Supreme Personality of Godhead. Thus the weapons of the demons had no tangible effects upon him. *(pp. 279–280)*

PLATE SEVEN

When the attempts of the demon Rākṣasas to kill Prahlāda Mahārāja were futile, the King of the demons, Hiraṇyakaśipu, being most fearful, began contriving other means to kill him. Hiraṇyakaśipu thought, "Although Prahlāda is only five years old, even at this young age he has given up his affectionate relationship with his father and mother. Prahlāda is so treacherous that he has become a devotee of Viṣṇu, who killed his uncle Hiraṇyākṣa. If a limb of one's body is poisoned by disease, it must be amputated so that the rest of the body may live happily. Similarly, even one's own son, if unfavorable, must be rejected, although born of one's own body." Thus Hiraṇyakaśipu planned a campaign to kill Prahlāda Mahārāja. He thought he would kill his son by throwing him beneath the feet of big elephants, throwing him among huge, fearful snakes, employing destructive spells, conjuring up illusory tricks, administering poison, starving him, exposing him to severe cold, winds, fire and water, throwing heavy stones to crush him, or hurling him from the top of a mountain. But Prahlāda Mahārāja, who was completely sinless, could not be harmed in any way. *(pp. 276–278, 282)*

CHAPTER ONE

The Supreme Lord Is Equal to Everyone

In this chapter, in response to a question by Mahārāja Parīkṣit, Śukadeva Gosvāmī gives his conclusions concerning how the Supreme Personality of Godhead, although the Supersoul, friend and protector of everyone, killed the Daityas, the demons, for the sake of Indra, the King of heaven. In his statements, he totally refutes the arguments of people in general who accuse the Supreme Lord of partiality. Śukadeva Gosvāmī proves that because the body of the conditioned soul is infected by the three qualities of nature, dualities arise such as enmity and friendship, attachment and detachment. For the Supreme Personality of Godhead, however, there are no such dualities. Even eternal time cannot control the activities of the Lord. Eternal time is created by the Lord, and it acts under His control. The Supreme Personality of Godhead, therefore, is always transcendental to the influence of the modes of nature, *māyā*, the Lord's external energy, which acts in creation and annihilation. Thus all the demons killed by the Supreme Lord attain salvation immediately.

The second question raised by Parīkṣit Mahārāja concerns how Śiśupāla, although inimical toward Kṛṣṇa from his very childhood and always blaspheming Kṛṣṇa, attained salvation in oneness when Kṛṣṇa killed him. Śukadeva Gosvāmī explains that because of their offenses at the feet of devotees, two attendants of the Lord in Vaikuṇṭha named Jaya and Vijaya became Hiraṇyakaśipu and Hiraṇyākṣa in Satya-yuga, Rāvaṇa and Kumbhakarṇa in the next *yuga*, Tretā-yuga, and Śiśupāla and Dantavakra at the end of Dvāpara-yuga. Because of their fruitive acts, Jaya and Vijaya agreed to become the Lord's enemies, and when killed in that mentality, they attained salvation in oneness. Thus even if one thinks of the Supreme Personality of Godhead in envy, he attains salvation. What then is to be said of devotees who always engage in the Lord's service with love and faith?

TEXT 1

श्रीराजोवाच
समः प्रियः सुहृद्ब्रह्मन् भूतानां भगवान् स्वयम् ।
इन्द्रस्यार्थे कथं दैत्यानवधीद्विषमो यथा ॥ १ ॥

śrī-rājovāca
samaḥ priyaḥ suhṛd brahman
bhūtānāṁ bhagavān svayam
indrasyārthe kathaṁ daityān
avadhīd viṣamo yathā

śrī-rājā uvāca—Mahārāja Parīkṣit said; *samaḥ*—equal; *priyaḥ*—beloved; *suhṛt*—friend; *brahman*—O *brāhmaṇa* (Śukadeva); *bhūtānām*—toward all living entities; *bhagavān*—the Supreme Lord, Viṣṇu; *svayam*—Himself; *indrasya*—of Indra; *arthe*—for the benefit; *katham*—how; *daityān*—the demons; *avadhīt*—killed; *viṣamaḥ*—partial; *yathā*—as if.

TRANSLATION

King Parīkṣit inquired: My dear brāhmaṇa, the Supreme Personality of Godhead, Viṣṇu, being everyone's well-wisher, is equal and extremely dear to everyone. How, then, did He become partial like a common man for the sake of Indra and thus kill Indra's enemies? How can a person equal to everyone be partial to some and inimical toward others?

PURPORT

In *Bhagavad-gītā* (9.29) the Lord says, *samo 'haṁ sarva-bhūteṣu na me dveṣyo 'sti na priyaḥ:* "I am equal to everyone. No one is dear to Me, nor is anyone My enemy." In the previous canto, however, it has been observed that the Lord sided with Indra by killing the demons on his account (*hata-putrā ditiḥ śakra-pārṣṇi-grāheṇa viṣṇunā*). Therefore, the Lord was clearly partial to Indra, although He is the Supersoul in everyone's heart. The soul is extremely dear to everyone, and similarly the

Supersoul is also dear to everyone. Thus there cannot be any faulty action on the part of the Supersoul. The Lord is always kind to all living entities, irrespective of form and situation, yet He took the side of Indra just like an ordinary friend. This was the subject of Parīkṣit Mahārāja's inquiry. As a devotee of Lord Kṛṣṇa, he knew very well that Kṛṣṇa cannot be partial to anyone, but when he saw that Kṛṣṇa acted as the enemy of the demons, he was somewhat doubtful. Therefore he posed this question to Śukadeva Gosvāmī for a clear answer.

A devotee cannot accept that Lord Viṣṇu has material qualifications. Mahārāja Parīkṣit knew perfectly well that Lord Viṣṇu, being transcendental, has nothing to do with material qualities, but to confirm his conviction he wanted to hear from the authority Śukadeva Gosvāmī. Śrīla Viśvanātha Cakravartī Ṭhākura says, *samasya kathaṁ vaiṣamyam:* since the Lord is equally disposed toward everyone, how can He be partial? *Priyasya katham asureṣu prīty-abhāvaḥ.* The Lord, being the Supersoul, is extremely dear to everyone. Why, then, should the Lord display unsympathetic behavior toward the *asuras?* How is this impartial? *Suhṛdaś ca kathaṁ teṣv asauhārdam.* Since the Lord says that He is *suhṛdaṁ sarva-bhūtānām,* the well-wisher of all living entities, how could He act with partiality by killing demons? These questions arose in the heart of Parīkṣit Mahārāja, and therefore he inquired from Śukadeva Gosvāmī.

TEXT 2

न ह्यस्यार्थः सुरगणैः साक्षान्निःश्रेयसात्मनः ।
नैवासुरेभ्यो विद्वेषो नोद्वेगश्चागुणस्य हि ॥ २ ॥

na hy asyārthaḥ sura-gaṇaiḥ
sākṣān niḥśreyasātmanaḥ
naivāsurebhyo vidveṣo
nodvegaś cāguṇasya hi

na—not; *hi*—certainly; *asya*—His; *arthaḥ*—benefit, interest; *sura-gaṇaiḥ*—with the demigods; *sākṣāt*—personally; *niḥśreyasa*—of the highest bliss; *ātmanaḥ*—whose nature; *na*—not; *eva*—certainly; *asurebhyaḥ*—for the demons; *vidveṣaḥ*—envy; *na*—not; *udvegaḥ*—

fear; *ca*—and; *aguṇasya*—who possesses no material qualities; *hi*—certainly.

TRANSLATION

Lord Viṣṇu Himself, the Supreme Personality of Godhead, is the reservoir of all pleasure. Therefore, what benefit would He derive from siding with the demigods? What interest would He fulfill in this way? Since the Lord is transcendental, why should He fear the asuras, and how could He be envious of them?

PURPORT

We should always remember the distinction between spiritual and material. That which is material is infected by material qualities, but these qualities cannot touch that which is spiritual, or transcendental. Kṛṣṇa is absolute, whether He is in the material world or spiritual world. When we see partiality in Kṛṣṇa, this vision is due to His external energy. Otherwise how could His enemies attain salvation after being killed by Him? Everyone who deals with the Supreme Personality of Godhead gradually acquires the qualities of the Lord. The more one advances in spiritual consciousness, the less he is affected by the duality of material qualities. The Supreme Lord, therefore, must certainly be freed from these qualities. His enmity and friendship are external features presented by the material energy. He is always transcendental. He is absolute, whether He kills or bestows His favor.

Envy and friendship arise in one who is imperfect. We fear our enemies because in the material world we are always in need of help. The Lord, however, does not need anyone's help, for He is *ātmārāma.* The Lord says in *Bhagavad-gītā* (9.26):

patraṁ puṣpaṁ phalaṁ toyaṁ
yo me bhaktyā prayacchati
tad ahaṁ bhakty-upahṛtam
aśnāmi prayatātmanaḥ

"If a devotee offers Me with devotion a little leaf, a flower, fruit or water, I shall accept it." Why does the Lord say this? Is He dependent on the offering of the devotee? He is not actually dependent, but He likes to be dependent upon His devotee. This is His mercy. Similarly, He does not fear the *asuras.* Thus there is no question of partiality in the Supreme Personality of Godhead.

TEXT 3

इति नः सुमहाभाग नारायणगुणान् प्रति ।
संशयः सुमहाञ्जातस्तद्भवांश्छेत्तुमर्हति ॥ ३ ॥

iti naḥ sumahā-bhāga
nārāyaṇa-guṇān prati
saṁśayaḥ sumahāñ jātas
tad bhavāṁś chettum arhati

iti—thus; *naḥ*—our; *su-mahā-bhāga*—O glorious one; *nārāyaṇa-guṇān*—the qualities of Nārāyaṇa; *prati*—toward; *saṁśayaḥ*—doubt; *su-mahān*—very great; *jātaḥ*—born; *tat*—that; *bhavān*—Your Lordship; *chettum arhati*—please dispel.

TRANSLATION

O greatly fortunate and learned brāhmaṇa, whether Nārāyaṇa is partial or impartial has become a subject of great doubt. Kindly dispel my doubt with positive evidence that Nārāyaṇa is always neutral and equal to everyone.

PURPORT

Since Lord Nārāyaṇa is absolute, His transcendental qualities are described as one. Thus His punishments and His offerings of favor are both of the same value. Essentially, His inimical actions are not displays of enmity toward His so-called enemies, but in the material field one thinks that Kṛṣṇa is favorable to devotees and unfavorable to nondevotees. When Kṛṣṇa finally instructs in *Bhagavad-gītā, sarva-dharmān parityajya mām ekaṁ śaraṇaṁ vraja,* this is meant not only for Arjuna but for every living entity within this universe.

TEXTS 4–5

श्रीऋषिरुवाच
साधु पृष्टं महाराज हरेश्चरितमद्भुतम् ।
यद् भागवतमाहात्म्यं भगवद्भक्तिवर्धनम् ॥ ४ ॥
गीयते परमं पुण्यमृषिभिर्नारदादिभिः ।
नत्वा कृष्णाय मुनये कथयिष्ये हरेः कथाम् ॥ ५ ॥

śrī-ṛṣir uvāca
sādhu pṛṣṭaṁ mahārāja
hareś caritam adbhutam
yad bhāgavata-māhātmyaṁ
bhagavad-bhakti-vardhanam

gīyate paramaṁ puṇyam
ṛṣibhir nāradādibhiḥ
natvā kṛṣṇāya munaye
kathayiṣye hareḥ kathām

śrī-ṛṣiḥ uvāca—the sage Śrī Śukadeva Gosvāmī said; *sādhu*—excellent; *pṛṣṭam*—inquiry; *mahā-rāja*—O great King; *hareḥ*—of the Supreme Lord, Hari; *caritam*—activities; *adbhutam*—wonderful; *yat*—from which; *bhāgavata*—of the Lord's devotee (Prahlāda); *māhātmyam*—the glories; *bhagavat-bhakti*—devotion to the Lord; *vardhanam*—increasing; *gīyate*—is sung; *paramam*—foremost; *puṇyam*—pious; *ṛṣibhiḥ*—by the sages; *nārada-ādibhiḥ*—headed by Śrī Nārada Muni; *natvā*—after offering obeisances; *kṛṣṇāya*—to Kṛṣṇa Dvaipāyana Vyāsa; *munaye*—the great sage; *kathayiṣye*—I shall narrate; *hareḥ*—of Hari; *kathām*—the topics.

TRANSLATION

The great sage Śukadeva Gosvāmī said: My dear King, you have put before me an excellent question. Discourses concerning the activities of the Lord, in which the glories of His devotees are also found, are extremely pleasing to devotees. Such wonderful topics

always counteract the miseries of the materialistic way of life. Therefore great sages like Nārada always speak upon Śrīmad-Bhāgavatam because it gives one the facility to hear and chant about the wonderful activities of the Lord. Let me offer my respectful obeisances unto Śrīla Vyāsadeva and then begin describing topics concerning the activities of Lord Hari.

PURPORT

In this verse Śukadeva Gosvāmī offers his respectful obeisances *kṛṣṇāya munaye,* which means to Kṛṣṇa Dvaipāyana Vyāsa. One must first offer one's respectful obeisances to one's spiritual master. Śukadeva Gosvāmī's spiritual master is his father, Vyāsadeva, and therefore he first offers his respectful obeisances to Kṛṣṇa Dvaipāyana Vyāsa and then begins describing topics of Lord Hari.

Whenever there is an opportunity to hear about the transcendental activities of the Lord, we must take it. Śrī Caitanya Mahāprabhu recommends, *kīrtanīyaḥ sadā hariḥ:* one should always engage in *kṛṣṇa-kathā* by chanting and talking about Kṛṣṇa and hearing about Him. That is the only occupation of a Kṛṣṇa conscious person.

TEXT 6

निर्गुणोऽपि ह्यजोऽव्यक्तो भगवान् प्रकृतेः परः ।
स्वमायागुणमाविश्य बाध्यबाधकतां गतः ॥ ६ ॥

nirguṇo 'pi hy ajo 'vyakto
bhagavān prakṛteḥ paraḥ
sva-māyā-guṇam āviśya
bādhya-bādhakatāṁ gataḥ

nirguṇaḥ—without material qualities; *api*—although; *hi*—certainly; *ajaḥ*—unborn; *avyaktaḥ*—unmanifest; *bhagavān*—the Supreme Lord; *prakṛteḥ*—to material nature; *paraḥ*—transcendental; *sva-māyā*—of His own energy; *guṇam*—material qualities; *āviśya*—entering; *bādhya*—obligation; *bādhakatām*—the condition of being obliged; *gataḥ*—accepts.

TRANSLATION

The Supreme Personality of Godhead, Viṣṇu, is always transcendental to material qualities, and therefore He is called nirguṇa, or without qualities. Because He is unborn, He does not have a material body to be subjected to attachment and hatred. Although the Lord is always above material existence, through His spiritual potency He appeared and acted like an ordinary human being, accepting duties and obligations, apparently like a conditioned soul.

PURPORT

So-called attachment, detachment and obligations pertain to the material nature, which is an emanation from the Supreme Personality of Godhead, but whenever the Lord descends and acts in this material world, He does so in His spiritual position. Although His activities materially appear different, spiritually they are absolute and nondifferent. Thus it is an imposition upon the Supreme Lord to say that He is envious of anyone or friendly to anyone.

In *Bhagavad-gītā* (9.11) the Lord clearly says, *avajānanti māṁ mūḍhā mānuṣīṁ tanum āśritam:* "Fools deride Me when I descend in a human form." Kṛṣṇa appears on this earth or within this universe without any change in His spiritual body or spiritual qualities. Indeed, He is never influenced by the material qualities. He is always free from such qualities, but He appears to act under material influence. This understanding is *āropita,* or an imposition. Therefore Kṛṣṇa says, *janma karma ca me divyam:* whatever He does, being always transcendental, has nothing to do with material qualities. *Evaṁ yo vetti tattvataḥ:* only devotees can understand the truth of how He acts. The fact is that Kṛṣṇa is never partial to anyone. He is always equal to everyone, but because of imperfect vision, influenced by material qualities, one imposes material qualities upon Kṛṣṇa, and when one does so he becomes a *mūḍha,* a fool. When one can properly understand the truth, one becomes devoted and *nirguṇa,* free from material qualities. Simply by understanding the activities of Kṛṣṇa one can become transcendental, and as soon as one is transcendental he is fit to be transferred to the transcendental world. *Tyaktvā dehaṁ punar janma naiti mām eti so 'rjuna:* one who understands the activities of the Lord in truth is transferred to the spiritual world after he gives up his material body.

TEXT 7

सत्त्वं रजस्तम इति प्रकृतेर्नात्मनो गुणाः ।
न तेषां युगपद्राजन् ह्रास उल्लास एव वा ॥ ७ ॥

sattvaṁ rajas tama iti
prakṛter nātmano guṇāḥ
na teṣāṁ yugapad rājan
hrāsa ullāsa eva vā

sattvam—the mode of goodness; *rajaḥ*—the mode of passion; *tamaḥ*—the mode of ignorance; *iti*—thus; *prakṛteḥ*—of material nature; *na*—not; *ātmanaḥ*—of the spirit soul; *guṇāḥ*—qualities; *na*—not; *teṣām*—of them; *yugapat*—simultaneously; *rājan*—O King; *hrāsaḥ*—diminution; *ullāsaḥ*—prominence; *eva*—certainly; *vā*—or.

TRANSLATION

My dear King Parīkṣit, the material qualities—sattva-guṇa, rajo-guṇa and tamo-guṇa—all belong to the material world and do not even touch the Supreme Personality of Godhead. These three guṇas cannot act by increasing or decreasing simultaneously.

PURPORT

The original position of the Supreme Personality of Godhead is one of equality. There is no question of His being influenced by *sattva-guṇa, rajo-guṇa* or *tamo-guṇa,* for these material qualities cannot touch the Supreme Lord. The Lord is therefore called the supreme *īśvara. Īśvaraḥ paramaḥ kṛṣṇaḥ:* He is the supreme controller. He controls the material qualities (*daivī hy eṣā guṇamayī mama māyā*). *Mayādhyakṣeṇa prakṛtiḥ sūyate:* material nature (*prakṛti*) works under His order. How, then, can He be under the qualities of *prakṛti*? Kṛṣṇa is never influenced by the material qualities. Therefore there is no question of partiality in the Supreme Personality of Godhead.

TEXT 8

जयकाले तु सत्त्वस्य देवर्षीन् रजसोऽसुरान् ।
तमसो यक्षरक्षांसि तत्कालानुगुणोऽभजत् ॥ ८ ॥

jaya-kāle tu sattvasya
devarṣīn rajaso 'surān
tamaso yakṣa-rakṣāṁsi
tat-kālānuguṇo 'bhajat

jaya-kāle—in the time of prominence; *tu*—indeed; *sattvasya*—of goodness; *deva*—the demigods; *ṛṣīn*—and the sages; *rajasaḥ*—of passion; *asurān*—the demons; *tamasaḥ*—of ignorance; *yakṣa-rakṣāṁsi*—the Yakṣas and Rākṣasas; *tat-kāla-anuguṇaḥ*—according to the particular time; *abhajat*—fostered.

TRANSLATION

When the quality of goodness is prominent, the sages and demigods flourish with the help of that quality, with which they are infused and surcharged by the Supreme Lord. Similarly, when the mode of passion is prominent the demons flourish, and when ignorance is prominent the Yakṣas and Rākṣasas flourish. The Supreme Personality of Godhead is present in everyone's heart, fostering the reactions of sattva-guṇa, rajo-guṇa and tamo-guṇa.

PURPORT

The Supreme Personality of Godhead is not partial to anyone. The conditioned soul is under the influence of the various modes of material nature, and behind material nature is the Supreme Personality of Godhead; but one's victory and loss under the influence of *sattva-guṇa, rajo-guṇa* and *tamo-guṇa* are reactions of these modes, not of the Supreme Lord's partiality. Śrīla Jīva Gosvāmī, in the *Bhāgavata-sandarbha*, has clearly said:

sattvādayo na santīśe
yatra ca prākṛtā guṇāḥ
sa śuddhaḥ sarva-śuddhebhyaḥ
pumān ādyaḥ prasīdatu

hlādinī sandhinī samvit
tvayy ekā sarva-saṁsthitau
hlāda-tāpa-karī miśrā
tvayi no guṇa-varjite

According to this statement of the *Bhāgavata-sandarbha*, the Supreme Lord, being always transcendental to the material qualities, is never affected by the influence of these qualities. This same characteristic is also present in the living being, but because he is conditioned by material nature, even the pleasure potency of the Lord is manifested in the conditioned soul as troublesome. In the material world the pleasure enjoyed by the conditioned soul is followed by many painful conditions. For instance, we have seen that in the two great wars, which were conducted by the *rajo-guṇa* and *tamo-guṇa*, both parties were actually ruined. The German people declared war against the English to ruin them, but the result was that both parties were ruined. Although the Allies were apparently victorious, at least on paper, actually neither of them were victorious. Therefore it should be concluded that the Supreme Personality of Godhead is not partial to anyone. Everyone works under the influence of various modes of material nature, and when the various modes are prominent, the demigods or demons appear victorious under the influence of these modes.

Everyone enjoys the fruits of his qualitative activities. This is also confirmed in *Bhagavad-gītā* (14.11–13):

sarva-dvāreṣu dehe 'smin
prakāśa upajāyate
jñānaṁ yadā tadā vidyād
vivṛddhaṁ sattvam ity uta

lobhaḥ pravṛttir ārambhaḥ
karmaṇām aśamaḥ spṛhā
rajasy etāni jāyante
vivṛddhe bharatarṣabha

aprakāśo 'pravṛttiś ca
pramādo moha eva ca

tamasy etāni jāyante
vivṛddhe kuru-nandana

"The manifestations of the modes of goodness can be experienced when all the gates of the body are illumined by knowledge.

"O chief of the Bhāratas, when there is an increase in the mode of passion, the symptoms of great attachment, uncontrollable desire, hankering, and intense endeavor develop.

"O son of Kuru, when there is an increase in the mode of ignorance, madness, illusion, inertia and darkness are manifested."

The Supreme Personality of Godhead, who is present in everyone's heart, simply gives the results of the increase in the various qualities, but He is impartial. He supervises victory and loss, but He does not take part in them.

The various modes of material nature do not work all at once. The interactions of these modes are exactly like seasonal changes. Sometimes there is an increment of *rajo-guṇa*, sometimes of *tamo-guṇa* and sometimes *sattva-guṇa*. Generally the demigods are surcharged with *sattva-guṇa*, and therefore when the demons and the demigods fight, the demigods are victorious because of the prominence of their *sattva-guṇa* qualities. However, this is not the partiality of the Supreme Lord.

TEXT 9

ज्योतिरादिरिवाभाति सङ्घातान्न विविच्यते ।
विदन्त्यात्मानमात्मस्थं मथित्वा कवयोऽन्ततः ॥९॥

jyotir-ādir ivābhāti
saṅghātān na vivicyate
vidanty ātmānam ātma-sthaṁ
mathitvā kavayo 'ntataḥ

jyotiḥ—fire; *ādiḥ*—and other elements; *iva*—just as; *ābhāti*—appear; *saṅghātāt*—from the bodies of demigods and others; *na*—not; *vivicyate*—are distinguished; *vidanti*—perceive; *ātmānam*—the Supersoul; *ātma-stham*—situated in the heart; *mathitvā*—by discerning; *kavayaḥ*—expert thinkers; *antataḥ*—within.

TRANSLATION

The all-pervading Personality of Godhead exists within the heart of every living being, and an expert thinker can perceive how He is present there to a large or small extent. Just as one can understand the supply of fire in wood, the water in a waterpot, or the sky within a pot, one can understand whether a living entity is a demon or a demigod by understanding that living entity's devotional performances. A thoughtful man can understand how much a person is favored by the Supreme Lord by seeing his actions.

PURPORT

In *Bhagavad-gītā* (10.41) the Lord says:

yad yad vibhūtimat sattvaṁ
śrīmad ūrjitam eva vā
tat tad evāvagaccha tvaṁ
mama tejo-'ṁśa-sambhavam

"Know that all beautiful, glorious and mighty creations spring from but a spark of My splendor." We have the practical experience of seeing that one person is able to do very wonderful things whereas another cannot do those same things and cannot even do things that require only a little common sense. Therefore, how much a devotee has been favored by the Supreme Personality of Godhead can be tested by the activities the devotee has performed. In *Bhagavad-gītā* (10.10) the Lord also says:

teṣāṁ satata-yuktānāṁ
bhajatāṁ prīti-pūrvakam
dadāmi buddhi-yogaṁ taṁ
yena mām upayānti te

"To those who are constantly devoted and who worship Me with love, I give the understanding by which they can come to Me." This is very practical. A teacher instructs the student if the student is capable of taking more and more instructions. Otherwise, in spite of being instructed by the teacher, the student cannot make strides in his understanding.

This has nothing to do with partiality. When Kṛṣṇa says *teṣāṁ satata-yuktānāṁ bhajatāṁ prīti-pūrvakam/ dadāmi buddhi-yogaṁ tam*, this indicates that Kṛṣṇa is prepared to give *bhakti-yoga* to everyone, but one must be capable of receiving it. That is the secret. Thus when a person exhibits wonderful devotional activities, a thoughtful man understands that Kṛṣṇa has been more favorable to this devotee.

This is not difficult to understand, but envious persons do not accept that Kṛṣṇa has bestowed His favor upon a particular devotee in accordance with his advanced position. Such foolish persons become envious and try to minimize an advanced devotee's activities. That is not Vaiṣṇavism. A Vaiṣṇava should appreciate the service rendered to the Lord by other Vaiṣṇavas. Therefore a Vaiṣṇava is described in *Śrīmad-Bhāgavatam* as *nirmatsara.* Vaiṣṇavas are never envious of other Vaiṣṇavas or of anyone else, and therefore they are called *nirmat-sarāṇāṁ satām.*

As *Bhagavad-gītā* informs us, one can understand how one is saturated with *sattva-guṇa, rajo-guṇa* or *tamo-guṇa.* In the examples given herewith, fire represents the mode of goodness. One can understand the constitution of a container for wood, petrol or other inflammable substances by the quantity of the fire. Similarly, water represents *rajo-guṇa,* the mode of passion. A small skin and the vast Atlantic Ocean both contain water, and by seeing the quantity of water in a container one can understand the size of the container. The sky represents the mode of ignorance. The sky is present in a small earthen pot and also in outer space. Thus by proper judgment one can see who is a *devatā,* or demigod, and who is an *asura,* Yakṣa or Rākṣasa according to the quantities of *sattva-guṇa, rajo-guṇa* and *tamo-guṇa.* One cannot judge whether a person is a *devatā,* an *asura* or a Rākṣasa by seeing him, but a sane man can understand this by the activities such a person performs. A general description is given in the *Padma Purāṇa: viṣṇu-bhaktaḥ smṛto daiva āsuras tad-viparyayaḥ.* A devotee of Lord Viṣṇu is a demigod, whereas an *asura* or Yakṣa is just the opposite. An *asura* is not a devotee of Lord Viṣṇu; instead, for his sense gratification he is a devotee of the demigods, *bhūtas, pretas* and so on. Thus one can judge who is a *devatā,* who is a Rākṣasa and who is an *asura* by how they conduct their activities.

The word *ātmānam* in this verse means *paramātmānam.* The

Paramātmā, or Supersoul, is situated in the core of everyone's heart (*antataḥ*). This is confirmed in *Bhagavad-gītā* (18.61). *Īśvaraḥ sarva-bhūtānāṁ hṛd-deśe 'rjuna tiṣṭhati.* The *īśvara*, the Supreme Personality of Godhead, being situated in everyone's heart, gives directions to everyone in terms of one's capabilities in taking the instructions. The instructions of *Bhagavad-gītā* are open to everyone, but some people understand them properly, whereas others understand them so improperly that they cannot even believe in the existence of Kṛṣṇa, although reading Kṛṣṇa's book. Although the *Gītā* says *śrī-bhagavān uvāca*, indicating that Kṛṣṇa spoke, they cannot understand Kṛṣṇa. This is due to their misfortune or incapability, which is caused by *rajo-guṇa* and *tamo-guṇa*, the modes of passion and ignorance. It is because of these modes that they cannot even understand Kṛṣṇa, whereas an advanced devotee like Arjuna understands Him and glorifies Him, saying, *paraṁ brahma paraṁ dhāma pavitraṁ paramaṁ bhavān:* "You are the Supreme Brahman, the supreme abode and purifier." Kṛṣṇa is open to everyone, but one needs the capability to understand Him.

By external features one cannot understand who is favored by Kṛṣṇa and who is not. According to one's attitude, Kṛṣṇa becomes one's direct adviser, or Kṛṣṇa becomes unknown. This is not Kṛṣṇa's partiality; it is His response to one's ability to understand Him. According to one's receptiveness—whether one be a *devatā*, *asura*, Yakṣa or Rākṣasa—Kṛṣṇa's quality is proportionately exhibited. This proportionate exhibition of Kṛṣṇa's power is misunderstood by less intelligent men to be Kṛṣṇa's partiality, but actually it is no such thing. Kṛṣṇa is equal to everyone, and according to one's ability to receive the favor of Kṛṣṇa, one advances in Kṛṣṇa consciousness. Śrīla Viśvanātha Cakravartī Ṭhākura gives a practical example in this connection. In the sky there are many luminaries. At night, even in darkness, the moon is extremely brilliant and can be directly perceived. The sun is also extremely brilliant. When covered by clouds, however, these luminaries are not distinctly visible. Similarly, the more one advances in *sattva-guṇa*, the more his brilliance is exhibited by devotional service, but the more one is covered by *rajo-guṇa* and *tamo-guṇa*, the less visible his brilliance, for he is covered by these qualities. The visibility of one's qualities does not depend on the partiality of the Supreme Personality of Godhead; it is due to various coverings in different proportions. Thus one can understand how far he has advanced in terms of *sattva-guṇa* and how much he is covered by *rajo-guṇa* and *tamo-guṇa.*

TEXT 10

यदा सिसृक्षुः पुर आत्मनः परो
रजः सृजत्येष पृथक् स्वमायया ।
सत्त्वं विचित्रासु रिरंसुरीश्वरः
शयिष्यमाणस्तम ईरयत्यसौ ॥१०॥

yadā sisṛkṣuḥ pura ātmanaḥ paro
rajaḥ sṛjaty eṣa pṛthak sva-māyayā
sattvaṁ vicitrāsu riraṁsur īśvaraḥ
śayiṣyamāṇas tama īrayaty asau

yadā—when; *sisṛkṣuḥ*—desiring to create; *puraḥ*—material bodies; *ātmanaḥ*—for the living entities; *paraḥ*—the Supreme Personality of Godhead; *rajaḥ*—the mode of passion; *sṛjati*—manifests; *eṣaḥ*—He; *pṛthak*—separately, predominantly; *sva-māyayā*—by His own creative energy; *sattvam*—the mode of goodness; *vicitrāsu*—in various types of bodies; *riraṁsuḥ*—desiring to act; *īśvaraḥ*—the Personality of Godhead; *śayiṣyamāṇaḥ*—being about to conclude; *tamaḥ*—the mode of ignorance; *īrayati*—causes to rise; *asau*—that Supreme.

TRANSLATION

When the Supreme Personality of Godhead creates different types of bodies, offering a particular body to each living entity according to his character and fruitive actions, the Lord revives all the qualities of material nature—sattva-guṇa, rajo-guṇa and tamo-guṇa. Then, as the Supersoul, He enters each body and influences the qualities of creation, maintenance and annihilation, using sattva-guṇa for maintenance, rajo-guṇa for creation and tamo-guṇa for annihilation.

PURPORT

Although material nature is conducted by the three qualities—*sattva-guṇa, rajo-guṇa* and *tamo-guṇa*—nature is not independent. As the Lord says in *Bhagavad-gītā* (9.10):

mayādhyakṣeṇa prakṛtiḥ
sūyate sa-carācaram
hetunānena kaunteya
jagad viparivartate

"This material nature is working under My direction, O son of Kuntī, and it is producing all moving and unmoving beings. By its rule this manifestation is created and annihilated again and again." The different changes in the material world take place as actions and reactions of the three *guṇas*, but above the three *guṇas* is their director, the Supreme Personality of Godhead. In the various types of bodies given to the living entities by material nature (*yantrārūḍhāni māyayā*), either *sattva-guṇa, rajo-guṇa* or *tamo-guṇa* is prominent. The body is produced by material nature according to the direction of the Supreme Personality of Godhead. Therefore it is said here, *yadā sisṛkṣuḥ pura ātmanaḥ paraḥ*, indicating that the body is certainly created by the Lord. *Karmaṇā daiva-netreṇa:* according to the *karma* of the living entity, a body is prepared under the Supreme Lord's supervision. Whether the body is of *sattva-guṇa, rajo-guṇa* or *tamo-guṇa*, everything is done by the direction of the Supreme Lord through the agency of the external energy (*pṛthak sva-māyayā*). In this way, in different types of bodies, the Lord (*īśvara*) gives directions as Paramātmā, and again, to destroy the body, He employs the *tamo-guṇa*. This is the way the living entities receive different types of bodies.

TEXT 11

कालं चरन्तं सृजतीश आश्रयं ।
प्रधानपुम्भ्यां नरदेव सत्यकृत् ॥११॥

kālaṁ carantaṁ sṛjatīśa āśrayaṁ
pradhāna-pumbhyāṁ nara-deva satya-kṛt

kālam—time; *carantam*—moving; *sṛjati*—creates; *īśaḥ*—the Supreme Personality of Godhead; *āśrayam*—shelter; *pradhāna*—for the material energy; *pumbhyām*—and the living entity; *nara-deva*—O ruler of men; *satya*—true; *kṛt*—creator.

TRANSLATION

O great King, the Supreme Personality of Godhead, the controller of the material and spiritual energies, who is certainly the creator of the entire cosmos, creates the time factor to allow the material energy and the living entity to act within the limits of time. Thus the Supreme Personality is never under the time factor nor under the material energy.

PURPORT

One should not think that the Lord is dependent on the time factor. He actually creates the situation by which material nature acts and by which the conditioned soul is placed under material nature. Both the conditioned soul and the material nature act within the time factor, but the Lord is not subject to the actions and reactions of time, for time has been created by Him. To be more clear, Śrīla Viśvanātha Cakravartī Ṭhākura says that creation, maintenance and annihilation are all under the supreme will of the Lord.

In *Bhagavad-gītā* (4.7) the Lord says:

yadā yadā hi dharmasya
glānir bhavati bhārata
abhyutthānam adharmasya
tadātmānaṁ sṛjāmy aham

"Whenever and wherever there is a decline in religious practice, O descendant of Bharata, and a predominant rise of irreligion—at that time I descend Myself." Since Kṛṣṇa, the Supreme Personality of Godhead, is the controller of everything, when He appears He is not within the limitations of material time (*janma karma ca me divyam*). In this verse the words *kālaṁ carantaṁ sṛjatīśa āśrayam* indicate that although the Lord acts within time, whether *sattva-guṇa, rajo-guṇa* or *tamo-guṇa* is prominent, one should not think that the Lord is under time's control.

Time is within His control, for He creates time to act in a certain way; He is not working under the control of time. The creation of the material world is one of the Lord's pastimes. Everything is fully under His control. Since creation takes place when *rajo-guṇa* is prominent, the Lord creates the necessary time to give facilities for *rajo-guṇa*. Similarly, He also creates the necessary times for maintenance and annihilation. Thus this verse establishes that the Lord is not under the limitations of time.

As stated in the *Brahma-saṁhitā, īśvaraḥ paramaḥ kṛṣṇaḥ:* Kṛṣṇa is the supreme controller. *Sac-cid-ānanda-vigrahaḥ:* He possesses a blissful, spiritual body. *Anādiḥ:* He is not subordinate to anything. As the Lord confirms in *Bhagavad-gītā* (7.7), *mattaḥ parataraṁ nānyat kiñcid asti dhanañjaya:* "O conqueror of wealth [Arjuna], there is no truth superior to Me." Nothing can be above Kṛṣṇa, for He is the controller and creator of everything.

The Māyāvādī philosophers say that this material world is *mithyā*, false, and that one should therefore not bother about this *mithyā* creation (*brahma satyaṁ jagan mithyā*). But this is not correct. Here it is said, *satya-kṛt:* whatever is created by the Supreme Personality of Godhead, *satyaṁ param*, cannot be called *mithyā.* The cause of the creation is *satya*, true, so how can the effect of the cause be *mithyā?* The very word *satya-kṛt* is used to establish that everything created by the Lord is factual, never false. The creation may be temporary, but it is not false.

TEXT 12

य एष राजन्नपि काल ईशिता
सत्त्वं सुरानीकमिवैधयत्यतः ।
तत्प्रत्यनीकानसुरान् सुरप्रियो
रजस्तमस्कान् प्रमिणोत्युरुश्रवाः ॥१२॥

ya eṣa rājann api kāla īśitā
sattvaṁ surānīkam ivaidhayaty ataḥ
tat-pratyanīkān asurān sura-priyo
rajas-tamaskān pramiṇoty uruśravāḥ

yaḥ—which; *eṣaḥ*—this; *rājan*—O King; *api*—even; *kālaḥ*—time; *īśitā*—the Supreme Lord; *sattvam*—the mode of goodness; *sura-*

anīkam—numbers of demigods; *iva*—certainly; *edhayati*—causes to increase; *ataḥ*—hence; *tat-pratyanīkān*—inimical to them; *asurān*—the demons; *sura-priyaḥ*—being the friend of the demigods; *rajaḥ-tamaskān*—covered by passion and ignorance; *praminoti*—destoys; *uru-śravāḥ*—whose glories are widespread.

TRANSLATION

O King, this time factor enhances the sattva-guṇa. Thus although the Supreme Lord is the controller, He favors the demigods, who are mostly situated in sattva-guṇa. Then the demons, who are influenced by tamo-guṇa, are annihilated. The Supreme Lord induces the time factor to act in different ways, but He is never partial. Rather, His activities are glorious, therefore He is called Uruśravā.

PURPORT

The Lord says in *Bhagavad-gītā* (9.29), *samo 'haṁ sarva-bhūteṣu na me dveṣyo 'sti na priyaḥ:* "I envy no one, nor am I partial to anyone. I am equal to all." The Supreme Personality of Godhead cannot be partial; He is always equal to everyone. Therefore when the demigods are favored and the demons killed, this is not His partiality but the influence of the time factor. A good example in this regard is that an electrician connects both a heater and a cooler to the same electrical energy. The cause of the heating and cooling is the electrician's manipulation of the electrical energy according to his desire, but factually the electrician has nothing to do with causing heat or cold, nor with the enjoyment or suffering that results.

There have been many historical incidents in which the Lord killed a demon, but the demon attained a higher position by the mercy of the Lord. Pūtanā is an example. Pūtanā's purpose was to kill Kṛṣṇa. *Aho bakī yaṁ stana-kāla-kūṭam.* She approached the house of Nanda Mahārāja with the purpose of killing Kṛṣṇa by smearing poison on her breast, yet when she was killed she attained the highest position, achieving the status of Kṛṣṇa's mother. Kṛṣṇa is so kind and impartial that because he sucked Pūtanā's breast, He immediately accepted her as His mother. This superfluous activity of killing Pūtanā did not diminish the

Lord's impartiality. He is *suhṛdaṁ sarva-bhūtānām*, the friend of everyone. Therefore partiality cannot apply to the character of the Supreme Personality of Godhead, who always maintains His position as the supreme controller. The Lord killed Pūtanā as an enemy, but because of His being the supreme controller, she attained an exalted position as His mother. Śrīla Madhva Muni therefore remarks, *kāle kāla-viṣaye 'pīśitā. dehādi-kāraṇatvāt surānīkam iva sthitaṁ sattvam.* Ordinarily a murderer is hanged, and in the *Manu-saṁhitā* it is said that a king bestows mercy upon a murderer by killing him, thus saving him from various kinds of suffering. Because of his sinful activities, such a murderer is killed by the mercy of the king. Kṛṣṇa, the supreme judge, deals with matters in a similar way because He is the supreme controller. The conclusion, therefore, is that the Lord is always impartial and always very kind to all living entities.

TEXT 13

अत्रैवोदाहृतः पूर्वमितिहासः सुरर्षिणा ।
प्रीत्या महाक्रतौ राजन् पृच्छतेऽजातशत्रवे ॥१३॥

atraivodāhṛtaḥ pūrvam
itihāsaḥ surarṣiṇā
prītyā mahā-kratau rājan
pṛcchate 'jāta-śatrave

atra—in this connection; *eva*—certainly; *udāhṛtaḥ*—was recited; *pūrvam*—previously; *itihāsaḥ*—an old story; *sura-ṛṣiṇā*—by the great sage Nārada; *prītyā*—with joy; *mahā-kratau*—at the great Rājasūya sacrifice; *rājan*—O King; *pṛcchate*—to the inquiring; *ajāta-śatrave*—Mahārāja Yudhiṣṭhira, who had no enemy.

TRANSLATION

Formerly, O King, when Mahārāja Yudhiṣṭhira was performing the Rājasūya sacrifice, the great sage Nārada, responding to his inquiry, recited historical facts showing how the Supreme Personality of Godhead is always impartial, even when killing demons. In this regard he gave a vivid example.

PURPORT

This relates to how the Lord exhibited His impartiality even when killing Śiśupāla in the arena of the Rājasūya *yajña* performed by Mahārāja Yudhiṣṭhira.

TEXTS 14–15

दृष्ट्वा महाद्भुतं राजा राजसूये महाक्रतौ ।
वासुदेवे भगवति सायुज्यं चेदिभूभुजः ॥१४॥
तत्रासीनं सुरऋषिं राजा पाण्डुसुतः क्रतौ ।
पप्रच्छ विस्मितमना मुनीनां शृण्वतामिदम् ॥१५॥

dṛṣṭvā mahādbhutaṁ rājā
rājasūye mahā-kratau
vāsudeve bhagavati
sāyujyaṁ cedibhū-bhujaḥ

tatrāsīnaṁ sura-ṛṣiṁ
rājā pāṇḍu-sutaḥ kratau
papraccha vismita-manā
munīnāṁ śṛṇvatām idam

dṛṣṭvā—after seeing; *mahā-adbhutam*—greatly wonderful; *rājā*—the King; *rājasūye*—called Rājasūya; *mahā-kratau*—at the great sacrifice; *vāsudeve*—into Vāsudeva; *bhagavati*—the Personality of Godhead; *sāyujyam*—merging; *cedibhū-bhujaḥ*—of Śiśupāla, the King of Cedi; *tatra*—there; *āsīnam*—seated; *sura-ṛṣim*—Nārada Muni; *rājā*—the King; *pāṇḍu-sutaḥ*—Yudhiṣṭhira, the son of Pāṇḍu; *kratau*—at the sacrifice; *papraccha*—asked; *vismita-manāḥ*—being struck with wonder; *munīnām*—in the presence of the sages; *śṛṇvatām*—listening; *idam*—this.

TRANSLATION

O King, at the Rājasūya sacrifice, Mahārāja Yudhiṣṭhira, the son of Mahārāja Pāṇḍu, personally saw Śiśupāla merge into the body of the Supreme Lord, Kṛṣṇa. Therefore, struck with wonder, he inquired about the reason for this from the great sage Nārada, who

was seated there. While he inquired, all the sages present also heard him ask his question.

TEXT 16

श्रीयुधिष्ठिर उवाच
अहो अत्यद्भुतं ह्येतद्दुर्लभैकान्तिनामपि ।
वासुदेवे परे तत्त्वे प्राप्तिश्चैद्यस्य विद्विषः ॥१६॥

śrī-yudhiṣṭhira uvāca
aho aty-adbhutaṁ hy etad
durlabhaikāntinām api
vāsudeve pare tattve
prāptiś caidyasya vidviṣaḥ

śrī-yudhiṣṭhiraḥ uvāca—Mahārāja Yudhiṣṭhira said; *aho*—oh; *ati-adbhutam*—very wonderful; *hi*—certainly; *etat*—this; *durlabha*—difficult to attain; *ekāntinām*—for the transcendentalists; *api*—even; *vāsudeve*—in Vāsudeva; *pare*—the supreme; *tattve*—Absolute Truth; *prāptiḥ*—the attainment; *caidyasya*—of Śiśupāla; *vidviṣaḥ*—envious.

TRANSLATION

Mahārāja Yudhiṣṭhira inquired: It is very wonderful that the demon Śiśupāla merged into the body of the Supreme Personality of Godhead even though extremely envious. This sāyujya-mukti is impossible to attain even for great transcendentalists. How then did the enemy of the Lord attain it?

PURPORT

There are two classes of transcendentalists—the *jñānīs* and the *bhaktas*. The *bhaktas* do not aspire to merge into the existence of the Lord, but the *jñānīs* do. Śiśupāla, however, was neither a *jñānī* nor a *bhakta*, yet simply by envy of the Lord he attained an exalted position by merging into the Lord's body. Certainly this was astonishing, and therefore Mahārāja Yudhiṣṭhira inquired about the cause for the Lord's mysterious mercy to Śiśupāla.

TEXT 17

एतद्वेदितुमिच्छामः सर्वे एव वयं मुने ।
भगवन्निन्दया वेनो द्विजैस्तमसि पातितः ॥१७॥

etad veditum icchāmaḥ
sarva eva vayaṁ mune
bhagavan-nindayā veno
dvijais tamasi pātitaḥ

etat—this; *veditum*—to know; *icchāmaḥ*—desire; *sarve*—all; *eva*—certainly; *vayam*—we; *mune*—O great sage; *bhagavat-nindayā*—because of blaspheming the Lord; *venaḥ*—Vena, the father of Pṛthu Mahārāja; *dvijaiḥ*—by the *brāhmaṇas; tamasi*—into hell; *pātitaḥ*—was thrown.

TRANSLATION

O great sage, we are all eager to know the cause for this mercy of the Lord. I have heard that formerly a king named Vena blasphemed the Supreme Personality of Godhead and that all the brāhmaṇas consequently obliged him to go to hell. Śiśupāla should also have been sent to hell. How then did he merge into the Lord's existence?

TEXT 18

दमघोषसुतः पाप आरभ्य कलभाषणात् ।
सम्प्रत्यमर्षी गोविन्दे दन्तवक्रश्च दुर्मतिः ॥१८॥

damaghoṣa-sutaḥ pāpa
ārabhya kala-bhāṣaṇāt
sampraty amarṣī govinde
dantavakraś ca durmatiḥ

damaghoṣa-sutaḥ—Śiśupāla, the son of Damaghoṣa; *pāpaḥ*—sinful; *ārabhya*—beginning; *kala-bhāṣaṇāt*—from the unclear speech of a child; *samprati*—even until now; *amarṣī*—envious; *govinde*—toward

Śrī Kṛṣṇa; *dantavakraḥ*—Dantavakra; *ca*—also; *durmatiḥ*—evil-minded.

TRANSLATION

From the very beginning of his childhood, when he could not even speak properly, Śiśupāla, the most sinful son of Damaghoṣa, began blaspheming the Lord, and he continued to be envious of Śrī Kṛṣṇa until death. Similarly, his brother Dantavakra continued the same habits.

TEXT 19

शपतोरसकृद्विष्णुं यद्ब्रह्म परमव्ययम् ।
श्वित्रो न जातो जिह्वायां नान्धं विविशतुस्तमः ॥१९॥

śapator asakṛd viṣṇuṁ
yad brahma param avyayam
śvitro na jāto jihvāyāṁ
nāndhaṁ viviśatus tamaḥ

śapatoḥ—of both Śiśupāla and Dantavakra, who were blaspheming; *asakṛt*—repeatedly; *viṣṇum*—Lord Kṛṣṇa; *yat*—which; *brahma param*—the Supreme Brahman; *avyayam*—without diminution; *śvitraḥ*—white leprosy; *na*—not; *jātaḥ*—appeared; *jihvāyām*—on the tongue; *na*—not; *andham*—dark; *viviśatuḥ*—they did enter; *tamaḥ*—hell.

TRANSLATION

Although these two men—Śiśupāla and Dantavakra—repeatedly blasphemed the Supreme Personality of Godhead, Lord Viṣṇu [Kṛṣṇa], the Supreme Brahman, they were quite healthy. Indeed, their tongues were not attacked by white leprosy, nor did they enter the darkest region of hellish life. We are certainly most surprised by this.

PURPORT

Kṛṣṇa is described by Arjuna in *Bhagavad-gītā* (10.12) as follows: *paraṁ brahma paraṁ dhāma pavitraṁ paramaṁ bhavān.* "You are the

Supreme Brahman, the supreme abode and purifier." Herein this is confirmed. *Viṣṇuṁ yad brahma param avyayam.* The Supreme Viṣṇu is Kṛṣṇa. Kṛṣṇa is the cause of Viṣṇu, not vice versa. Similarly, Brahman is not the cause of Kṛṣṇa; Kṛṣṇa is the cause of Brahman. Therefore Kṛṣṇa is the Parabrahman (*yad brahma param avyayam*).

TEXT 20

कथं तस्मिन् भगवति दुरवग्राह्यधामनि ।
पश्यतां सर्वलोकानां लयमीयतुरञ्जसा ॥२०॥

kathaṁ tasmin bhagavati
duravagrāhya-dhāmani
paśyatāṁ sarva-lokānāṁ
layam īyatur añjasā

katham—how; *tasmin*—that; *bhagavati*—in the Supreme Personality of Godhead; *duravagrāhya*—difficult to attain; *dhāmani*—whose nature; *paśyatām*—looked on; *sarva-lokānām*—while all the people; *layam īyatuḥ*—became absorbed; *añjasā*—easily.

TRANSLATION

How was it possible for Śiśupāla and Dantavakra, in the presence of many exalted persons, to enter very easily into the body of Kṛṣṇa, whose nature is difficult to attain?

PURPORT

Śiśupāla and Dantavakra were formerly Jaya and Vijaya, the doorkeepers of Vaikuṇṭha. Merging into the body of Kṛṣṇa was not their final destination. For some time they remained merged, and later they received the liberations of *sārūpya* and *sālokya*, living on the same planet as the Lord in the same bodily form. The *śāstras* give evidence that if one blasphemes the Supreme Lord, his punishment is to remain in hellish life for many millions of years more than one suffers by killing many *brāhmaṇas*. Śiśupāla, however, instead of entering hellish life, immediately and very easily received *sāyujya-mukti*. That such a privilege had been offered to Śiśupāla was not merely a story. Everyone saw it happen; there was no scarcity of evidence. How did it happen? Mahārāja Yudhiṣṭhira was very much surprised.

TEXT 21

एतद् भ्राम्यति मे बुद्धिर्दीपार्चिरिव वायुना ।
ब्रूह्येतदद्भुततमं भगवान्ह्यत्र कारणम् ॥२१॥

etad bhrāmyati me buddhir
dīpārcir iva vāyunā
brūhy etad adbhutatamaṁ
bhagavān hy atra kāraṇam

etat—concerning this; *bhrāmyati*—is flickering; *me*—my; *buddhiḥ*—intelligence; *dīpa-arciḥ*—the flame of a candle; *iva*—like; *vāyunā*—by the wind; *brūhi*—please tell; *etat*—this; *adbhutatamam*—most wonderful; *bhagavān*—possessing all knowledge; *hi*—indeed; *atra*—here; *kāraṇam*—the cause.

TRANSLATION

This matter is undoubtedly very wonderful. Indeed, my intelligence has become disturbed, just as the flame of a candle is disturbed by a blowing wind. O Nārada Muni, you know everything. Kindly let me know the cause of this wonderful event.

PURPORT

The *śāstras* enjoin, *tad-vijñānārthaṁ sa gurum evābhigacchet:* when one is perplexed by the difficult problems of life, to solve them one must approach a *guru* like Nārada or his representative in the disciplic succession. Mahārāja Yudhiṣṭhira therefore requested Nārada to explain the cause for such a wonderful event.

TEXT 22

श्रीबादरायणिरुवाच
राज्ञस्तद्वच आकर्ण्य नारदो भगवानृषिः ।
तुष्टः प्राह तमाभाष्य शृण्वत्यास्तत्सदः कथाः ॥२२॥

śrī-bādarāyaṇir uvāca
rājñas tad vaca ākarṇya
nārado bhagavān ṛṣiḥ
tuṣṭaḥ prāha tam ābhāṣya
śṛṇvatyās tat-sadaḥ kathāḥ

śrī-bādarāyaṇiḥ uvāca—Śrī Śukadeva Gosvāmī said; *rājñaḥ*—of the King (Yudhiṣṭhira); *tat*—those; *vacaḥ*—words; *ākarṇya*—after hearing; *nāradaḥ*—Nārada Muni; *bhagavān*—powerful; *ṛṣiḥ*—sage; *tuṣṭaḥ*—being satisfied; *prāha*—spoke; *tam*—him; *ābhāṣya*—after addressing; *śṛṇvatyāḥ tat-sadaḥ*—in the presence of the assembly members; *kathāḥ*—the topics.

TRANSLATION

Śrī Śukadeva Gosvāmī said: After hearing the request of Mahārāja Yudhiṣṭhira, Nārada Muni, the most powerful spiritual master, who knew everything, was very pleased. Thus he replied in the presence of everyone taking part in the yajña.

TEXT 23

श्रीनारद उवाच
निन्दनस्तवसत्कारन्यक्कारार्थं कलेवरम् ।
प्रधानपरयो राजन्नविवेकेन कल्पितम् ॥२३॥

śrī-nārada uvāca
nindana-stava-satkāra-
nyakkārārthaṁ kalevaram
pradhāna-parayo rājann
avivekena kalpitam

śrī-nāradaḥ uvāca—Śrī Nārada Muni said; *nindana*—blasphemy; *stava*—praise; *satkāra*—honor; *nyakkāra*—dishonor; *artham*—for the purpose of; *kalevaram*—body; *pradhāna-parayoḥ*—of nature and the Supreme Personality of Godhead; *rājan*—O King; *avivekena*—without discrimination; *kalpitam*—created.

TRANSLATION

The great sage Śrī Nāradajī said: O King, blasphemy and praise, chastisement and respect, are experienced because of ignorance. The body of the conditioned soul is planned by the Lord for suffering in the material world through the agency of the external energy.

PURPORT

In *Bhagavad-gītā* (18.61) it is said:

īśvaraḥ sarva-bhūtānāṁ
hṛd-deśe 'rjuna tiṣṭhati
bhrāmayan sarva-bhūtāni
yantrārūḍhāni māyayā

"The Supreme Lord is situated in everyone's heart, O Arjuna, and is directing the wanderings of all living entities, who are seated as on a machine, made of material energy." A material body is manufactured by the external energy according to the direction of the Supreme Personality of Godhead. The conditioned soul, being seated on this machine, wanders throughout the universe, and because of his bodily conception of life he only suffers. Actually the suffering of being blasphemed and the enjoyment of being praised, the acceptance of a good welcome or of chastisement by harsh words, are felt in the material conception of life; but since the body of the Supreme Personality of Godhead is not material but *sac-cid-ānanda-vigraha,* He is unaffected by insults or greetings, blasphemy or prayers. Being always unaffected and complete, He does not feel extra pleasure when offered nice prayers by the devotee, although the devotee benefits by offering prayers to the Lord. Indeed, the Lord is very kind to His so-called enemy because one who always thinks of the Personality of Godhead as an enemy also benefits, although he thinks of the Lord adversely. If a conditioned soul, thinking of the Lord as an enemy or a friend, somehow or other becomes attached to the Lord, he receives great benefit.

TEXT 24

हिंसा तदभिमानेन दण्डपारुष्ययोर्यथा ।
वैषम्यमिह भूतानां ममाहमिति पार्थिव ॥२४॥

hiṁsā tad-abhimānena
daṇḍa-pāruṣyayor yathā
vaiṣamyam iha bhūtānāṁ
mamāham iti pārthiva

hiṁsā—suffering; *tat*—of this; *abhimānena*—by the false conception; *daṇḍa-pāruṣyayoḥ*—when there is punishment and chastisement; *yathā*—just as; *vaiṣamyam*—misconception; *iha*—here (in this body); *bhūtānām*—of the living entities; *mama-aham*—mine and I; *iti*—thus; *pārthiva*—O lord of the earth.

TRANSLATION

My dear King, the conditioned soul, being in the bodily conception of life, considers his body to be his self and considers everything in relationship with the body to be his. Because he has this wrong conception of life, he is subjected to dualities like praise and chastisement.

PURPORT

Only when a conditioned soul accepts the body as himself does he feel the effects of chastisement or praise. Then he determines one person to be his enemy and another his friend and wants to chastise the enemy and welcome the friend. This creation of friends and enemies is a result of one's bodily conception of life.

TEXT 25

यन्निबद्धोऽभिमानोऽयं तद्वधात्प्राणिनां वधः ।
तथा न यस्य कैवल्यादभिमानोऽखिलात्मनः ।
परस्य दमकर्तुर्हि हिंसा केनास्य कल्प्यते ॥२५॥

yan-nibaddho 'bhimāno 'yaṁ
tad-vadhāt prāṇināṁ vadhaḥ
tathā na yasya kaivalyād
abhimāno 'khilātmanaḥ
parasya dama-kartur hi
hiṁsā kenāsya kalpyate

yat—in which; *nibaddhaḥ*—bound; *abhimānaḥ*—false conception; *ayam*—this; *tat*—of that (body); *vadhāt*—from the annihilation; *prāṇinām*—of the living beings; *vadhaḥ*—annihilation; *tathā*—similarly; *na*—not; *yasya*—of whom; *kaivalyāt*—because of being absolute, one without a second; *abhimānaḥ*—false conception; *akhila-ātmanaḥ*—of the Supersoul of all living entities; *parasya*—the Supreme Personality of Godhead; *dama-kartuḥ*—the supreme controller; *hi*—certainly; *hiṁsā*—harm; *kena*—how; *asya*—His; *kalpyate*—is performed.

TRANSLATION

Because of the bodily conception of life, the conditioned soul thinks that when the body is annihilated the living being is annihilated. Lord Viṣṇu, the Supreme Personality of Godhead, is the supreme controller, the Supersoul of all living entities. Because He has no material body, He has no false conception of "I and mine." It is therefore incorrect to think that He feels pleasure or pain when blasphemed or offered prayers. This is impossible for Him. Thus He has no enemy and no friend. When He chastises the demons it is for their good, and when He accepts the prayers of the devotees it is for their good. He is affected neither by prayers nor by blasphemy.

PURPORT

Because of being covered by material bodies, the conditioned souls, including even greatly learned scholars and falsely educated professors, all think that as soon as the body is finished, everything is finished. This is due to their bodily conception of life. Kṛṣṇa has no such bodily conception, nor is His body different from His self. Therefore, since Kṛṣṇa has no material conception of life, how can He be affected by material prayers and accusations? Kṛṣṇa's body is described herewith as *kaivalya*, nondifferent from Himself. Since everyone has a material bodily conception of life, if Kṛṣṇa had such a conception what would be the difference between Kṛṣṇa and the conditioned soul? Kṛṣṇa's instructions in *Bhagavad-gītā* are accepted as final because He does not possess a material body. As soon as one has a material body he has four deficiencies, but since Kṛṣṇa does not possess a material body, He has no deficiencies. He is always spiritually conscious and blissful. *Īśvaraḥ paramaḥ kṛṣṇaḥ sac-cid-ānanda-vigrahaḥ:* His form is eternal, blissful knowledge. *Sac-cid-ānanda-vigrahaḥ, ānanda-cinmaya-rasa* and *kaivalya* are the same.

Kṛṣṇa can expand Himself as Paramātmā in the core of everyone's heart. In *Bhagavad-gītā* (13.3) this is confirmed. *Kṣetrajñaṁ cāpi māṁ viddhi sarva-kṣetreṣu bhārata:* the Lord is the Paramātmā—the *ātmā* or Superself of all individual souls. Therefore it must naturally be concluded that He has no defective bodily conceptions. Although situated in everyone's body, He has no bodily conception of life. He is always free from such conceptions, and thus He cannot be affected by anything in relation to the material body of the *jīva.*

Kṛṣṇa says in *Bhagavad-gītā* (16.19):

tān ahaṁ dviṣataḥ krūrān
saṁsāreṣu narādhamān
kṣipāmy ajasram aśubhān
āsurīṣv eva yoniṣu

"Those who are envious and mischievous, who are the lowest among men, are cast by Me into the ocean of material existence, into various demoniac species of life." Whenever the Lord punishes persons like demons, however, such punishment is meant for the good of the conditioned soul. The conditioned soul, being envious of the Supreme Personality of Godhead, may accuse Him, saying, "Kṛṣṇa is bad, Kṛṣṇa is a thief" and so on, but Kṛṣṇa, being kind to all living entities, does not consider such accusations. Instead, He takes account of the conditioned soul's chanting of "Kṛṣṇa, Kṛṣṇa" so many times. He sometimes punishes such demons for one life by putting them in a lower species, but then, when they have stopped accusing Him, they are liberated in the next life because of chanting Kṛṣṇa's name constantly. Blaspheming the Supreme Lord or His devotee is not at all good for the conditioned soul, but Kṛṣṇa, being very kind, punishes the conditioned soul in one life for such sinful activities and then takes him back home, back to Godhead. The vivid example for this is Vṛtrāsura, who was formerly Citraketu Mahārāja, a great devotee. Because he derided Lord Śiva, the foremost of all devotees, he had to accept the body of a demon called Vṛtra, but then he was taken back to Godhead. Thus when Kṛṣṇa punishes a demon or conditioned soul, He stops that soul's habit of blaspheming Him, and when the soul becomes completely pure, the Lord takes him back to Godhead.

TEXT 26

तस्माद्वैरानुबन्धेन निर्वैरेण भयेन वा ।
स्नेहात्कामेन वा युञ्ज्यात् कथञ्चिन्नेक्षते पृथक् ॥२६॥

tasmād vairānubandhena
nirvaireṇa bhayena vā
snehāt kāmena vā yuñjyāt
kathañcin nekṣate pṛthak

tasmāt—therefore; *vaira-anubandhena*—by constant enmity; *nirvaireṇa*—by devotion; *bhayena*—by fear; *vā*—or; *snehāt*—from affection; *kāmena*—by lusty desires; *vā*—or; *yuñjyāt*—one should concentrate; *kathañcit*—somehow or other; *na*—not; *īkṣate*—sees; *pṛthak*—something else.

TRANSLATION

Therefore by enmity or by devotional service, by fear, by affection or by lusty desire—by all of these or any one of them—if a conditioned soul somehow or other concentrates his mind upon the Lord, the result is the same, for the Lord, because of His blissful position, is never affected by enmity or friendship.

PURPORT

From this verse one should not conclude that because Kṛṣṇa is unaffected by favorable prayers or unfavorable blasphemy one should therefore blaspheme the Supreme Lord. This is not the regulative principle. *Bhakti-yoga* means *ānukūlyena kṛṣṇānuśīlanam:* one should serve Kṛṣṇa very favorably. This is the real injunction. Here it is said that although an enemy thinks of Kṛṣṇa unfavorably, the Lord is unaffected by such antidevotional service. Thus He offers His benedictions even to Śiśupāla and similarly inimical conditioned souls. This does not mean, however, that one should be inimical toward the Lord. The stress is given to the favorable execution of devotional service, not purposeful blasphemy of the Lord. It is said:

nindāṁ bhagavataḥ śṛṇvaṁs
tat-parasya janasya vā
tato nāpaiti yaḥ so 'pi
yāty adhaḥ sukṛtāc cyutaḥ

One who hears blasphemy of the Supreme Personality of Godhead or His devotees should immediately take action or should leave. Otherwise he will be put into hellish life perpetually. There are many such injunctions. Therefore as a regulative principle one should not be unfavorable toward the Lord but always favorably inclined toward Him.

Śiśupāla's achievement of oneness with the Supreme Lord was different because Jaya and Vijaya, from the very beginning of their material existence, were ordained to treat the Supreme Lord as an enemy for three lives and then return home, back to Godhead. Jaya and Vijaya inwardly knew that Kṛṣṇa is the Supreme Personality of Godhead, but they purposely became His enemies to be delivered from material life. From the very beginning of their lives they thought of Lord Kṛṣṇa as an enemy, and even though blaspheming Lord Kṛṣṇa, they chanted the holy name of Kṛṣṇa constantly along with their inimical thoughts. Thus they were purified because of chanting the holy name of Kṛṣṇa. It is to be understood that even a blasphemer can be freed from sinful activities by chanting the holy name of the Lord. Certainly, therefore, freedom is assured for a devotee who is always favorable to the service of the Lord. This will be clear from the following verse. By rapt attention fixed upon Kṛṣṇa, one is purified, and thus one is delivered from material life.

Śrīla Viśvanātha Cakravartī Ṭhākura has very nicely explained the word *bhayena,* which means "by fear." When the *gopīs* went to Kṛṣṇa in the dead of night, they certainly feared chastisement by their relatives—their husbands, brothers and fathers—but nonetheless, not caring for their relatives, they went to Kṛṣṇa. There was certainly fear, but this fear could not check their devotional service to Kṛṣṇa.

One should not mistakenly think that Lord Kṛṣṇa must be worshiped by an inimical attitude like that of Śiśupāla. The injunction is *ānukūlyasya grahaṇaṁ prātikūlyasya varjanam:* one should give up unfavorable activities and accept only favorable conditions in devotional service. Generally, if one blasphemes the Supreme Personality of Godhead he is punished. As the Lord says in *Bhagavad-gītā* (16.19):

tān ahaṁ dviṣataḥ krūrān
saṁsāreṣu narādhamān
kṣipāmy ajasram aśubhān
āsurīṣv eva yoniṣu

There are many such injunctions. One should not try to worship Kṛṣṇa unfavorably; otherwise he must be punished, at least for one life, to be purified. As one should not try to be killed by embracing an enemy, a tiger or a snake, one should not blaspheme the Supreme Personality of Godhead and become His enemy in order to be put into hellish life.

The purpose of this verse is to emphasize that even the enemy of the Lord can be delivered, not to speak of His friend. Śrīla Madhvācārya also says in many ways that one should not blaspheme Lord Viṣṇu through one's mind, words or actions, for a blasphemer will go to hellish life along with his forefathers.

karmaṇā manasā vācā
yo dviṣyād viṣṇum avyayam
majjanti pitaras tasya
narake śāśvatīḥ samāḥ

In *Bhagavad-gītā* (16.19–20) the Lord says:

tān ahaṁ dviṣataḥ krūrān
saṁsāreṣu narādhamān
kṣipāmy ajasram aśubhān
āsurīṣv eva yoniṣu

āsurīṁ yonim āpannā
mūḍhā janmani janmani
mām aprāpyaiva kaunteya
tato yānty adhamāṁ gatim

"Those who are envious and mischievous, who are the lowest among men, are cast by Me into the ocean of material existence, into various demoniac species of life. Attaining repeated birth amongst the species of demoniac life, such persons can never approach Me. Gradually they sink down to the most abominable type of existence." One who blasphemes the Lord is put into a family of *asuras*, in which there is every chance of forgetting the service of the Lord. Lord Kṛṣṇa further states in *Bhagavad-gītā* (9.11–12):

avajānanti māṁ mūḍhā
mānuṣīṁ tanum āśritam
paraṁ bhāvam ajānanto
mama bhūta-maheśvaram

Mūḍhas, rascals, blaspheme the Supreme Lord because He appears exactly like a human being. They do not know the unlimited opulence of the Supreme Personality of Godhead.

moghāśā mogha-karmāṇo
mogha-jñānā vicetasaḥ
rākṣasīm āsurīṁ caiva
prakṛtiṁ mohinīṁ śritāḥ

Anything done by those who have taken the attitude of enemies will be baffled (*moghāśāḥ*). If these enemies try to be liberated or to merge into the existence of Brahman, if they desire to be elevated to the higher planetary systems as *karmīs*, or even if they desire to return home, back to Godhead, they will certainly be baffled.

As for Hiraṇyakaśipu, although he was extremely inimical toward the Supreme Personality of Godhead, he always thought of his son, who was a great devotee. Therefore by the grace of his son, Prahlāda Mahārāja, Hiraṇyakaśipu was also delivered by the Supreme Personality of Godhead.

hiraṇyakaśipuś cāpi
bhagavan-nindayā tamaḥ
vivakṣur atyagāt sūnoḥ
prahlādasyānubhāvataḥ

The conclusion is that one should not give up pure devotional service. For one's own benefit, one should not imitate Hiraṇyakaśipu or Śiśupāla. This is not the way to achieve success.

TEXT 27

यथा वैरानुबन्धेन मर्त्यस्तन्मयतामियात् ।
न तथा भक्तियोगेन इति मे निश्चिता मतिः ॥२७॥

yathā vairānubandhena
martyas tan-mayatām iyāt
na tathā bhakti-yogena
iti me niścitā matiḥ

yathā—as; *vaira-anubandhena*—by constant enmity; *martyaḥ*—a person; *tat-mayatām*—absorption in Him; *iyāt*—may attain; *na*—not; *tathā*—in a like manner; *bhakti-yogena*—by devotional service; *iti*—thus; *me*—my; *niścitā*—definite; *matiḥ*—opinion.

TRANSLATION

Nārada Muni continued: By devotional service one cannot achieve such intense absorption in thought of the Supreme Personality of Godhead as one can through enmity toward Him. That is my opinion.

PURPORT

Śrīmān Nārada Muni, the topmost pure devotee, praises Kṛṣṇa's enemies like Śiśupāla because their minds are always completely absorbed in Kṛṣṇa. Indeed, he thinks himself deficient in the inspiration of being feelingly absorbed in Kṛṣṇa consciousness. This does not mean, however, that the enemies of Kṛṣṇa are more elevated than Kṛṣṇa's pure devotees. In the *Caitanya-caritāmṛta* (*Ādi* 5.205) Kṛṣṇadāsa Kavirāja Gosvāmī also thinks of himself in such a humble way:

jagāi mādhāi haite muñi se pāpiṣṭha
purīṣera kīṭa haite muñi se laghiṣṭha

"I am a worse sinner than Jagāi and Mādhāi and am even lower than the worms in the stool." A pure devotee always thinks himself more deficient than everyone else. If a devotee approaches Śrīmatī Rādhārāṇī to offer some service to Kṛṣṇa, even Śrīmatī Rādhārāṇī thinks that the devotee is greater than She. Thus Nārada Muni says that according to his opinion the enemies of Kṛṣṇa are better situated because they are fully absorbed in thoughts of Kṛṣṇa in terms of killing Him, just as a very lusty man always thinks of women and their association.

The essential point in this connection is that one should be fully absorbed in thoughts of Kṛṣṇa, twenty-four hours a day. There are many devotees in *rāga-mārga*, which is exhibited in Vṛndāvana. Whether in *dāsya-rasa, sakhya-rasa, vātsalya-rasa* or *mādhurya-rasa*, all the devotees of Kṛṣṇa are always overwhelmed by thoughts of Kṛṣṇa. When Kṛṣṇa is away from Vṛndāvana tending the cows in the forest, the *gopīs*, in the *mādhurya-rasa*, are always absorbed in thoughts of how Kṛṣṇa walks in the forest. The soles of His feet are so soft that the *gopīs* would not dare keep His lotus feet on their soft breasts. Indeed, they consider their breasts a very hard place for the lotus feet of Kṛṣṇa, yet those lotus feet wander in the forest, which is full of thorny plants. The *gopīs* are absorbed in such thoughts at home, although Kṛṣṇa is away from them. Similarly, when Kṛṣṇa plays with His young friends, mother Yaśodā is very much disturbed by thoughts that Kṛṣṇa, because of always playing and not taking His food properly, must be getting weak. These are examples of the exalted ecstasy felt in Kṛṣṇa's service as manifested in Vṛndāvana. This service is indirectly praised by Nārada Muni in this verse. Especially for the conditioned soul, Nārada Muni recommends that one somehow or other be absorbed in thoughts of Kṛṣṇa, for that will save one from all the dangers of material existence. Full absorption in thought of Kṛṣṇa is the highest platform of *bhakti-yoga*.

TEXTS 28–29

कीटः पेशस्कृता रुद्धः कुड्यायां तमनुस्मरन् ।
संरम्भभययोगेन विन्दते तत्स्वरूपताम् ॥२८॥
एवं कृष्णे भगवति मायामनुज ईश्वरे ।
वैरेण पूतपाप्मानस्तमापुरनुचिन्तया ॥२९॥

kīṭaḥ peśaskṛtā ruddhaḥ
kuḍyāyāṁ tam anusmaran
saṁrambha-bhaya-yogena
vindate tat-svarūpatām

evaṁ kṛṣṇe bhagavati
māyā-manuja īśvare
vaireṇa pūta-pāpmānas
tam āpur anucintayā

kīṭaḥ—the grassworm; *peśaskṛtā*—by a bee; *ruddhaḥ*—confined; *kuḍyāyām*—in a hole in a wall; *tam*—that (bee); *anusmaran*—thinking of; *saṁrambha-bhaya-yogena*—through intense fear and enmity; *vindate*—attains; *tat*—of that bee; *sva-rūpatām*—the same form; *evam*—thus; *kṛṣṇe*—in Kṛṣṇa; *bhagavati*—the Personality of Godhead; *māyā-manuje*—who appeared by His own energy in His eternal humanlike form; *īśvare*—the Supreme; *vaireṇa*—by enmity; *pūta-pāpmānaḥ*—those purified of sins; *tam*—Him; *āpuḥ*—attained; *anucintayā*—by thinking of.

TRANSLATION

A grassworm confined in a hole of a wall by a bee always thinks of the bee in fear and enmity and later becomes a bee simply because of such remembrance. Similarly, if the conditioned souls somehow or other think of Kṛṣṇa, who is sac-cid-ānanda-vigraha, they will become free from their sins. Whether thinking of Him as their worshipable Lord or an enemy, because of constantly thinking of Him they will regain their spiritual bodies.

PURPORT

In *Bhagavad-gītā* (4.10) the Lord says:

vīta-rāga-bhaya-krodhā
man-mayā mām upāśritāḥ
bahavo jñāna-tapasā
pūtā mad-bhāvam āgatāḥ

"Being freed from attachment, fear and anger, being fully absorbed in Me and taking refuge in Me, many, many persons in the past became purified by knowledge of Me—and thus they all attained transcendental love for Me." There are two ways of constantly thinking of Kṛṣṇa—as a devotee and as an enemy. A devotee, of course, by his knowledge and *tapasya*, becomes free from fear and anger and becomes a pure devotee. Similarly, an enemy, although thinking of Kṛṣṇa inimically, thinks of Him constantly and also becomes purified. This is confirmed elsewhere in *Bhagavad-gītā* (9.30), where the Lord says:

api cet sudurācāro
bhajate mām ananya-bhāk
sādhur eva sa mantavyaḥ
samyag vyavasito hi saḥ

"Even if one commits the most abominable actions, if he engages in devotional service he is to be considered saintly because he is properly situated." A devotee undoubtedly worships the Lord with rapt attention. Similarly, if an enemy (*sudurācāraḥ*) always thinks of Kṛṣṇa, he also becomes a purified devotee. The example given here concerns the grassworm that becomes beelike because of constantly thinking of the bee that forces it to enter a hole. By always thinking of the bee in fear, the grassworm starts to become a bee. This is a practical example. Lord Kṛṣṇa appears within this material world for two purposes—*paritrāṇāya sādhūnāṁ vināśāya ca duṣkṛtām:* to protect the devotees and annihilate the demons. The *sādhus* and devotees certainly think of the Lord always, but *duṣkṛtīs*, the demons like Kaṁsa and Śiśupāla, also think of Kṛṣṇa in terms of killing Him. By thinking of Kṛṣṇa, both the demons and devotees attain liberation from the clutches of material *māyā*.

This verse uses the word *māyā-manuje*. When Kṛṣṇa, the Supreme Personality of Godhead, appears in His original spiritual potency (*sambhavāmy ātma-māyayā*), He is not forced to accept a form made by material nature. Therefore the Lord is addressed as *īśvara*, the controller of *māyā*. He is not controlled by *māyā*. When a demon continuously thinks of Kṛṣṇa because of enmity toward Him, he is certainly freed from the sinful reactions of his life. To think of Kṛṣṇa in any way, in terms of His name, form, qualities, paraphernalia or anything pertaining to Him, is beneficial for everyone. *Śṛṇvatāṁ sva-kathāḥ kṛṣṇaḥ puṇya-śravaṇa-kīrtanaḥ*. Thinking of Kṛṣṇa, hearing the holy name of Kṛṣṇa or hearing the pastimes of Kṛṣṇa will make one pure, and then he will become a devotee. Our Kṛṣṇa consciousness movement is therefore trying to introduce the system of somehow or other letting everyone hear the holy name of Kṛṣṇa and take Kṛṣṇa's *prasāda.* Thus one will gradually become a devotee, and his life will be successful.

TEXT 30

कामाद् द्वेषाद्भयात्स्नेहाद्यथा भक्त्येश्वरे मनः ।
आवेश्य तदघं हित्वा बहवस्तद्गतिं गताः ॥३०॥

kāmād dveṣād bhayāt snehād
yathā bhaktyeśvare manaḥ
āveśya tad-aghaṁ hitvā
bahavas tad-gatiṁ gatāḥ

kāmāt—from lust; *dveṣāt*—from hatred; *bhayāt*—from fear; *snehāt*—from affection; *yathā*—as well as; *bhaktyā*—by devotion; *īśvare*—in the Supreme; *manaḥ*—the mind; *āveśya*—absorbing; *tat*—of that; *agham*—sin; *hitvā*—giving up; *bahavaḥ*—many; *tat*—of that; *gatim*—path of liberation; *gatāḥ*—attained.

TRANSLATION

Many, many persons have attained liberation simply by thinking of Kṛṣṇa with great attention and giving up sinful activities. This great attention may be due to lusty desires, inimical feelings, fear, affection or devotional service. I shall now explain how one receives Kṛṣṇa's mercy simply by concentrating one's mind upon Him.

PURPORT

As stated in *Śrīmad-Bhāgavatam* (10.33.39):

vikrīḍitaṁ vraja-vadhūbhir idaṁ ca viṣṇoḥ
śraddhānvito 'nuśṛṇuyād atha varṇayed yaḥ
bhaktiṁ parāṁ bhagavati pratilabhya kāmaṁ
hṛd-rogam āśv apahinoty acireṇa dhīraḥ

If a bona fide listener hears of Kṛṣṇa's pastimes with the *gopīs,* which seem to be lusty affairs, the lusty desires in his heart, which constitute the heart disease of the conditioned soul, will be vanquished, and he will become a most exalted devotee of the Lord. If one who hears of the *gopīs'* lusty behavior with Kṛṣṇa becomes free from lusty desires, certainly the *gopīs* who approached Kṛṣṇa became free from all such desires. Similarly, Śiśupāla and others who were very much envious of Kṛṣṇa and who constantly thought of Kṛṣṇa became free from envy. Nanda Mahārāja and mother Yaśodā were fully absorbed in Kṛṣṇa consciousness because of affection. When the mind is somehow or other fully absorbed in Kṛṣṇa, the material part is very soon vanquished, and the spiritual part—attraction to Kṛṣṇa—becomes manifest. This indirectly confirms that if one thinks of Kṛṣṇa enviously, simply because of thinking of Kṛṣṇa he becomes free from all sinful reactions and thus becomes a pure devotee. Examples of this are given in the following verse.

TEXT 31

गोप्यः कामाद्भयात्कंसो द्वेषाच्चैद्यादयो नृपाः ।
सम्बन्धाद् वृष्णयः स्नेहाद्यूयं भक्त्या वयं विभो ॥३१॥

gopyaḥ kāmād bhayāt kaṁso
dveṣāc caidyādayo nṛpāḥ
sambandhād vṛṣṇayaḥ snehād
yūyaṁ bhaktyā vayaṁ vibho

gopyaḥ—the *gopīs; kāmāt*—out of lusty desires; *bhayāt*—out of fear; *kaṁsaḥ*—King Kaṁsa; *dveṣāt*—out of envy; *caidya-ādayaḥ*—Śiśupāla and others; *nṛpāḥ*—kings; *sambandhāt*—out of kinship; *vṛṣṇayaḥ*—the Vṛṣṇis or the Yādavas; *snehāt*—out of affection; *yūyam*—you (the Pāṇḍavas); *bhaktyā*—by devotional service; *vayam*—we; *vibho*—O great King.

TRANSLATION

My dear King Yudhiṣṭhira, the gopīs by their lusty desires, Kaṁsa by his fear, Śiśupāla and other kings by envy, the Yadus by their familial relationship with Kṛṣṇa, you Pāṇḍavas by your great affection for Kṛṣṇa, and we, the general devotees, by our devotional service, have obtained the mercy of Kṛṣṇa.

PURPORT

Different persons achieve different types of *mukti—sāyujya, sālokya, sārūpya, sāmīpya* and *sārṣṭi*—according to their own intense desire, which is called *bhāva*. Thus it is described here that the *gopīs*, by their lusty desires, which were based upon their intense love for Kṛṣṇa, became the most beloved devotees of the Lord. Although the *gopīs* at Vṛndāvana expressed their lusty desires in relationship with a paramour (*parakīya-rasa*), they actually had no lusty desires. This is significant of spiritual advancement. Their desires appeared lusty, but actually they were not the lusty desires of the material world. *Caitanya-caritāmṛta* compares the desires of the spiritual and material world to gold and iron. Both gold and iron are metal, but there is a vast difference in their value. The lusty desires of the *gopīs* for Kṛṣṇa are compared to gold, and material lusty desires are compared to iron.

Kaṁsa and other enemies of Kṛṣṇa merged into the existence of Brahman, but why should Kṛṣṇa's friends and devotees have the same position? Kṛṣṇa's devotees attain the association of the Lord as His constant companions, either in Vṛndāvana or in the Vaikuṇṭha planets. Similarly, although Nārada Muni wanders in the three worlds, he has exalted devotion for Nārāyaṇa (*aiśvaryamān*). The Vṛṣṇis and Yadus and the father and mother of Kṛṣṇa in Vṛndāvana all have familial relationships with Kṛṣṇa; Kṛṣṇa's foster father and mother in Vṛndāvana, however, are more exalted than Vasudeva and Devakī.

TEXT 32

कतमोऽपि न वेनः स्यात्पञ्चानां पुरुषं प्रति ।
तस्मात् केनाप्युपायेन मनः कृष्णे निवेशयेत् ॥३२॥

katamo 'pi na venaḥ syāt
pañcānāṁ puruṣaṁ prati
tasmāt kenāpy upāyena
manaḥ kṛṣṇe niveśayet

katamaḥ api—anyone; *na*—not; *venaḥ*—the atheistic King Vena; *syāt*—would adopt; *pañcānām*—of the five (previously mentioned); *puruṣam*—the Supreme Personality of Godhead; *prati*—in regard to;

tasmāt—therefore; *kenāpi*—by any; *upāyena*—means; *manaḥ*—the mind; *kṛṣṇe*—in Kṛṣṇa; *niveśayet*—one should fix.

TRANSLATION

Somehow or other, one must consider the form of Kṛṣṇa very seriously. Then, by one of the five different processes mentioned above, one can return home, back to Godhead. Atheists like King Vena, however, being unable to think of Kṛṣṇa's form in any of these five ways, cannot attain salvation. Therefore, one must somehow think of Kṛṣṇa, whether in a friendly way or inimically.

PURPORT

Impersonalists and atheists always try to circumvent the form of Kṛṣṇa. Great politicians and philosophers of the modern age even try to banish Kṛṣṇa from *Bhagavad-gītā.* Consequently, for them there is no salvation. But Kṛṣṇa's enemies think, "Here is Kṛṣṇa, my enemy. I have to kill Him." They think of Kṛṣṇa in His actual form, and thus they attain salvation. Devotees, therefore, who constantly think of Kṛṣṇa's form, are certainly liberated. The only business of the Māyāvādī atheists is to make Kṛṣṇa formless, and consequently, because of this severe offense at the lotus feet of Kṛṣṇa, they cannot expect salvation. Śrīla Viśvanātha Cakravartī Ṭhākura says in this connection: *tena śiśupālādi-bhinnaḥ pratikūla-bhāvaṁ didhīṣur yena iva narakaṁ yātīti bhāvaḥ.* Except for Śiśupāla, those who go against the regulative principles cannot attain salvation and are surely destined for hellish life. The regulative principle is that one must always think of Kṛṣṇa, whether as a friend or enemy.

TEXT 33

मातृष्वस्रेयो वश्चैद्यो दन्तवक्रश्च पाण्डव ।
पार्षदप्रवरौ विष्णोर्विप्रशापात्पदच्युतौ ॥३३॥

mātṛ-ṣvasreyo vaś caidyo
dantavakraś ca pāṇḍava
pārṣada-pravarau viṣṇor
vipra-śāpāt pada-cyutau

mātṛ-svasreyaḥ—the son of the mother's sister (Śiśupāla); *vaḥ*—your; *caidyaḥ*—King Śiśupāla; *dantavakraḥ*—Dantavakra; *ca*—and; *pāṇḍava*—O Pāṇḍava; *parṣada-pravarau*—two exalted attendants; *viṣṇoḥ*—of Viṣṇu; *vipra*—by *brāhmaṇas; śāpāt*—because of a curse; *pada*—from their position in Vaikuṇṭha; *cyutau*—fallen.

TRANSLATION

Nārada Muni continued: O best of the Pāṇḍavas, your two cousins Śiśupāla and Dantavakra, the sons of your maternal aunt, were formerly associates of Lord Viṣṇu, but because they were cursed by brāhmaṇas, they fell from Vaikuṇṭha to this material world.

PURPORT

Śiśupāla and Dantavakra were not ordinary demons, but were formerly personal associates of Lord Viṣṇu. They apparently fell to this material world, but actually they came to assist the Supreme Personality of Godhead by nourishing His pastimes within this world.

TEXT 34

श्रीयुधिष्ठिर उवाच
कीदृशः कस्य वा शापो हरिदासाभिमर्शनः ।
अश्रद्धेय इवाभाति हरेरेकान्तिनां भवः ॥३४॥

śrī-yudhiṣṭhira uvāca
kīdṛśaḥ kasya vā śāpo
hari-dāsābhimarśanaḥ
aśraddheya ivābhāti
harer ekāntināṁ bhavaḥ

śrī-yudhiṣṭhiraḥ uvāca—Mahārāja Yudhiṣṭhira said; *kīdṛśaḥ*—what kind of; *kasya*—whose; *vā*—or; *śāpaḥ*—curse; *hari-dāsa*—the servant of Hari; *abhimarśanaḥ*—overcoming; *aśraddheyaḥ*—incredible; *iva*—as if; *ābhāti*—appears; *hareḥ*—of Hari; *ekāntinām*—of those exclusively devoted as exalted attendants; *bhavaḥ*—birth.

TRANSLATION

Mahārāja Yudhiṣṭhira inquired: What kind of great curse could affect even liberated viṣṇu-bhaktas, and what sort of person could curse even the Lord's associates? For unflinching devotees of the Lord to fall again to this material world is impossible. I cannot believe this.

PURPORT

In *Bhagavad-gītā* (8.16) the Lord clearly states, *mām upetya tu kaunteya punar janma na vidyate:* one who is purified of material contamination and returns home, back to Godhead, does not return to this material world. Elsewhere in *Bhagavad-gītā* (4.9) Kṛṣṇa says:

janma karma ca me divyam
evaṁ yo vetti tattvataḥ
tyaktvā dehaṁ punar janma
naiti mām eti so 'rjuna

"One who knows the transcendental nature of My appearance and activities does not, upon leaving the body, take his birth again in this material world, but attains My eternal abode, O Arjuna." Mahārāja Yudhiṣṭhira, therefore, was surprised that a pure devotee could return to this material world. This is certainly a very important question.

TEXT 35

देहेन्द्रियासुहीनानां वैकुण्ठपुरवासिनाम् ।
देहसम्बन्धसम्बद्धमेतदाख्यातुमर्हसि ॥३५॥

dehendriyāsu-hīnānāṁ
vaikuṇṭha-pura-vāsinām
deha-sambandha-sambaddham
etad ākhyātum arhasi

deha—of a material body; *indriya*—material senses; *asu*—life breath; *hīnānām*—of those devoid; *vaikuṇṭha-pura*—of Vaikuṇṭha; *vāsinām*—of the residents; *deha-sambandha*—in a material body; *sambaddham*—bondage; *etat*—this; *ākhyātum arhasi*—please describe.

TRANSLATION

The bodies of the inhabitants of Vaikuṇṭha are completely spiritual, having nothing to do with the material body, senses or life air. Therefore, kindly explain how associates of the Personality of Godhead were cursed to descend in material bodies like ordinary persons.

PURPORT

This very significant question would be difficult for an ordinary person to answer, but Nārada Muni, being an authority, could answer it. Therefore Mahārāja Yudhiṣṭhira inquired from him, saying, *etad ākhyātum arhasi:* "only you can explain the reason." From authoritative sources it can be discerned that associates of Lord Viṣṇu who descend from Vaikuṇṭha do not actually fall. They come with the purpose of fulfilling the desire of the Lord, and their descent to this material world is comparable to that of the Lord. The Lord comes to this material world through the agency of His internal potency, and similarly, when a devotee or associate of the Lord descends to this material world, he does so through the action of the spiritual energy. Any pastime conducted by the Supreme Personality of Godhead is an arrangement by *yogamāyā,* not *mahāmāyā.* Therefore it is to be understood that when Jaya and Vijaya descended to this material world, they came because there was something to be done for the Supreme Personality of Godhead. Otherwise it is a fact that no one falls from Vaikuṇṭha.

Of course, a living entity who desires *sāyujya-mukti* remains in Kṛṣṇa's Brahman effulgence, which is dependent on Kṛṣṇa's body (*brahmaṇo hi pratiṣṭhāham*). Such an impersonalist who takes shelter of the Brahman effulgence must surely fall down. This is stated in the *śāstra* (*Bhāg.* 10.2.32):

ye 'nye 'ravindākṣa vimukta-māninas
tvayy asta-bhāvād aviśuddha-buddhayaḥ
āruhya kṛcchreṇa paraṁ padaṁ tataḥ
patanty adho 'nādṛta-yuṣmad-aṅghrayaḥ

"O Lord, the intelligence of those who think themselves liberated but who have no devotion is impure. Even though they rise to the highest point of liberation by dint of severe penances and austerities, they are sure to fall down again into material existence, for they do not take shelter at Your lotus feet." The impersonalists cannot reach the Vaikuṇṭha planets to become associates of the Lord, and therefore, according to their desires, Kṛṣṇa gives them *sāyujya-mukti.* However, since *sāyujya-mukti* is partial *mukti,* they must fall again to this material world. When it is said that the individual soul falls from Brahmaloka, this applies to the impersonalist.

From authoritative sources it is learned that Jaya and Vijaya were sent to this material world to fulfill the Lord's desire to fight. The Lord also sometimes wants to fight, but who can fight with the Lord but a very confidential devotee of the Lord? Jaya and Vijaya descended to this world to fulfill the Lord's desire. Therefore in each of their three births—first as Hiraṇyākṣa and Hiraṇyakaśipu, second as Rāvaṇa and Kumbhakarṇa, and third as Śiśupāla and Dantavakra—the Lord personally killed them. In other words, these associates of the Lord, Jaya and Vijaya, descended to the material world to serve the Lord by fulfilling His desire to fight. Otherwise, as Mahārāja Yudhiṣṭhira says, *aśraddheya ivābhāti:* the statement that a servant of the Lord could fall from Vaikuṇṭha seems unbelievable. How Jaya and Vijaya came to this material world is explained by Nārada Muni as follows.

TEXT 36

श्रीनारद उवाच
एकदा ब्रह्मणः पुत्रा विष्णुलोकं यदृच्छया ।
सनन्दनादयो जग्मुश्चरन्तो भुवनत्रयम् ॥३६॥

śrī-nārada uvāca
ekadā brahmaṇaḥ putrā
viṣṇu-lokaṁ yadṛcchayā
sanandanādayo jagmuś
caranto bhuvana-trayam

śrī-nāradaḥ uvāca—Śrī Nārada Muni said; *ekadā*—once upon a time; *brahmaṇaḥ*—of Lord Brahmā; *putrāḥ*—the sons; *viṣṇu*—of Lord Viṣṇu; *lokam*—the planet; *yadṛcchayā*—by chance; *sanandana-*

ādayaḥ—Sanandana and the others; *jagmuḥ*—went; *carantaḥ*—traveling about; *bhuvana-trayam*—the three worlds.

TRANSLATION

The great saint Nārada said: Once upon a time when the four sons of Lord Brahmā named Sanaka, Sanandana, Sanātana and Sanat-kumāra were wandering throughout the three worlds, they came by chance to Viṣṇuloka.

TEXT 37

पञ्चषड्ढायनार्भाभाः पूर्वेषामपि पूर्वजाः ।
दिग्वाससः शिशून् मत्वा द्वाःस्थौ तान् प्रत्यषेधताम् ॥ ३७॥

pañca-ṣaḍḍhāyanārbhābhāḥ
pūrveṣām api pūrvajāḥ
dig-vāsasaḥ śiśūn matvā
dvāḥ-sthau tān pratyaṣedhatām

pañca-ṣaṭ-dhā—five or six years; *āyana*—approaching; *arbha-ābhāḥ*—like boys; *pūrveṣām*—the ancients of the universe (Marīci and the rest); *api*—even though; *pūrva-jāḥ*—born before; *dik-vāsasaḥ*—being naked; *śiśūn*—children; *matvā*—thinking; *dvāḥ-sthau*—the two gate guards, Jaya and Vijaya; *tān*—them; *pratyaṣedhatām*—forbade.

TRANSLATION

Although these four great sages were older than Brahmā's other sons like Marīci, they appeared like small naked children only five or six years old. When Jaya and Vijaya saw them trying to enter Vaikuṇṭhaloka, these two gatekeepers, thinking them ordinary children, forbade them to enter.

PURPORT

In this regard, Śrīla Madhvācārya says in his *Tantra-sāra:*

dvāḥ-sthāv ity anenādhikāra-sthatvam uktam

adhikāra-sthitāś caiva
vimuktāś ca dvidhā janāḥ
viṣṇu-loka-sthitās teṣāṁ
vara-śāpādi-yoginaḥ

adhikāra-sthitāṁ muktiṁ
niyataṁ prāpnuvanti ca
vimukty-anantaraṁ teṣāṁ
vara-śāpādayo nanu

dehendriyāsu-yuktaś ca
pūrvaṁ paścān na tair yutāḥ
apy abhimānibhis teṣāṁ
devaiḥ svātmottamair yutāḥ

The purport is that the personal associates of Lord Viṣṇu in Vaikuṇṭhaloka are always liberated souls. Even if sometimes cursed or blessed, they are always liberated and never contaminated by the material modes of nature. Before their liberation to Vaikuṇṭhaloka they possessed material bodies, but once they come to Vaikuṇṭha they no longer have them. Therefore even if the associates of Lord Viṣṇu sometimes descend as if cursed, they are always liberated.

TEXT 38

अशपन् कुपिता एवं युवां वासं न चार्हथः ।
रजस्तमोभ्यां रहिते पादमूले मधुद्विषः ।
पापिष्ठामासुरीं योनिं बालिशौ यातमाश्वतः ॥३८॥

aśapan kupitā evaṁ
yuvāṁ vāsaṁ na cārhathaḥ
rajas-tamobhyāṁ rahite
pāda-mūle madhudviṣaḥ
pāpiṣṭhām āsurīṁ yoniṁ
bāliśau yātam āśv ataḥ

aśapan—cursed; *kupitāḥ*—being full of anger; *evam*—thus; *yuvām*—you two; *vāsam*—residence; *na*—not; *ca*—and; *arhathaḥ*—deserve; *rajaḥ-tamobhyām*—from passion and ignorance; *rahite*—free; *pāda-mūle*—at the lotus feet; *madhu-dviṣaḥ*—of Viṣṇu, the slayer of the Madhu demon; *pāpiṣṭhām*—most sinful; *āsurīm*—demoniac; *yonim*—to a womb; *bāliśau*—O you two fools; *yātam*—go; *āśu*—quickly hereafter; *ataḥ*—therefore.

TRANSLATION

Thus checked by the doorkeepers Jaya and Vijaya, Sanandana and the other great sages very angrily cursed them. "You two foolish doorkeepers," they said. "Being agitated by the material qualities of passion and ignorance, you are unfit to live at the shelter of Madhudviṣa's lotus feet, which are free from such modes. It would be better for you to go immediately to the material world and take your birth in a family of most sinful asuras."

TEXT 39

एवं शप्तौ स्वभवनात् पतन्तौ तौ कृपालुभिः ।
प्रोक्तौ पुनर्जन्मभिर्वां त्रिभिर्लोकाय कल्पताम् ॥३९॥

evaṁ śaptau sva-bhavanāt
patantau tau kṛpālubhiḥ
proktau punar janmabhir vāṁ
tribhir lokāya kalpatām

evam—thus; *śaptau*—being cursed; *sva-bhavanāt*—from their abode, Vaikuṇṭha; *patantau*—falling down; *tau*—those two (Jaya and Vijaya); *kṛpālubhiḥ*—by the merciful sages (Sanandana, etc.); *proktau*—addressed; *punaḥ*—again; *janmabhiḥ*—with births; *vām*—your; *tribhiḥ*—three; *lokāya*—for the position; *kalpatām*—let it be possible.

TRANSLATION

While Jaya and Vijaya, thus cursed by the sages, were falling to the material world, they were addressed as follows by the same

sages, who were very kind to them. "O doorkeepers, after three births you will be able to return to your positions in Vaikuṇṭha, for then the duration of the curse will have ended."

TEXT 40

जज्ञाते तौ दितेः पुत्रौ दैत्यदानववन्दितौ ।
हिरण्यकशिपुर्ज्येष्ठो हिरण्याक्षोऽनुजस्ततः ॥४०॥

jajñāte tau diteḥ putrau
daitya-dānava-vanditau
hiraṇyakaśipur jyeṣṭho
hiraṇyākṣo 'nujas tataḥ

jajñāte—were born; *tau*—the two; *diteḥ*—of Diti; *putrau*—the sons; *daitya-dānava*—by all the demons; *vanditau*—being worshiped; *hiraṇyakaśipuḥ*—Hiraṇyakaśipu; *jyeṣṭhaḥ*—the elder; *hiraṇyākṣaḥ*—Hiraṇyākṣa; *anujaḥ*—the younger; *tataḥ*—thereafter.

TRANSLATION

These two associates of the Lord—Jaya and Vijaya—later descended to the material world, taking birth as the two sons of Diti, Hiraṇyakaśipu being the elder and Hiraṇyākṣa the younger. They were very much respected by the Daityas and Dānavas [demoniac species].

TEXT 41

हतो हिरण्यकशिपुर्हरिणा सिंहरूपिणा ।
हिरण्याक्षो धरोद्धारे बिभ्रता शौकरं वपुः ॥४१॥

hato hiraṇyakaśipur
hariṇā siṁha-rūpiṇā
hiraṇyākṣo dharoddhāre
bibhratā śaukaraṁ vapuḥ

hataḥ—killed; *hiraṇyakaśipuḥ*—Hiraṇyakaśipu; *hariṇā*—by Hari, Viṣṇu; *siṁha-rūpiṇā*—in the form of a lion (Lord Narasiṁha);

hiraṇyākṣaḥ—Hiraṇyākṣa; *dharā-uddhāre*—to lift the earth; *bibhratā*—assuming; *śaukaram*—the boarlike; *vapuḥ*—form.

TRANSLATION

Appearing as Nṛsiṁhadeva, the Supreme Personality of Godhead, Śrī Hari, killed Hiraṇyakaśipu. When the Lord delivered the planet earth, which had fallen in the Garbhodaka Ocean, Hiraṇyākṣa tried to hinder Him, and then the Lord, as Varāha, killed Hiraṇyākṣa.

TEXT 42

हिरण्यकशिपुः पुत्रं प्रह्लादं केशवप्रियम् ।
जिघांसुरकरोन्नाना यातना मृत्युहेतवे ॥४२॥

hiraṇyakaśipuḥ putraṁ
prahlādaṁ keśava-priyam
jighāṁsur akaron nānā
yātanā mṛtyu-hetave

hiraṇyakaśipuḥ—Hiraṇyakaśipu; *putram*—son; *prahlādam*—Prahlāda Mahārāja; *keśava-priyam*—the beloved devotee of Keśava; *jighāṁsuḥ*—desirous of killing; *akarot*—enacted; *nānā*—various; *yātanāḥ*—tortures; *mṛtyu*—death; *hetave*—to cause.

TRANSLATION

Desiring to kill his son Prahlāda, who was a great devotee of Lord Viṣṇu, Hiraṇyakaśipu tortured him in many ways.

TEXT 43

तं सर्वभूतात्मभूतं प्रशान्तं समदर्शनम् ।
भगवत्तेजसा स्पृष्टं नाशक्नोद्धन्तुमुद्यमैः ॥४३॥

taṁ sarva-bhūtātma-bhūtaṁ
praśāntaṁ sama-darśanam

bhagavat-tejasā spṛṣṭaṁ
nāśaknod dhantum udyamaiḥ

tam—Him; *sarva-bhūta-ātma-bhūtam*—the soul in all entities; *praśāntam*—peaceful and without hatred, etc.; *sama-darśanam*—equal to everyone; *bhagavat-tejasā*—with the power of the Supreme Personality of Godhead; *spṛṣṭam*—protected; *na*—not; *aśaknot*—was able; *hantum*—to kill; *udyamaiḥ*—by great attempts and various weapons.

TRANSLATION

The Lord, the Supersoul of all living entities, is sober, peaceful and equal to everyone. Since the great devotee Prahlāda was protected by the Lord's potency, Hiraṇyakaśipu was unable to kill him, in spite of endeavoring to do so in various ways.

PURPORT

In this verse the word *sarva-bhūtātma-bhūtam* is very significant. *Īśvaraḥ sarva-bhūtānāṁ hṛd-deśe 'rjuna tiṣṭhati:* the Lord is equally situated in the core of everyone's heart. Thus He cannot be envious of anyone or friendly to anyone; for Him everyone is the same. Although He is sometimes seen to punish someone, this is exactly like a father's punishing his child for the child's welfare. The Supreme Lord's punishment is also a manifestation of the Lord's equality. Therefore the Lord is described as *praśāntaṁ sama-darśanam.* Although the Lord has to execute His will properly, He is equipoised in all circumstances. He is equally disposed toward everyone.

TEXT 44

ततस्तौ राक्षसौ जातौ केशिन्यां विश्रवःसुतौ ।
रावणः कुम्भकर्णश्च सर्वलोकोपतापनौ ॥४४॥

tatas tau rākṣasau jātau
keśinyāṁ viśravaḥ-sutau
rāvaṇaḥ kumbhakarṇaś ca
sarva-lokopatāpanau

tataḥ—thereafter; *tau*—the two doorkeepers (Jaya and Vijaya); *rākṣasau*—demons; *jātau*—born; *keśinyām*—in the womb of Keśinī; *viśravaḥ-sutau*—the sons of Viśravā; *rāvaṇaḥ*—Rāvaṇa; *kumbhakarṇaḥ*—Kumbhakarṇa; *ca*—and; *sarva-loka*—to all people; *upatāpanau*—giving misery.

TRANSLATION

Thereafter the same Jaya and Vijaya, the two doorkeepers of Lord Viṣṇu, took birth as Rāvaṇa and Kumbhakarṇa, begotten by Viśravā in the womb of Keśinī. They were extremely troublesome to all the people of the universe.

TEXT 45

तत्रापि राघवो भूत्वा न्यहनच्छापमुक्तये ।
रामवीर्यं श्रोष्यसि त्वं मार्कण्डेयमुखात् प्रभो ॥४५॥

tatrāpi rāghavo bhūtvā
nyahanac chāpa-muktaye
rāma-vīryaṁ śroṣyasi tvaṁ
mārkaṇḍeya-mukhāt prabho

tatra api—thereupon; *rāghavaḥ*—as Lord Rāmacandra; *bhūtvā*—manifesting; *nyahanat*—killed; *śāpa-muktaye*—for freedom from the curse; *rāma-vīryam*—the prowess of Lord Rāma; *śroṣyasi*—will hear; *tvam*—you; *mārkaṇḍeya-mukhāt*—from the lips of the sage Mārkaṇḍeya; *prabho*—O lord.

TRANSLATION

Nārada Muni continued: My dear King, just to relieve Jaya and Vijaya of the brāhmaṇas' curse, Lord Rāmacandra appeared in order to kill Rāvaṇa and Kumbhakarṇa. It will be better for you to hear narrations about Lord Rāmacandra's activities from Mārkaṇḍeya.

TEXT 46

तावत्र क्षत्रियौ जातौ मातृष्वस्रात्मजौ तव ।
अधुना शापनिर्मुक्तौ कृष्णचक्रहतांहसौ ॥४६॥

tāv atra kṣatriyau jātau
mātṛ-ṣvasrātmajau tava
adhunā śāpa-nirmuktau
kṛṣṇa-cakra-hatāṁhasau

tau—the two; *atra*—here, in the third birth; *kṣatriyau*—*kṣatriyas* or kings; *jātau*—born; *mātṛ-svasṛ-ātma-jau*—the sons of the mother's sister; *tava*—your; *adhunā*—now; *śāpa-nirmuktau*—freed from the curse; *kṛṣṇa-cakra*—by the disc weapon of Kṛṣṇa; *hata*—destroyed; *aṁhasau*—whose sins.

TRANSLATION

In their third birth, the same Jaya and Vijaya appeared in a family of kṣatriyas as your cousins, the sons of your aunt. Because Lord Kṛṣṇa has struck them with His disc, all their sinful reactions have been destroyed, and now they are free from the curse.

PURPORT

In their last birth, Jaya and Vijaya did not become demons or Rākṣasas. Instead they took birth in a very exalted *kṣatriya* family related to Kṛṣṇa's family. They became first cousins of Lord Kṛṣṇa and were practically on an equal footing with Him. By personally killing them with His own disc, Lord Kṛṣṇa destroyed whatever sinful reactions were left in them because of the curse of the *brāhmaṇas*. Nārada Muni explained to Mahārāja Yudhiṣṭhira that by entering Kṛṣṇa's body, Śiśupāla reentered Vaikuṇṭhaloka as the Lord's associate. Everyone had seen this incident.

TEXT 47

वैरानुबन्धतीव्रेण ध्यानेनाच्युतसात्मताम् ।
नीतौ पुनर्हरेः पार्श्वं जग्मतुर्विष्णुपार्षदौ ॥४७॥

vairānubandha-tīvreṇa
dhyānenācyuta-sātmatām
nītau punar hareḥ pārśvaṁ
jagmatur viṣṇu-pārṣadau

vaira-anubandha—bond of hatred; *tīvreṇa*—consisting of acute; *dhyānena*—by meditation; *acyuta-sātmatām*—to the effulgence of the infallible Lord; *nītau*—attained; *punaḥ*—again; *hareḥ*—of Hari; *pārśvam*—the proximity; *jagmatuḥ*—they reached; *viṣṇu-pārṣadau*—the gatekeeper associates of Viṣṇu.

TRANSLATION

These two associates of Lord Viṣṇu—Jaya and Vijaya—maintained a feeling of enmity for a very long time. Because of always thinking of Kṛṣṇa in this way, they regained the shelter of the Lord, having returned home, back to Godhead.

PURPORT

Whatever their position, certainly Jaya and Vijaya always thought of Kṛṣṇa. Therefore at the end of the *mauṣala-līlā*, these two associates of the Lord returned to Kṛṣṇa. There is no difference between Kṛṣṇa's body and Nārāyaṇa's body. Therefore although they visibly entered the body of Kṛṣṇa, they actually reentered Vaikuṇṭhaloka as the doorkeepers of Lord Viṣṇu. Through Lord Kṛṣṇa's body, they returned to Vaikuṇṭha, although they seemed to have attained *sāyujya-mukti* in Kṛṣṇa's body.

TEXT 48

श्रीयुधिष्ठिर उवाच
विद्वेषो दयिते पुत्रे कथमासीन्महात्मनि ।
ब्रूहि मे भगवन्येन प्रह्लादस्याच्युतात्मता ॥४८॥

śrī-yudhiṣṭhira uvāca
vidveṣo dayite putre
katham āsīn mahātmani
brūhi me bhagavan yena
prahlādasyācyutātmatā

śrī-yudhiṣṭhiraḥ uvāca—Mahārāja Yudhiṣṭhira said; *vidveṣaḥ*—hatred; *dayite*—for his own beloved; *putre*—son; *katham*—how; *āsīt*—there was; *mahā-ātmani*—the great soul, Prahlāda; *brūhi*—please tell; *me*—unto me; *bhagavan*—O exalted sage; *yena*—by which; *prahlādasya*—of Prahlāda Mahārāja; *acyuta*—to Acyuta; *ātmatā*—great attachment.

TRANSLATION

Mahārāja Yudhiṣṭhira inquired: O my lord, Nārada Muni, why was there such enmity between Hiraṇyakaśipu and his beloved son Prahlāda Mahārāja? How did Prahlāda Mahārāja become such a great devotee of Lord Kṛṣṇa? Kindly explain this to me.

PURPORT

All the devotees of Lord Kṛṣṇa are called *acyutātmā* because they follow in the footsteps of Prahlāda Mahārāja. Acyuta refers to the infallible Lord Viṣṇu, whose heart is always infallible. Because the devotees are attached to the Infallible, they are called *acyutātmā.*

Thus end the Bhaktivedanta purports of the Seventh Canto, First Chapter, of the Śrīmad-Bhāgavatam, *entitled "The Supreme Lord Is Equal to Everyone."*

CHAPTER TWO

Hiraṇyakaśipu, King of the Demons

As described in this chapter, after the annihilation of Hiraṇyākṣa, Hiraṇyākṣa's sons and his brother Hiraṇyakaśipu were very much aggrieved. Hiraṇyakaśipu reacted very sinfully by trying to diminish the religious activities of people in general. However, he instructed his nephews about a history just to diminish their aggrievement.

When the Supreme Personality of Godhead appeared as the boar and killed Hiraṇyakaśipu's brother Hiraṇyākṣa, Hiraṇyakaśipu was very much aggrieved. In anger, he accused the Supreme Personality of Godhead of being partial to His devotees and derided the Lord's appearance as Varāha to kill his brother. He began to agitate all the demons and Rākṣasas and disturb the ritualistic ceremonies of the peaceful sages and other inhabitants of earth. For want of the performance of *yajña,* sacrifice, the demigods began wandering unseen on earth.

After finishing the ritualistic funeral ceremonies of his brother, Hiraṇyakaśipu began speaking to his nephews, quoting from the *śāstras* about the truth of life. To pacify them, he spoke as follows: "My dear nephews, for heroes to die before the enemy is glorious. According to their different fruitive activities, living entities come together within this material world and are again separated by the laws of nature. We should always know, however, that the spirit soul, which is different from the body, is eternal, inadjustable, pure, all-pervading and aware of everything. When bound by the material energy, the soul takes birth in higher or lower species of life according to varying association and in this way receives various types of bodies in which to suffer or enjoy. One's affliction by the conditions of material existence is the cause of happiness and distress; there are no other causes, and one should not be aggrieved upon seeing the superficial actions of *karma.*"

Hiraṇyakaśipu then related a historical incident concerning a King Suyajña who resided in the country named Uśīnara. When the King was killed, his queens, overwhelmed with grief, received instructions, which

Hiraṇyakaśipu quoted to his nephews. Hiraṇyakaśipu related an account of a *kuliṅga* bird pierced by the arrow of a hunter while lamenting for his wife, who had also been shot by the same hunter. By narrating these stories, Hiraṇyakaśipu pacified his nephews and other relatives and relieved them of lamentation. Thus having been pacified, Diti and Ruṣābhānu, Hiraṇyakaśipu's mother and sister-in-law, engaged their minds in spiritual understanding.

TEXT 1

श्रीनारद उवाच

भ्रातर्येवं विनिहते हरिणा क्रोडमूर्तिना ।
हिरण्यकशिपू राजन् पर्यतप्यद्रुषा शुचा ॥ १ ॥

śrī-nārada uvāca
bhrātary evaṁ vinihate
hariṇā kroḍa-mūrtinā
hiraṇyakaśipū rājan
paryatapyad ruṣā śucā

śrī-nāradaḥ uvāca—Śrī Nārada Muni said; *bhrātari*—when the brother (Hiraṇyākṣa); *evam*—thus; *vinihate*—was killed; *hariṇā*—by Hari; *kroḍa-mūrtinā*—in the form of the boar, Varāha; *hiraṇya-kaśipuḥ*—Hiraṇyakaśipu; *rājan*—O King; *paryatapyat*—was afflicted; *ruṣā*—by anger; *śucā*—by grief.

TRANSLATION

Śrī Nārada Muni said: My dear King Yudhiṣṭhira, when Lord Viṣṇu, in the form of Varāha, the boar, killed Hiraṇyākṣa, Hiraṇyākṣa's brother Hiraṇyakaśipu was extremely angry and began to lament.

PURPORT

Yudhiṣṭhira had inquired from Nārada Muni why Hiraṇyakaśipu was so envious of his own son Prahlāda. Nārada Muni began narrating the story by explaining how Hiraṇyakaśipu had become a staunch enemy of Lord Viṣṇu.

TEXT 2

आह चेदं रुषा पूर्णः सन्दष्टदशनच्छदः ।
कोपोज्ज्वलद्भ्यां चक्षुर्भ्यां निरीक्षन् धूम्रमम्बरम् ॥२॥

āha cedaṁ ruṣā pūrṇaḥ
sandaṣṭa-daśana-cchadaḥ
kopojjvaladbhyāṁ cakṣurbhyāṁ
nirīkṣan dhūmram ambaram

āha—said; *ca*—and; *idam*—this; *ruṣā*—with anger; *pūrṇaḥ*—full; *sandaṣṭa*—bitten; *daśana-chadaḥ*—whose lips; *kopa-ujjvaladbhyām*—blazing with anger; *cakṣurbhyām*—with eyes; *nirīkṣan*—looking over; *dhūmram*—smoky; *ambaram*—the sky.

TRANSLATION

Filled with rage and biting his lips, Hiraṇyakaśipu gazed at the sky with eyes that blazed in anger, making the whole sky smoky. Thus he began to speak.

PURPORT

As usual, the demon is envious of the Supreme Personality of Godhead and inimical toward Him. These were Hiraṇyakaśipu's external bodily features as he considered how to kill Lord Viṣṇu and devastate His kingdom, Vaikuṇṭhaloka.

TEXT 3

करालदंष्ट्रोग्रदृष्ट्या दुष्प्रेक्ष्यभ्रुकुटीमुखः ।
शूलमुद्यम्य सदसि दानवानिदमब्रवीत् ॥ ३ ॥

karāla-daṁṣṭrogra-dṛṣṭyā
duṣprekṣya-bhrukuṭī-mukhaḥ
śūlam udyamya sadasi
dānavān idam abravīt

karāla-daṁṣṭra—with terrible teeth; *ugra-dṛṣṭyā*—and fierce glance; *duṣprekṣya*—horrible to see; *bhru-kuṭī*—with frowning eyebrows; *mukhaḥ*—whose face; *śūlam*—trident; *udyamya*—raising; *sadasi*—in the assembly; *dānavān*—to the demons; *idam*—this; *abravīt*—spoke.

TRANSLATION

Exhibiting his terrible teeth, fierce glance and frowning eyebrows, terrible to see, he took up his weapon, a trident, and thus began speaking to his associates, the assembled demons.

TEXT 4–5

भो भो दानवदैतेया द्विमूर्धंस्त्र्यक्ष शम्बर ।
शतबाहो हयग्रीव नमुचे पाक इल्वल ॥ ४ ॥
विप्रचित्ते मम वचः पुलोमन् शकुनादयः ।
शृणुतानन्तरं सर्वे क्रियतामाशु मा चिरम् ॥ ५ ॥

bho bho dānava-daiteyā
dvimūrdhaṁs tryakṣa śambara
śatabāho hayagrīva
namuce pāka ilvala

vipracitte mama vacaḥ
puloman śakunādayaḥ
śṛṇutānantaraṁ sarve
kriyatām āśu mā ciram

bhoḥ—O; *bhoḥ*—O; *dānava-daiteyāḥ*—Dānavas and Daityas; *dvi-mūrdhan*—Dvimūrdha (two-headed); *tri-akṣa*—Tryakṣa (three-eyed); *śambara*—Śambara; *śata-bāho*—Śatabāhu (hundred-armed); *haya-grīva*—Hayagrīva (horse-headed); *namuce*—Namuci; *pāka*—Pāka; *il-vala*—Ilvala; *vipracitte*—Vipracitti; *mama*—my; *vacaḥ*—words; *pulo-man*—Puloma; *śakuna*—Śakuna; *ādayaḥ*—and others; *śṛṇuta*—just hear; *anantaram*—after that; *sarve*—all; *kriyatām*—let it be done; *āśu*—quickly; *mā*—do not; *ciram*—delay.

TRANSLATION

O Dānavas and Daityas! O Dvimūrdha, Tryakṣa, Śambara and Śatabāhu! O Hayagrīva, Namuci, Pāka and Ilvala! O Vipracitti, Puloman, Śakuna and other demons! All of you, kindly hear me attentively and then act according to my words without delay.

TEXT 6

सपत्नैर्घातितः क्षुद्रैर्भ्राता मे दयितः सुहृत् ।
पार्ष्णिग्राहेण हरिणा समेनाप्युपधावनैः ॥ ६ ॥

sapatnair ghātitaḥ kṣudrair
bhrātā me dayitaḥ suhṛt
pārṣṇi-grāheṇa hariṇā
samenāpy upadhāvanaiḥ

sapatnaiḥ—by the enemies*; *ghātitaḥ*—killed; *kṣudraiḥ*—insignificant in power; *bhrātā*—brother; *me*—my; *dayitaḥ*—very dear; *suhṛt*—well-wisher; *pārṣṇi-grāheṇa*—attacking from the rear; *hariṇā*—by the Supreme Personality of Godhead; *samena*—equal to everyone (both the demigods and demons); *api*—although; *upadhāvanaiḥ*—by the worshipers, the demigods.

TRANSLATION

My insignificant enemies the demigods have combined to kill my very dear and obedient well-wisher, my brother Hiraṇyākṣa. Although the Supreme Lord, Viṣṇu, is always equal to both of us—namely, the demigods and the demons—this time, being devoutly worshiped by the demigods, He has taken their side and helped them kill Hiraṇyākṣa.

---

*Both the demons and demigods understand the Supreme Personality of Godhead to be the supreme master, but the demigods follow the master whereas the demons defy Him. Thus the demigods and demons are compared to the two co-wives of one husband. Each wife is the *sapatnī* (co-wife) of the other, and therefore the word *sapatnaiḥ* is used here.

PURPORT

As stated in *Bhagavad-gītā* (9.29), *samo 'haṁ sarva-bhūteṣu:* the Lord is equal to all living entities. Since the demigods and demons are both living entities, how is it possible that the Lord was partial to one class of living beings and opposed to another? Actually it is not possible for the Lord to be partial. Nonetheless, since the demigods, the devotees, always strictly follow the Supreme Lord's orders, because of sincerity they are victorious over the demons, who know that the Supreme Lord is Viṣṇu but do not follow His instructions. Because of constantly remembering the Supreme Personality of Godhead, Viṣṇu, the demons generally attain *sāyujya-mukti* after death. The demon Hiraṇyakaśipu accused the Lord of being partial because the demigods worshiped Him, but in fact the Lord, like the government, is not partial at all. The government is not partial to any citizen, but if a citizen is law-abiding he receives abundant opportunities from the state laws to live peacefully and fulfill his real interests.

TEXTS 7–8

तस्य त्यक्तस्वभावस्य घृणेर्मायावनौकसः ।
भजन्तं भजमानस्य बालस्येवास्थिरात्मनः ॥ ७ ॥
मच्छूलभिन्नग्रीवस्य भूरिणा रुधिरेण वै ।
असृक्प्रियं तर्पयिष्ये भ्रातरं मे गतव्यथः ॥ ८ ॥

tasya tyakta-svabhāvasya
ghṛṇer māyā-vanaukasaḥ
bhajantaṁ bhajamānasya
bālasyevāsthirātmanaḥ

mac-chūla-bhinna-grīvasya
bhūriṇā rudhireṇa vai
asṛk-priyaṁ tarpayiṣye
bhrātaraṁ me gata-vyathaḥ

tasya—of Him (the Supreme Personality of Godhead); *tyakta-svabhāvasya*—who has given up His natural position (of being equal to everyone); *ghṛṇeḥ*—most abominable; *māyā*—under the influence of the illusory energy; *vana-okasaḥ*—behaving exactly like an animal in the jungle; *bhajantam*—unto the devotee engaged in devotional service; *bhajamānasya*—being worshiped; *bālasya*—a child; *iva*—like; *asthira-ātmanaḥ*—who is always restless and changing; *mat*—my; *śūla*—by the trident; *bhinna*—separated; *grīvasya*—whose neck; *bhūriṇā*—profuse; *rudhireṇa*—by blood; *vai*—indeed; *asṛk-priyam*—who was fond of blood; *tarpayiṣye*—I shall please; *bhrātaram*—brother; *me*—my; *gata-vyathaḥ*—becoming peaceful myself.

TRANSLATION

The Supreme Personality of Godhead has given up His natural tendency of equality toward the demons and demigods. Although He is the Supreme Person, now, influenced by māyā, He has assumed the form of a boar to please His devotees, the demigods, just as a restless child leans toward someone. I shall therefore sever Lord Viṣṇu's head from His trunk by my trident, and with the profuse blood from His body I shall please my brother Hiraṇyākṣa, who was so fond of sucking blood. Thus shall I too be peaceful.

PURPORT

The defect of the demoniac mentality is expressed in this verse very clearly. Hiraṇyakaśipu thought that Viṣṇu also becomes partial, like a child whose mind is not steady or resolute. The Lord can change His mind at any time, Hiraṇyakaśipu thought, and therefore His words and activities are like those of children. Actually, because the demons are ordinary human beings, their minds change, and being materially conditioned, they think that the Supreme Personality of Godhead is conditioned also. As the Lord says in *Bhagavad-gītā* (9.11), *avajānanti māṁ mūḍhā mānuṣīṁ tanum āśritam:* "Fools deride Me when I descend in a human form."

Demons always think that Viṣṇu can be killed. Therefore, being absorbed in thoughts of Viṣṇu's form to kill Him, at least they have the opportunity to think of Viṣṇu unfavorably. Although they are not devotees, their thinking of Viṣṇu is effective, and thus they generally attain *sāyujya-mukti.* Because the demons consider the Supreme Lord an ordinary living being, they think that they can kill Lord Viṣṇu as one might kill an ordinary person. Another fact disclosed herein is that demons are very much fond of sucking blood. Indeed, all of them are meat-eaters and bloodsuckers.

Hiraṇyakaśipu accused the Supreme Lord of having a restless mind like that of a small child who can be induced to do anything if simply offered some cakes and *lāḍḍus*. Indirectly, this indicates the true position of the Supreme Personality of Godhead, who says in *Bhagavad-gītā* (9.26):

patraṁ puṣpaṁ phalaṁ toyaṁ
yo me bhaktyā prayacchati
tad ahaṁ bhakty-upahṛtam
aśnāmi prayatātmanaḥ

"If one offers Me with love and devotion a leaf, a flower, fruit or water, I will accept it." The Lord accepts the offerings of devotees because of their transcendental love. Because they are in love with the Supreme Lord, they do not eat anything without offering it first to the Lord. The Lord does not hanker for a small leaf or flower; He has enough to eat. Indeed, He is feeding all living entities. Nonetheless, because He is very merciful and is *bhakta-vatsala*, very favorable to the devotees, He certainly eats whatever they offer Him with love and devotion. This quality should not be misjudged to be childish. The highest quality of the Supreme Lord is that He is *bhakta-vatsala;* in other words, He is always extremely pleased with His devotees. As for the word *māyā*, when used in reference to the dealings of the Supreme Personality of Godhead and His devotees, this word means "affection." The actions of the Lord to favor His devotees are not disqualifications but signs of His natural affection.

As for *rudhira*, or the blood of Lord Viṣṇu, since there is no possibility of severing Lord Viṣṇu's head from His body, there is no question of blood. But the garland that decorates Viṣṇu's body is as red as blood. When the demons achieve *sāyujya-mukti* and leave behind their sinful activities, they are blessed by Viṣṇu's garland, which is red like blood. After attaining *sāyujya-mukti*, the demons are sometimes promoted to the Vaikuṇṭha world, where they receive the reward of the Lord's garland *prasāda*.

TEXT 9

तस्मिन् कूटेऽहिते नष्टे कृत्तमूले वनस्पतौ ।
विटपा इव शुष्यन्ति विष्णुप्राणा दिवौकसः ॥ ९ ॥

tasmin kūṭe 'hite naṣṭe
kṛtta-mūle vanas-patau
viṭapā iva śuṣyanti
viṣṇu-prāṇā divaukasaḥ

tasmin—when He; *kūṭe*—the most deceitful; *ahite*—enemy; *naṣṭe*—is finished; *kṛtta-mūle*—having its roots cut off; *vanas-patau*—a tree; *viṭapāḥ*—the branches and leaves; *iva*—like; *śuṣyanti*—dry up; *viṣṇu-prāṇāḥ*—whose life is Lord Viṣṇu; *diva-okasaḥ*—the demigods.

TRANSLATION

When the root of a tree is cut and the tree falls down, its branches and twigs automatically dry up. Similarly, when I have killed this diplomatic Viṣṇu, the demigods, for whom Lord Viṣṇu is the life and soul, will lose the source of their life and wither away.

PURPORT

The difference between the demigods and the demons is here explained. The demigods always follow the instructions of the Supreme Personality of Godhead, whereas the demons simply plan to disturb or kill Him. Nevertheless, sometimes the demons very much appreciate the full dependence of the demigods upon the mercy of the Lord. This is indirect glorification of the demigods by the demons.

TEXT 10

तावद्यात भुवं यूयं ब्रह्मक्षत्रसमेधिताम् ।
सूदयध्वं तपोयज्ञस्वाध्यायव्रतदानिनः ॥१०॥

tāvad yāta bhuvaṁ yūyaṁ
brahma-kṣatra-samedhitām

sūdayadhvaṁ tapo-yajña-
svādhyāya-vrata-dāninaḥ

tāvat—as long as (I am engaged in the matter of killing Viṣṇu); *yāta*—go; *bhuvam*—to the planet earth; *yūyam*—all of you; *brahma-kṣatra*—of the *brāhmaṇas* and *kṣatriyas; samedhitām*—made prosperous by the activities (brahminical culture and Vedic government); *sūdayadhvam*—just destroy; *tapaḥ*—the performers of austerities; *yajña*—sacrifices; *svādhyāya*—study of Vedic knowledge; *vrata*—the regulative vows; *dāninaḥ*—and those giving charity.

TRANSLATION

While I am engaged in the business of killing Lord Viṣṇu, go down to the planet earth, which is flourishing due to brahminical culture and a kṣatriya government. These people engage in austerity, sacrifice, Vedic study, regulative vows, and charity. Destroy all the people thus engaged!

PURPORT

Hiraṇyakaśipu's main purpose was to disturb the demigods. He planned first to kill Lord Viṣṇu so that with Lord Viṣṇu's death the demigods would automatically weaken and die. Another of his plans was to disturb the residents of the planet earth. The peace and prosperity of the residents of earth, and all the other planets, were maintained by the *brāhmaṇas* and *kṣatriyas.* The Lord says in *Bhagavad-gītā* (4.13), *cātur-varṇyaṁ mayā sṛṣṭaṁ guṇa-karma-vibhāgaśaḥ:* "According to the three modes of material nature and the work ascribed to them, the four divisions of human society were created by Me." On all the planets there are different types of residents, but the Lord recommends, referring especially to the planet earth, which is inhabited by human beings, that society be divided into four *varṇas*—*brāhmaṇa, kṣatriya, vaiśya* and *śūdra.* Before the advent of Lord Kṛṣṇa on this earth, it is understood that the earth was managed by the *brāhmaṇas* and *kṣatriyas.* The duty of the *brāhmaṇas* is to cultivate *śamaḥ* (peacefulness), *damaḥ* (self-control), *titikṣā* (tolerance), *satyam* (truthfulness), *śaucam* (cleanliness) and *ārjavam* (simplicity), and then to advise the *kṣatriya* kings how to rule the country or planet. Following the instructions of the *brāhmaṇas,* the *kṣatriyas* should engage the populace in austerity, sacrifices, Vedic study and adherence to the rules and regulations established by Vedic principles. They should also arrange for charity to be given to the *brāhmaṇas, sannyāsīs* and temples. This is the godly arrangement of brahminical culture.

People are inclined to offer *yajña* because unless sacrifices are offered there will be insufficient rain (*yajñād bhavati parjanyaḥ*), which will hamper agricultural activities (*parjanyād anna-sambhavaḥ*). By introducing brahminical culture, therefore, a *kṣatriya* government should engage people in performing *yajña,* studying the *Vedas* and giving charity. Thus the people will receive their necessities for life very easily, and there will be no disturbances in society. In this regard, Lord Kṛṣṇa says in *Bhagavad-gītā* (3.12):

iṣṭān bhogān hi vo devā
dāsyante yajña-bhāvitāḥ
tair dattān apradāyaibhyo
yo bhuṅkte stena eva saḥ

"In charge of the various necessities of life, the demigods, being satisfied by the performance of *yajña* [sacrifice], supply all necessities to man. But he who enjoys these gifts, without offering them to the demigods in return, is certainly a thief."

The demigods are authorized supplying agents who act on behalf of the Supreme Personality of Godhead, Viṣṇu. Therefore, they must be satisfied by the performance of prescribed *yajñas.* In the *Vedas,* there are different kinds of *yajñas* prescribed for different kinds of demigods, but all are ultimately offered to the Supreme Personality of Godhead. For one who cannot understand what the Personality of Godhead is, sacrifice to the demigods is recommended. According to the different material qualities of the persons concerned, different types of *yajñas* are recommended in the *Vedas.* Worship of different demigods is also on the same basis—namely, according to different qualities. For example, the meat-eaters are recommended to worship the goddess Kālī, the ghastly form of material nature, and before the goddess the sacrifice of animals is recommended. But for those in the mode of goodness, the transcendental worship of Viṣṇu is recommended. Ultimately, all *yajñas* are meant for gradual promotion to the transcendental position. For ordinary men, at least five *yajñas*, known as *pañca-mahāyajña*, are necessary.

One should know, however, that all the necessities of life that human society requires are supplied by the demigod agents of the Lord. No one can manufacture anything. Consider, for example, all the eatables of human society. These eatables include grains, fruits, vegetables, milk and sugar for persons in the mode of goodness, and also eatables for the nonvegetarians, such as meats, none of which can be manufactured by men. Then again, take for example, heat, light, water and air, which are also necessities of life—none of them can be manufactured by human society. Without the Supreme Lord, there can be no profuse sunlight, moonlight, rainfall or breeze, without which no one can live. Obviously, our life is dependent on supplies from the Lord. Even for our manufacturing enterprises, we require so many raw materials like metal, sulphur, mercury, manganese and so many essentials—all of which are supplied by the agents of the Lord, with the purpose that we should make proper use of them to keep ourselves fit and healthy for the purpose of self-realization, leading to the ultimate goal of life, namely, liberation from the material struggle for existence. This aim of life is attained by performance of *yajñas*. If we forget the purpose of human life and simply take supplies from the agents of the Lord for sense gratification and become more and more entangled in material existence, which is not the purpose of creation, certainly we become thieves, and therefore we are punished by the laws of material nature. A society of thieves can never be happy, for they have no aim in life. The gross materialist thieves have no ultimate goal of life. They are simply directed to sense gratification; nor do they have knowledge of how to perform *yajñas*. Lord Caitanya, however, inaugurated the easiest performance of *yajña*, namely the *saṅkīrtana-yajña*, which can be performed by anyone in the world who accepts the principles of Kṛṣṇa consciousness.

Hiraṇyakaśipu planned to kill the inhabitants of earth so that *yajña* would stop and the demigods, being disturbed, would die automatically when Lord Viṣṇu, the *yajñeśvara*, was killed. These were the demoniac plans of Hiraṇyakaśipu, who was expert in such activities.

TEXT 11

विष्णुर्द्विजक्रियामूलो यज्ञो धर्ममयः पुमान् ।
देवर्षिपितृभूतानां धर्मस्य च परायणम् ॥११॥

viṣṇur dvija-kriyā-mūlo
yajño dharmamayaḥ pumān
devarṣi-pitṛ-bhūtānāṁ
dharmasya ca parāyaṇam

viṣṇuḥ—Lord Viṣṇu, the Supreme Personality of Godhead; *dvija*—of the *brāhmaṇas* and *kṣatriyas; kriyā-mūlaḥ*—whose root is the performance of *yajña* and the ritualistic ceremonies mentioned in the *Vedas; yajñaḥ*—personified *yajña* (Lord Viṣṇu, who is known as the *yajña-puruṣa*); *dharma-mayaḥ*—full of religious principles; *pumān*—the Supreme Person; *deva-ṛṣi*—of the demigods and great *ṛṣis* like Vyāsadeva and Nārada; *pitṛ*—of the forefathers; *bhūtānām*—and of all other living entities; *dharmasya*—of the religious principles; *ca*—also; *parāyaṇam*—the shelter.

TRANSLATION

The basic principle of brahminical culture is to satisfy Lord Viṣṇu, the personification of sacrificial and ritualistic ceremonies. Lord Viṣṇu is the personified reservoir of all religious principles, and He is the shelter of all the demigods, the great pitās, and the people in general. When the brāhmaṇas are killed, no one will exist to encourage the kṣatriyas to perform yajñas, and thus the demigods, not being appeased by yajña, will automatically die.

PURPORT

Since Viṣṇu is the central point of brahminical culture, Hiraṇyakaśipu's plan was to kill Viṣṇu, for if Viṣṇu were killed, naturally the brahminical culture would also be lost. With brahminical culture lost, *yajña* would no longer be performed, and for want of *yajña* the regular distribution of rainfall would cease (*yajñād bhavati parjanyaḥ*). Thus there would be disturbances all over the world, and naturally the demigods would be defeated. From this verse we get a clear indication of how human society is disturbed when the Vedic Āryan civilization is killed and the Vedic ritualistic ceremonies performed by the *brāhmaṇas* are stopped. *Kalau śūdra-sambhavaḥ:* because the population of the modern world consists mostly of *śūdras*, the brahminical culture is now lost and is extremely difficult to reestablish in a proper way. Therefore Lord Caitanya has recommended the chanting of the holy name of the Lord, which will revive brahminical culture very easily.

harer nāma harer nāma
harer nāmaiva kevalam
kalau nāsty eva nāsty eva
nāsty eva gatir anyathā

Because of the increment in demoniac population, people have lost brahminical culture. Nor is there a *kṣatriya* government. Instead, the government is a democracy in which any *śūdra* can be voted into taking up the governmental reigns and capture the power to rule. Because of the poisonous effects of Kali-yuga, the *śāstra* (*Bhāg.* 12.2.13) says, *dasyu-prāyeṣu rājasu:* the government will adopt the policies of *dasyus*, or plunderers. Thus there will be no instructions from the *brāhmaṇas*, and even if there are brahminical instructions, there will be no *kṣatriya* rulers who can follow them. Aside from Satya-yuga, even formerly, in the days when demons were flourishing, Hiraṇyakaśipu planned to destroy the brahminical culture and the *kṣatriya* government and thus create chaos all over the world. Although in Satya-yuga this plan was very difficult to execute, in Kali-yuga, which is full of *śūdras* and demons, the brahminical culture is lost and can be revived only by the chanting of the *mahā-mantra.* Therefore the Kṛṣṇa consciousness movement, or the Hare Kṛṣṇa movement, has been inaugurated to revive brahminical culture very easily so that people may become happy and peaceful in this life and prepare for elevation in the next. In this regard, Śrīla Madhvācārya quotes this verse from the *Brahmāṇḍa Purāṇa:*

vipra-yajñādi-mūlaṁ tu
harir ity āsuraṁ matam
harir eva hi sarvasya
mūlaṁ samyaṅ mato nṛpa

"O King, the demons think that Hari, Lord Viṣṇu, exists because of the *brāhmaṇas* and *yajña*, but factually Hari is the cause of everything including the *brāhmaṇas* and *yajña*." Therefore, through the popularizing of *hari-kīrtana*, or the *saṅkīrtana* movement, the brahminical culture and *kṣatriya* government will automatically come back, and people will be extremely happy.

TEXT 12

यत्र यत्र द्विजा गावो वेदा वर्णाश्रमक्रियाः ।
तं तं जनपदं यात सन्दीपयत वृश्चत ॥१२॥

yatra yatra dvijā gāvo
vedā varṇāśrama-kriyāḥ
taṁ taṁ janapadaṁ yāta
sandīpayata vṛścata

yatra yatra—wherever; *dvijāḥ*—the *brāhmaṇas; gāvaḥ*—the protected cows; *vedāḥ*—the Vedic culture; *varṇa-āśrama*—of the Āryan civilization of four *varṇas* and four *āśramas; kriyāḥ*—the activities; *tam tam*—that; *jana-padam*—to the city or town; *yāta*—go; *sandīpayata*—set fire; *vṛścata*—cut down (all the trees).

TRANSLATION

Immediately go wherever there is good protection for the cows and brāhmaṇas and wherever the Vedas are studied in terms of the varṇāśrama principles. Set fire to those places and cut from the roots the trees there, which are the source of life.

PURPORT

The picture of a proper human civilization is indirectly described here. In a perfect human civilization there must be a class of men fully trained as perfect *brāhmaṇas*. Similarly, there must be *kṣatriyas* to rule the country very nicely according to the injunctions of the *śāstras*, and there must be *vaiśyas* who can protect the cows. The word *gāvaḥ* indicates that cows should be given protection. Because the Vedic civilization is lost, cows are not protected, but instead indiscriminately killed in slaughterhouses. Such are the acts of demons. Therefore this is a demoniac civilization. The *varṇāśrama-dharma* mentioned here is essential for human civilization. Unless there is a *brāhmaṇa* to guide, a *kṣatriya* to rule perfectly, and a perfect *vaiśya* to produce food and protect the cows, how will people live peacefully? It is impossible.

Another point is that trees also should be given protection. During its lifetime, a tree should not be cut for industrial enterprises. In Kali-yuga, trees are indiscriminately and unnecessarily cut for industry, in particular for paper mills that manufacture a profuse quantity of paper for the publication of demoniac propaganda, nonsensical literature, huge quantities of newspapers and many other paper products. This is a sign of a demoniac civilization. The cutting of trees is prohibited unless necessary for the service of Lord Viṣṇu. *Yajñārthāt karmaṇo 'nyatra loko 'yaṁ karma-bandhanaḥ:* "Work done as a sacrifice for Lord Viṣṇu must be performed, otherwise work binds one to this material world." But if the paper mills stop producing paper, one may argue, how can our ISKCON literature be published? The answer is that the paper mills should manufacture paper only for the publication of ISKCON literature because ISKCON literature is published for the service of Lord Viṣṇu. This literature clarifies our relationship with Lord Viṣṇu, and therefore the publication of ISKCON literature is the performance of *yajña. Yajñārthāt karmaṇo 'nyatra loko 'yaṁ karma-bandhanaḥ. Yajña* must be performed, as indicated by the superior authorities. The cutting of trees simply to manufacture paper for the publication of unwanted literature is the greatest sinful act.

TEXT 13

इति ते भर्तृनिर्देशमादाय शिरसादृताः ।
तथा प्रजानां कदनं विदधुः कदनप्रियाः ॥१३॥

iti te bhartṛ-nirdeśam
ādāya śirasādṛtāḥ
tathā prajānāṁ kadanaṁ
vidadhuḥ kadana-priyāḥ

iti—thus; *te*—they; *bhartṛ*—of the master; *nirdeśam*—the direction; *ādāya*—receiving; *śirasā*—with their heads; *ādṛtāḥ*—respecting;

tathā—so also; *prajānām*—of all the citizens; *kadanam*—persecution; *vidadhuḥ*—executed; *kadana-priyāḥ*—who are expert in persecuting others.

TRANSLATION

Thus the demons, being fond of disastrous activities, took Hiraṇyakaśipu's instructions on their heads with great respect and offered him obeisances. According to his directions, they engaged in envious activities directed against all living beings.

PURPORT

The followers of demoniac principles, as described here, are thoroughly envious of the general populace. In the present day, scientific advancement exemplifies such envy. The discovery of nuclear energy has been disastrous to people in general because demons all over the world are manufacturing nuclear weapons. The word *kadana-priyāḥ* is very significant in this regard. The demoniac persons who want to kill the Vedic culture are extremely envious of the feeble citizens, and they act in such a way that ultimately their discoveries will be inauspicious for everyone (*jagato 'hitāḥ*). The Sixteenth Chapter of *Bhagavad-gītā* fully explains how the demons engage in sinful activities for the destruction of the populace.

TEXT 14

पुरग्रामव्रजोद्यानक्षेत्रारामाश्रमाकरान् ।
खेटखर्वटघोषांश्च ददहुः पत्तनानि च ॥१४॥

pura-grāma-vrajodyāna-
kṣetrārāmāśramākarān
kheṭa-kharvaṭa-ghoṣāṁś ca
dadahuḥ pattanāni ca

pura—cities and towns; *grāma*—villages; *vraja*—pasturing grounds; *udyāna*—gardens; *kṣetra*—agricultural fields; *ārāma*—natural forests; *āśrama*—hermitages of saintly persons; *ākarān*—and mines (that produce valuable metals to maintain brahminical culture); *kheṭa*—farm villages; *kharvaṭa*—mountain villages; *ghoṣān*—the little villages of cowherds; *ca*—and; *dadahuḥ*—they burned; *pattanāni*—the capitals; *ca*—also.

TRANSLATION

The demons set fire to the cities, villages, pasturing grounds, cowpens, gardens, agricultural fields and natural forests. They burned the hermitages of the saintly persons, the important mines that produced valuable metals, the residential quarters of the agriculturalists, the mountain villages, and the villages of the cow protectors, the cowherd men. They also burned the government capitals.

PURPORT

The word *udyāna* refers to places where trees are especially grown to produce fruits and flowers, which are most important for human civilization. Kṛṣṇa says in *Bhagavad-gītā* (9.26):

patraṁ puṣpaṁ phalaṁ toyaṁ
yo me bhaktyā prayacchati
tad ahaṁ bhakty-upahṛtam
aśnāmi prayatātmanaḥ

"If one offers Me with love and devotion a leaf, a flower, fruit or water, I will accept it." Fruits and flowers are very much pleasing to the Lord. If one wants to please the Supreme Personality of Godhead, he can simply offer fruits and flowers, and the Lord will be pleased to accept them. Our only duty is to please the Supreme Godhead (*saṁsiddhir hari-toṣaṇam*). Whatever we do and whatever our occupation, our main purpose should be to please the Supreme Lord. All the paraphernalia mentioned in this verse is especially meant for the satisfaction of the Lord, not the satisfaction of one's senses. The government—indeed, the entire society—should be structured in such a way that everyone can be trained to satisfy the Supreme Personality of Godhead. But unfortunately, especially in this age, *na te viduḥ svārtha-gatiṁ hi viṣṇum:* people do not know that the highest goal of human life is to please Lord Viṣṇu. On the contrary, like demons, they simply plan to kill Viṣṇu and be happy by sense gratification.

TEXT 15

केचित्खनित्रैर्बिभिदुः सेतुप्राकारगोपुरान् ।
आजीव्यांश्चिच्छिदुर्वृक्षान् केचित्परशुपाणयः ।
प्रादहञ् शरणान्येके प्रजानां ज्वलितोल्मुकैः ॥१५॥

kecit khanitrair bibhiduḥ
setu-prākāra-gopurān
ājīvyāṁś cicchidur vṛkṣān
kecit paraśu-pāṇayaḥ
prādahañ śaraṇāny eke
prajānāṁ jvalitolmukaiḥ

kecit—some of the demons; *khanitraiḥ*—with digging instruments; *bibhiduḥ*—broke to pieces; *setu*—bridges; *prākāra*—protective walls; *gopurān*—city gates; *ājīvyān*—the source of livelihood; *cicchiduḥ*—cut down; *vṛkṣān*—trees; *kecit*—some; *paraśu-pāṇayaḥ*—taking axes in hand; *prādahan*—burned down; *śaraṇāni*—the dwellings; *eke*—other demons; *prajānām*—of the citizens; *jvalita*—blazing; *ulmukaiḥ*—with firebrands.

TRANSLATION

Some of the demons took digging instruments and broke down the bridges, the protective walls and the gates [gopuras] of the cities. Some took axes and began cutting the important trees that produced mango, jackfruit and other sources of food. Some of the demons took firebrands and set fire to the residential quarters of the citizens.

PURPORT

The cutting of trees is generally prohibited. In particular, trees that produce nice fruit for the maintenance of human society should not be cut. In different countries there are different types of fruit trees. In India the mango and jackfruit trees are prominent, and in other places there are mango trees, jackfruit trees, coconut trees and berry trees. Any tree that produces nice fruit for the maintenance of the people should not be cut at all. This is a śāstric injunction.

TEXT 16

एवं विप्रकृते लोके दैत्येन्द्रानुचरैर्मुहुः ।
दिवं देवाः परित्यज्य भुवि चेरुरलक्षिताः ॥१६॥

evaṁ viprakṛte loke
daityendrānucarair muhuḥ
divaṁ devāḥ parityajya
bhuvi cerur alakṣitāḥ

evam—thus; *viprakṛte*—being disturbed; *loke*—when all the people; *daitya-indra-anucaraiḥ*—by the followers of Hiraṇyakaśipu, the King of the Daityas; *muhuḥ*—again and again; *divam*—the heavenly planets; *devāḥ*—the demigods; *parityajya*—giving up; *bhuvi*—on the planet earth; *ceruḥ*—wandered (to see the extent of the disturbances); *alakṣitāḥ*—unseen by the demons.

TRANSLATION

Thus disturbed again and again by the unnatural occurrences caused by the followers of Hiraṇyakaśipu, all the people had to cease the activities of Vedic culture. Not receiving the results of yajña, the demigods also became disturbed. They left their residential quarters in the heavenly planets and, unobserved by the demons, began wandering on the planet earth to see the disasters.

PURPORT

As stated in *Bhagavad-gītā*, the performance of *yajña* brings reciprocal good fortune for both the human beings and the demigods. When the performances of *yajña* were stopped by the disturbances of the demons, the demigods were naturally bereft of the results of *yajña* and hampered in executing their respective duties. Therefore they came down to the planet earth to see how people had become disturbed and to consider what to do.

TEXT 17

हिरण्यकशिपुर्भ्रातुः सम्परेतस्य दुःखितः ।
कृत्वा कटोदकादीनि भ्रातृपुत्रानसान्त्वयत् ॥१७॥

hiraṇyakaśipur bhrātuḥ
samparetasya duḥkhitaḥ
kṛtvā kaṭodakādīni
bhrātṛ-putrān asāntvayat

hiraṇyakaśipuḥ—Hiraṇyakaśipu; *bhrātuḥ*—of the brother; *samparetasya*—deceased; *duḥkhitaḥ*—being very much distressed; *kṛtvā*—performing; *kaṭodaka-ādīni*—ceremonies observed after a death; *bhrātṛ-putrān*—the sons of his brother; *asāntvayat*—pacified.

TRANSLATION

After performing the ritualistic observances for the death of his brother, Hiraṇyakaśipu, being extremely unhappy, tried to pacify his nephews.

TEXTS 18–19

शकुनिं शम्बरं धृष्टिं भूतसन्तापनं वृकम् ।
कालनाभं महानाभं हरिश्मश्रुमथोत्कचम् ॥१८॥
तन्मातरं रुषाभानुं दितिं च जननीं गिरा ।
श्लक्ष्णया देशकालज्ञ इदमाह जनेश्वर ॥१९॥

śakuniṁ śambaraṁ dhṛṣṭiṁ
bhūtasantāpanaṁ vṛkam
kālanābhaṁ mahānābhaṁ
hariśmaśrum athotkacam

tan-mātaraṁ ruṣābhānuṁ
ditiṁ ca jananīṁ girā
ślakṣṇayā deśa-kāla-jña
idam āha janeśvara

śakunim—Śakuni; *śambaram*—Śambara; *dhṛṣṭim*—Dhṛṣṭi; *bhūtasantāpanam*—Bhūtasantāpana; *vṛkam*—Vṛka; *kālanābham*—Kālanābha; *mahānābham*—Mahānābha; *hariśmaśrum*—Hariśmaśru; *atha*—as well as; *utkacam*—Utkaca; *tat-mātaram*—their mother; *ruṣābhānum*—Ruṣābhānu; *ditim*—Diti; *ca*—and; *jananīm*—his own mother; *girā*—by words; *ślakṣṇayā*—very sweet; *deśa-kāla-jñaḥ*—who was expert in understanding the time and situation; *idam*—this; *āha*—said; *jana-īśvara*—O King.

TRANSLATION

O King, Hiraṇyakaśipu was extremely angry, but since he was a great politician, he knew how to act according to the time and situation. With sweet words he began pacifying his nephews, whose names were Śakuni, Śambara, Dhṛṣṭi, Bhūtasantāpana, Vṛka, Kālanābha, Mahānābha, Hariśmaśru and Utkaca. He also consoled their mother, his sister-in-law, Ruṣābhānu, as well as his own mother, Diti. He spoke to them all as follows.

TEXT 20

श्रीहिरण्यकशिपुरुवाच

अम्बाम्ब हे वधूः पुत्रा वीरं मार्हथ शोचितुम् ।
रिपोरभिमुखे श्लाघ्यः शूराणां वध ईप्सितः ॥२०॥

śrī-hiraṇyakaśipur uvāca
ambāmba he vadhūḥ putrā
vīraṁ mārhatha śocitum
ripor abhimukhe ślāghyaḥ
śūrāṇāṁ vadha īpsitaḥ

śrī-hiraṇyakaśipuḥ uvāca—Hiraṇyakaśipu said; *amba amba*—my mother, my mother; *he*—O; *vadhūḥ*—my sister-in-law; *putrāḥ*—O sons of my brother; *vīram*—the hero; *mā*—not; *arhatha*—you deserve; *śocitum*—to lament about; *ripoḥ*—of the enemy; *abhimukhe*—in front; *ślāghyaḥ*—glorious; *śūrāṇām*—of those who are actually great; *vadhaḥ*—killing; *īpsitaḥ*—desired.

TRANSLATION

Hiraṇyakaśipu said: My dear mother, sister-in-law and nephews, you should not lament for the death of the great hero, for a hero's death in front of his enemy is glorious and desirable.

TEXT 21

भूतानामिह संवासः प्रपायामिव सुव्रते ।
दैवेनैकत्र नीतानामुन्नीतानां स्वकर्मभिः ॥२१॥

bhūtānām iha saṁvāsaḥ
prapāyām iva suvrate
daivenaikatra nītānām
unnītānāṁ sva-karmabhiḥ

bhūtānām—of all living entities; *iha*—in this material world; *saṁvāsaḥ*—the living together; *prapāyām*—in a place for drinking cold water; *iva*—like; *su-vrate*—O my gentle mother; *daivena*—by the superior arrangement; *ekatra*—in one place; *nītānām*—of those brought; *unnītānām*—of those led apart; *sva-karmabhiḥ*—by their own reactions.

TRANSLATION

My dear mother, in a restaurant or place for drinking cold water, many travelers are brought together, and after drinking water they continue to their respective destinations. Similarly, living entities join together in a family, and later, as a result of their own actions, they are led apart to their destinations.

PURPORT

prakṛteḥ kriyamāṇāni
guṇaiḥ karmāṇi sarvaśaḥ
ahaṅkāra-vimūḍhātmā
kartāham iti manyate

"The bewildered soul, under the influence of the three modes of material nature, thinks himself the doer of activities, which are in actuality carried out by nature." (Bg. 3.27) All living entities act exactly according to the directions of *prakṛti*, material nature, because in the material world we are fully under a higher control. All the living entities in this material world have come here only because they wanted to be equal to

Kṛṣṇa in enjoyment and have thus been sent here to be conditioned by material nature in different degrees. In the material world a so-called family is a combination of several persons in one home to fulfill the terms of their imprisonment. As criminal prisoners scatter as soon as their terms are over and they are released, all of us who have temporarily assembled as family members will continue to our respective destinations. Another example given is that family members are like straws carried together by the waves of a river. Sometimes such straws mix together in whirlpools, and later, dispersed again by the same waves, they float alone in the water.

Although Hiraṇyakaśipu was a demon, he had Vedic knowledge and understanding. Thus the advice given to his family members—his sister-in-law, mother and nephews—was quite sound. The demons are considered highly elevated in knowledge, but because they do not use their good intelligence for the service of the Lord, they are called demons. The demigods, however, act very intelligently to satisfy the Supreme Personality of Godhead. This is confirmed in *Śrīmad-Bhāgavatam* (1.2.13) as follows:

ataḥ pumbhir dvija-śreṣṭhā
varṇāśrama-vibhāgaśaḥ
svanuṣṭhitasya dharmasya
saṁsiddhir hari-toṣaṇam

"O best among the twiceborn, it is therefore concluded that the highest perfection one can achieve, by discharging his prescribed duties [*dharma*] according to caste divisions and orders of life, is to please the Lord Hari." To become a demigod or to become godly, whatever one's occupation, one must satisfy the Supreme Personality of Godhead.

TEXT 22

नित्य आत्माव्ययः शुद्धः सर्वगः सर्ववित्परः ।
धत्तेऽसावात्मनो लिङ्गं मायया विसृजन्गुणान् ॥२२॥

nitya ātmāvyayaḥ śuddhaḥ
sarvagaḥ sarva-vit paraḥ

dhatte 'sāv ātmano liṅgaṁ
māyayā visṛjan guṇān

nityaḥ—eternal; *ātmā*—spirit soul; *avyayaḥ*—inexhaustible; *śuddhaḥ*—with no material tinge; *sarva-gaḥ*—qualified to go anywhere in the material or spiritual worlds; *sarva-vit*—full of knowledge; *paraḥ*—transcendental to material conditions; *dhatte*—accepts; *asau*—that *ātmā*, or living being; *ātmanaḥ*—of the self; *liṅgam*—a body; *māyayā*—by the material energy; *visṛjan*—creating; *guṇān*—various material qualities.

TRANSLATION

The spirit soul, the living entity, has no death, for he is eternal and inexhaustible. Being free from material contamination, he can go anywhere in the material or spiritual worlds. He is fully aware and completely different from the material body, but because of being misled by misuse of his slight independence, he is obliged to accept subtle and gross bodies created by the material energy and thus be subjected to so-called material happiness and distress. Therefore, no one should lament for the passing of the spirit soul from the body.

PURPORT

Hiraṇyakaśipu very intelligently described the position of the soul. The soul is never the body, but is always completely different from the body. Being eternal and inexhaustible, the soul has no death, but when the same pure soul desires to enjoy the material world independently, he is placed under the conditions of material nature and must therefore accept a certain type of body and suffer the pains and pleasures thereof. This is also described by Kṛṣṇa in *Bhagavad-gītā* (13.22). *Kāraṇaṁ guṇa-saṅgo 'sya sad-asad-yoni-janmasu:* the living entity is born in different families or species of life because of being infected by the modes of material nature. When conditioned by material nature, the living entity must accept a certain type of body, which is offered by nature under the direction of the Supreme Lord.

īśvaraḥ sarva-bhūtānāṁ
hṛd-deśe 'rjuna tiṣṭhati

bhrāmayan sarva-bhūtāni
yantrārūḍhāni māyayā

"The Supreme Lord is situated in everyone's heart, O Arjuna, and is directing the wanderings of all living entities, who are seated as on a machine, made of the material energy." (Bg. 18.61) The body is just like a machine, and according to the living entity's *karma*, he is offered a particular type of machine to move here and there under the control of material nature. This continues until he surrenders to the Supreme Personality of Godhead (*mām eva ye prapadyante māyām etāṁ taranti te*). Until he surrenders, the conditioned soul is carried from life to life by the arrangement of material nature.

TEXT 23

यथाम्भसा प्रचलता तरवोऽपि चला इव ।
चक्षुषा भ्राम्यमाणेन दृश्यते चलतीव भूः ॥२३॥

yathāmbhasā pracalatā
taravo 'pi calā iva
cakṣuṣā bhrāmyamāṇena
dṛśyate calatīva bhūḥ

yathā—just as; *ambhasā*—by water; *pracalatā*—moving; *taravaḥ*—the trees (on the bank of the river); *api*—also; *calāḥ*—moving; *iva*—as if; *cakṣuṣā*—by the eye; *bhrāmyamāṇena*—moving; *dṛśyate*—is seen; *calatī*—moving; *iva*—as if; *bhūḥ*—the ground.

TRANSLATION

Because of the movements of the water, the trees on the bank of a river, when reflected on the water, seem to move. Similarly, when the eyes move because of some mental derangement, the land appears to move also.

PURPORT

Sometimes, because of mental derangement, the land appears to be moving. A drunkard, for example, or a person with heart disease, sometimes feels that the land is moving. Similarly, the reflections of trees in a flowing river also appear to move. These are the actions of *māyā*. Actually the living entity does not move (*sthāṇur acalo 'yam*). The living entity does not take birth or accept death, but because of the transient subtle and gross bodies, the living entity appears to move from one place to another or be dead and gone forever. As the great Bengali Vaiṣṇava poet, Jagadānanda Paṇḍita, has said:

piśācī pāile yena mati-cchanna haya
māyā-grasta jīvera haya se bhāva udaya

According to this statement from the *Prema-vivarta*, when a living entity is conditioned by material nature, he is exactly like a person haunted by a ghost. One should therefore understand the fixed position of the spirit soul and how he is carried away by the waves of material nature to different bodies and different situations under lamentation and hankering. One achieves the success of life when he understands the constitutional position of his self and is undisturbed by the conditions created by material nature (*prakṛteḥ kriyamāṇāni guṇaiḥ karmāṇi sarvaśaḥ*).

TEXT 24

एवं गुणैर्भ्राम्यमाणे मनस्यविकलः पुमान् ।
याति तत्साम्यतां भद्रे ह्यलिङ्गो लिङ्गवानिव ।।२४।।

evaṁ guṇair bhrāmyamāṇe
manasy avikalaḥ pumān
yāti tat-sāmyatāṁ bhadre
hy aliṅgo liṅgavān iva

evam—in this way; *guṇaiḥ*—by the modes of material nature; *bhrāmyamāṇe*—when shaken; *manasi*—the mind; *avikalaḥ*—changeless; *pumān*—the living entity; *yāti*—approaches; *tat-sāmyatām*—the same condition of agitation as the mind; *bhadre*—O my gentle mother; *hi*—indeed; *aliṅgaḥ*—without a subtle or gross body; *liṅga-vān*—possessing a material body; *iva*—as if.

TRANSLATION

In the same way, O my gentle mother, when the mind is agitated by the movements of the modes of material nature, the living entity, although freed from all the different phases of the subtle and gross bodies, thinks that he has changed from one condition to another.

PURPORT

As stated in *Śrīmad-Bhāgavatam* (10.84.13):

yasyātma-buddhiḥ kuṇape tri-dhātuke
sva-dhīḥ kalatrādiṣu bhauma-ijya-dhīḥ
yat-tīrtha-buddhiḥ salile na karhicij
janeṣv abhijñeṣu sa eva go-kharaḥ

"A human being who identifies the body made of three elements as the self, who considers the by-products of the body to be his kinsmen, who considers the land of his birth worshipable, and who goes to a place of pilgrimage simply to bathe rather than to meet men of transcendental knowledge there, is to be considered like a cow or an ass." Although Hiraṇyakaśipu was a great demon, he was not as foolish as the population of the modern world. Hiraṇyakaśipu had clear knowledge of the spirit soul and the subtle and gross bodies, but now we are so degraded that everyone, including the exalted scientists, philosophers and other leaders, is under the bodily conception of life, which is condemned in the *śāstras. Sa eva go-kharaḥ:* such persons are nothing but cows and asses.

Hiraṇyakaśipu advised his family members that although the gross body of his brother Hiraṇyākṣa was dead and they were aggrieved because of this, they should not lament for the great soul of Hiraṇyākṣa, who had already attained his next destination. *Ātmā,* the spirit soul, is always unchanged (*avikalaḥ pumān*). We are spirit souls, but when carried away by mental activities (*manodharma*), we suffer from so-called material conditions of life. This generally happens to nondevotees. *Harāv abhaktasya kuto mahad-guṇāḥ:* nondevotees may possess exalted material qualities, but because they are foolish they have no good qualifications. The designations of the conditioned soul in the material world are decorations of the dead body. The conditioned soul has no information of the spirit and its exalted existence beyond the effects of the material condition.

TEXTS 25–26

एष आत्मविपर्यासो ह्यलिङ्गे लिङ्गभावना ।
एष प्रियाप्रियैर्योगो वियोगः कर्मसंसृतिः ॥२५॥
सम्भवश्च विनाशश्च शोकश्च विविधः स्मृतः ।
अविवेकश्च चिन्ता च विवेकास्मृतिरेव च ॥२६॥

eṣa ātma-viparyāso
hy aliṅge liṅga-bhāvanā
eṣa priyāpriyair yogo
viyogaḥ karma-saṁsṛtiḥ

sambhavaś ca vināśaś ca
śokaś ca vividhaḥ smṛtaḥ
avivekaś ca cintā ca
vivekāsmṛtir eva ca

esaḥ—this; *ātma-viparyāsaḥ*—bewilderment of the living being; *hi*—indeed; *aliṅge*—in that which does not possess a material body; *liṅga-bhāvanā*—accepting the material body to be the self; *eṣaḥ*—this; *priya*—with those who are very dear; *apriyaiḥ*—and with those who are not dear (enemies, those not in the family, etc.); *yogaḥ*—connection; *viyogaḥ*—separation; *karma*—the fruits of action; *saṁsṛtiḥ*—the material condition of life; *sambhavaḥ*—accepting birth; *ca*—and; *vināśaḥ*—accepting death; *ca*—and; *śokaḥ*—lamentation; *ca*—and; *vividhaḥ*—varieties; *smṛtaḥ*—mentioned in scripture; *avivekaḥ*—lack of discrimination; *ca*—and; *cintā*—anxiety; *ca*—also; *viveka*—of proper discrimination; *asmṛtiḥ*—forgetfulness; *eva*—indeed; *ca*—also.

TRANSLATION

In his bewildered state, the living entity, accepting the body and mind to be the self, considers some people to be his kinsmen and

others to be outsiders. Because of this misconception, he suffers. Indeed, the accumulation of such concocted material ideas is the cause of suffering and so-called happiness in the material world. The conditioned soul thus situated must take birth in different species and work in various types of consciousness, thus creating new bodies. This continued material life is called saṁsāra. Birth, death, lamentation, foolishness and anxiety are due to such material considerations. Thus we sometimes come to a proper understanding and sometimes fall again to a wrong conception of life.

TEXT 27

अत्राप्युदाहरन्तीममितिहासं पुरातनम् ।
यमस्य प्रेतबन्धूनां संवादं तं निबोधत ॥२७॥

atrāpy udāharantīmam
itihāsaṁ purātanam
yamasya preta-bandhūnāṁ
saṁvādaṁ taṁ nibodhata

atra—in this connection; *api*—indeed; *udāharanti*—they cite; *imam*—this; *itihāsam*—history; *purātanam*—very old; *yamasya*—of Yamarāja, the superintendent of death, who gives judgment after death; *preta-bandhūnām*—of the friends of a dead man; *saṁvādam*—discussion; *tam*—that; *nibodhata*—try to understand.

TRANSLATION

In this regard, an example is given from an old history. This involves a discourse between Yamarāja and the friends of a dead person. Please hear it attentively.

PURPORT

The words *itihāsaṁ purātanam* mean "an old history." The *Purāṇas* are not chronologically recorded, but the incidents mentioned in the *Purāṇas* are actual histories of bygone ages. *Śrīmad-Bhāgavatam* is the *Mahā-purāṇa*, the essence of all the *Purāṇas*. The Māyāvādī scholars do not accept the *Purāṇas*, but Śrīla Madhvācārya and all other authorities accept them as the authoritative histories of the world.

TEXT 28

उशीनरेष्वभूद्राजा सुयज्ञ इति विश्रुतः ।
सपत्नैर्निहतो युद्धे ज्ञातयस्तमुपासत ॥२८॥

uśīnareṣv abhūd rājā
suyajña iti viśrutaḥ
sapatnair nihato yuddhe
jñātayas tam upāsata

uśīnareṣu—in the state known as Uśīnara; *abhūt*—there was; *rājā*—a king; *suyajñaḥ*—Suyajña; *iti*—thus; *viśrutaḥ*—celebrated; *sapatnaiḥ*—by enemies; *nihataḥ*—killed; *yuddhe*—in war; *jñātayaḥ*—the kinsmen; *tam*—him; *upāsata*—sat around.

TRANSLATION

In the state known as Uśīnara there was a celebrated king named Suyajña. When the King was killed in battle by his enemies, his kinsmen sat down around the dead body and began to lament the death of their friend.

TEXTS 29–31

विशीर्णरत्नकवचं विभ्रष्टाभरणस्रजम् ।
शरनिर्भिन्नहृदयं शयानमसृगाविलम् ॥२९॥
प्रकीर्णकेशं ध्वस्ताक्षं रभसा दष्टदच्छदम् ।
रजःकुण्ठमुखाम्भोजं छिन्नायुधभुजं मृधे ॥३०॥
उशीनरेन्द्रं विधिना तथा कृतं
पतिं महिष्यः प्रसमीक्ष्य दुःखिताः ।
हताः स्म नाथेति करैरुरो भृशं
घ्नन्त्यो मुहुस्तत्पदयोरुपापतन् ॥३१॥

viśīrṇa-ratna-kavacaṁ
vibhraṣṭābharaṇa-srajam
śara-nirbhinna-hṛdayaṁ
śayānam asṛg-āvilam

prakīrṇa-keśaṁ dhvastākṣaṁ
rabhasā daṣṭa-dacchadam
rajaḥ-kuṇṭha-mukhāmbhojaṁ
chinnāyudha-bhujaṁ mṛdhe

uśīnarendraṁ vidhinā tathā kṛtaṁ
patiṁ mahiṣyaḥ prasamīkṣya duḥkhitāḥ
hatāḥ sma nātheti karair uro bhṛśaṁ
ghnantyo muhus tat-padayor upāpatan

viśīrṇa—scattered here and there; *ratna*—made of jewels; *kavacam*—protective armor; *vibhraṣṭa*—fallen off; *ābharaṇa*—ornaments; *srajam*—garlands; *śara-nirbhinna*—pierced by arrows; *hṛdayam*—the heart; *śayānam*—lying down; *asṛk-āvilam*—smeared with blood; *prakīrṇa-keśam*—his hair loosened and scattered; *dhvasta-akṣam*—his eyes obscured; *rabhasā*—with anger; *daṣṭa*—bitten; *dac-chadam*—his lips; *rajaḥ-kuṇṭha*—covered with dust; *mukha-ambhojam*—his face, which had formerly resembled a lotus flower; *chinna*—cut off; *āyudha-bhujam*—his arms and weapons; *mṛdhe*—on the battlefield; *uśīnara-indram*—the master of the state of Uśīnara; *vidhinā*—by providence; *tathā*—thus; *kṛtam*—forced into this position; *patim*—the husband; *mahiṣyaḥ*—the queens; *prasamīkṣya*—seeing; *duḥkhitāḥ*—very much aggrieved; *hatāḥ*—killed; *sma*—certainly; *nātha*—O husband; *iti*—thus; *karaiḥ*—with the hands; *uraḥ*—the breast; *bhṛśam*—constantly; *ghnantyaḥ*—pounding; *muhuḥ*—again and again; *tat-padayoḥ*—at the feet of the King; *upāpatan*—fell down.

TRANSLATION

His golden, bejeweled armor smashed, his ornaments and garlands fallen from their places, his hair scattered and his eyes lusterless, the slain King lay on the battlefield, his entire body

smeared with blood, his heart pierced by the arrows of the enemy. When he died he had wanted to show his prowess, and thus he had bitten his lips, and his teeth remained in that position. His beautiful lotuslike face was now black and covered with dust from the battlefield. His arms, with his sword and other weapons, were cut and broken. When the queens of the King of Uśīnara saw their husband lying in that position, they began crying, "O lord, now that you have been killed, we also have been killed." Repeating these words again and again, they fell down, pounding their breasts, at the feet of the dead King.

PURPORT

As stated here, *rabhasā daṣṭa-dacchadam:* the dead King, while fighting in anger, bit his lips to show his prowess, but nonetheless he was killed by providence (*vidhinā*). This proves that we are controlled by higher authorities; our personal power or endeavor is not always supreme. We must therefore accept the position offered to us by the order of the Supreme.

TEXT 32

रुदत्य उच्चैर्दयिताङ्घ्रिपङ्कजं
सिञ्चन्त्य अस्रैः कुचकुङ्कुमारुणैः ।
विस्रस्तकेशाभरणाः शुचं नृणां
सृजन्त्य आक्रन्दनया विलेपिरे ॥३२॥

rudatya uccair dayitāṅghri-paṅkajaṁ
siñcantya asraiḥ kuca-kuṅkumāruṇaiḥ
visrasta-keśābharaṇāḥ śucaṁ nṛṇāṁ
sṛjantya ākrandanayā vilepire

rudatyaḥ—crying; *uccaiḥ*—very loudly; *dayita*—of their beloved husband; *aṅghri-paṅkajam*—the lotus feet; *siñcantyaḥ*—moistening; *asraiḥ*—with tears; *kuca-kuṅkuma-aruṇaiḥ*—which were red from the *kuṅkuma* covering their breasts; *visrasta*—scattered; *keśa*—hair; *ābharaṇāḥ*—and ornaments; *śucam*—grief; *nṛṇām*—of the people in general; *sṛjantyaḥ*—creating; *ākrandanayā*—by crying very pitiably; *vilepire*—began to lament.

TRANSLATION

As the queens loudly cried, their tears glided down their breasts, becoming reddened by kuṅkuma powder, and fell upon the lotus feet of their husband. Their hair became disarrayed, their ornaments fell, and in a way that evoked sympathy from the hearts of others, the queens began lamenting their husband's death.

TEXT 33

अहो विधात्राकरुणेन नः प्रभो
भवान् प्रणीतो दृगगोचरां दशाम् ।
उशीनराणामसि वृत्तिदः पुरा
कृतोऽधुना येन शुचां विवर्धनः ॥३३॥

aho vidhātrākaruṇena naḥ prabho
bhavān praṇīto dṛg-agocarāṁ daśām
uśīnarāṇām asi vṛttidaḥ purā
kṛto 'dhunā yena śucāṁ vivardhanaḥ

aho—alas; *vidhātrā*—by providence; *akaruṇena*—who is merciless; *naḥ*—our; *prabho*—O lord; *bhavān*—Your Lordship; *praṇītaḥ*—taken away; *dṛk*—of sight; *agocarām*—beyond the range; *daśām*—to a state; *uśīnarāṇām*—to the inhabitants of the state of Uśīnara; *asi*—you were; *vṛtti-daḥ*—giving livelihood; *purā*—formerly; *kṛtaḥ*—finished; *adhunā*—now; *yena*—by whom; *śucām*—of lamentation; *vivardhanaḥ*—increasing.

TRANSLATION

O lord, you have now been removed by cruel providence to a state beyond our sight. You had previously sustained the livelihood of the inhabitants of Uśīnara, and thus they were happy, but your condition now is the cause of their unhappiness.

TEXT 34

त्वया कृतज्ञेन वयं महीपते
कथं विना स्याम सुहृत्तमेन ते ।
तत्रानुयानं तव वीर पादयोः
शुश्रूषतीनां दिश यत्र यास्यसि ॥३४॥

tvayā kṛtajñena vayaṁ mahī-pate
kathaṁ vinā syāma suhṛttamena te
tatrānuyānaṁ tava vīra pādayoḥ
śuśrūṣatīnāṁ diśa yatra yāsyasi

tvayā—you; *kṛtajñena*—a most grateful personality; *vayam*—we; *mahī-pate*—O King; *katham*—how; *vinā*—without; *syāma*—shall exist; *suhṛt-tamena*—the best of our friends; *te*—of you; *tatra*—there; *anuyānam*—the following; *tava*—of you; *vīra*—O hero; *pādayoḥ*—of the lotus feet; *śuśrūṣatīnām*—of those engaging in the service; *diśa*—please order; *yatra*—where; *yāsyasi*—you will go.

TRANSLATION

O King, O hero, you were a very grateful husband and the most sincere friend of all of us. How shall we exist without you? O hero, wherever you are going, please direct us there so that we may follow in your footsteps and engage again in your service. Let us go along with you!

PURPORT

Formerly, a *kṣatriya* king was generally the husband of many wives, and after the death of the king, especially in the battlefield, all the queens would agree to accept *saha-māraṇa*, dying with the husband who was their life. When Pāṇḍu Mahārāja, the father of the Pāṇḍavas, died, his two wives—namely, the mother of Yudhiṣṭhira, Bhīma and Arjuna and the mother of Nakula and Sahadeva—were both ready to die in the fire with their husband. Later, after a compromise was arranged, Kuntī stayed alive to care for the little children, and the other wife, Mādrī, was allowed to die with her husband. This system of *saha-māraṇa* continued in India even until the time of British rule, but later it was discouraged, since the attitude of wives gradually changed with the advancement of Kali-yuga. Thus the system of *saha-māraṇa* has practically been abolished. Nevertheless, within the past fifty years I have seen the wife of a medical practitioner voluntarily accept death immediately when her husband died. Both the husband and wife were taken in procession in the mourning cart. Such intense love of a chaste wife for her husband is a special case.

TEXT 35

एवं विलपतीनां वै परिगृह्य मृतं पतिम् ।
अनिच्छतीनां निर्हारमर्कोऽस्तं संन्यवर्तत ॥३५॥

evaṁ vilapatīnāṁ vai
parigṛhya mṛtaṁ patim
anicchatīnāṁ nirhāram
arko 'staṁ sannyavartata

evam—thus; *vilapatīnām*—of the lamenting queens; *vai*—indeed; *parigṛhya*—taking on their laps; *mṛtam*—the dead; *patim*—husband; *anicchatīnām*—not desiring; *nirhāram*—the carrying out of the body for the funeral ceremony; *arkaḥ*—the sun; *astam*—the setting position; *sannyavartata*—passed away.

TRANSLATION

The time was appropriate for the body to be burned, but the queens, not allowing it to be taken away, continued lamenting for the dead body, which they kept on their laps. In the meantime, the sun completed its movements for setting in the west.

PURPORT

According to the Vedic system, if a person dies during the daytime it is customary for his funeral ceremony to be performed before the sun sets, regardless of whether he is burned or buried, and if he dies at night the funeral must be completed before the next sunrise. Apparently the queens continued lamenting for the dead body, the lump of matter, and would not allow it to be taken away for burning. This illustrates the strong grip of illusion among foolish persons who consider the body the self. Women are generally considered less intelligent. Because of ignorance only, the queens thought of the dead body as their husband and somehow or other thought that if the body were kept their husband would remain with them. Such a conception of the self is certainly for *go-khara*—cows and asses. We have actually seen that sometimes when a cow's calf has died the milkman cheats the cow by presenting before her the dead body of her calf. Thus the cow, who would not otherwise allow milking, licks the dead body of the calf and allows herself to be milked. This substantiates the description of the *śāstra* that a foolish man in the bodily concept of life is like a cow. Not only do foolish men and women consider the body the self, but we have even seen that the dead body of a so-called *yogī* was kept for days by his disciples, who thought that their *guru* was in *samādhi*. When decomposition began and a bad smell unfortunately began to overwhelm the yogic power, the disciples allowed the dead body of the so-called *yogī* to be burned. Thus the bodily concept of life is extremely strong among foolish persons, who are compared to cows and asses. Nowadays, great scientists are trying to freeze dead bodies so that in the future these frozen bodies may again be brought to life. The incident narrated by Hiraṇyakaśipu from history must have taken place millions of years ago because Hiraṇyakaśipu lived millions of years ago and was even then quoting from history. Thus the incident occurred before Hiraṇyakaśipu's lifetime, but the same ignorance in the bodily concept of life is still prevalent, not only among laymen but even among scientists who think they will be able to revive frozen corpses.

Apparently the queens did not want to deliver the dead body for burning because they were afraid of dying with the dead body of their husband.

TEXT 36

तत्र ह प्रेतबन्धूनामाश्रुत्य परिदेवितम् ।
आह तान् बालको भूत्वा यमः स्वयमुपागतः ॥३६॥

tatra ha preta-bandhūnām
āśrutya paridevitam

āha tān bālako bhūtvā
yamaḥ svayam upāgataḥ

tatra—there; *ha*—certainly; *preta-bandhūnām*—of the friends and relatives of the dead King; *āśrutya*—hearing; *paridevitam*—the loud lamentation (so loud that it could be heard from the planet of Yamarāja); *āha*—said; *tān*—unto them (the lamenting queens); *bālakaḥ*—a boy; *bhūtvā*—becoming; *yamaḥ*—Yamarāja, the superintendent of death; *svayam*—personally; *upāgataḥ*—after coming.

TRANSLATION

While the queens were lamenting for the dead body of the King, their loud cries were heard even from the abode of Yamarāja. Assuming the body of a boy, Yamarāja personally approached the relatives of the dead body and advised them as follows.

PURPORT

Sometimes the living entity is forced to give up his body and enter another one according to the judgment of Yamarāja. It is difficult, however, for the conditioned soul to enter another body unless the present dead body is annihilated through cremation or some other means. The living being has attachment for the present body and does not want to enter another, and thus in the interim he remains a ghost. If a living being who has already left his body has been pious, Yamarāja, just to give him relief, will give him another body. Since the living being in the body of the King had some attachment to his body, he was hovering as a ghost, and therefore Yamarāja, as a special consideration, approached the lamenting relatives to instruct them personally. Yamarāja approached them as a child because a child is not restricted but is granted admittance anywhere, even to the palace of a king. Besides this, the child was speaking philosophy. People are very much interested in hearing philosophy when it is spoken by a child.

TEXT 37

श्रीयम उवाच

अहो अमीषां वयसाधिकानां
विपश्यतां लोकविधिं विमोहः ।

यत्रागतस्तत्र गतं मनुष्यं
स्वयं सधर्मा अपि शोचन्त्यपार्थम् ॥३७॥

śrī-yama uvāca
aho amīṣāṁ vayasādhikānāṁ
vipaśyatāṁ loka-vidhiṁ vimohaḥ
yatrāgatas tatra gataṁ manuṣyaṁ
svayaṁ sadharmā api śocanty apārtham

śrī-yamaḥ uvāca—Śrī Yamarāja said; *aho*—alas; *amīṣām*—of these; *vayasā*—by age; *adhikānām*—of those advanced; *vipaśyatām*—seeing every day; *loka-vidhim*—the law of nature (that everyone dies); *vimohaḥ*—the bewilderment; *yatra*—from where; *āgataḥ*—came; *tatra*—there; *gatam*—returned; *manuṣyam*—the man; *svayam*—themselves; *sa-dharmāḥ*—similar in nature (prone to die); *api*—although; *śocanti*—they lament; *apārtham*—uselessly.

TRANSLATION

Śrī Yamarāja said: Alas, how amazing it is! These persons, who are older than me, have full experience that hundreds and thousands of living entities have taken birth and died. Thus they should understand that they also are apt to die, yet still they are bewildered. The conditioned soul comes from an unknown place and returns after death to that same unknown place. There is no exception to this rule, which is conducted by material nature. Knowing this, why do they uselessly lament?

PURPORT

The Lord says in *Bhagavad-gītā* (2.28):

avyaktādīni bhūtāni
vyakta-madhyāni bhārata
avyakta-nidhanāny eva
tatra kā paridevanā

"All created beings are unmanifest in their beginning, manifest in their interim state, and unmanifest again when they are annihilated. So what need is there for lamentation?"

Accepting that there are two classes of philosophers, one believing in the existence of the soul and the other not believing in its existence, there is no cause for lamentation in either case. Nonbelievers in the existence of the soul are called atheists by followers of Vedic wisdom. Yet even if for argument's sake we accept the atheistic theory, there is still no cause for lamentation. Apart from the separate existence of the soul, the material elements remain unmanifested before creation. From this subtle state of unmanifestation comes manifestation, just as from ether, air is generated; from air, fire is generated; from fire, water is generated; and from water, earth becomes manifested. From the earth, many varieties of manifestations take place. For example, a big skyscraper is manifested from the earth. When it is dismantled, the manifestation becomes again unmanifested and remains as atoms in the ultimate stage. The law of conservation of energy remains, but in the course of time things are manifested and unmanifested—that is the difference. Then what cause is there for lamentation, in either manifestation or unmanifestation? Somehow or other, even in the unmanifested stage, things are not lost. Both at the beginning and at the end, all elements remain unmanifested, and this does not make any real material difference.

If we accept the Vedic conclusion as stated in the *Bhagavad-gītā* (*antavanta ime dehāḥ*) that these material bodies are perishable in due course of time (*nityasyoktāḥ śarīriṇaḥ*) but that the soul is eternal, then we must remember always that the body is like a dress; therefore why lament the changing of a dress? The material body has no factual existence in relation to the eternal soul. It is something like a dream. In a dream we may think of flying in the sky or sitting on a chariot as a king, but when we wake up we can see that we are neither in the sky nor seated on the chariot. The Vedic wisdom encourages self-realization on the basis of the nonexistence of the material body. Therefore, in either case, whether one believes in the existence of the soul or one does not believe in the existence of the soul, there is no cause for lamentation for loss of the body.

In the *Mahābhārata* it is said, *adarśanād ihāyātaḥ punaś cādarśanaṁ gataḥ.* This statement could support the theory of the atheistic scientist that the child in the womb of the mother has no life but is simply a lump of matter. To follow this theory, if the lump of matter is aborted by a surgical operation, no life is killed; the body of a child is like a tumor, and if a tumor is operated upon and thrown away, no sin is involved. The same argument could be put forward in regard to the King and his queens. The body of the King was manifested from an unmanifested source, and again it became unmanifested from manifestation. Since the manifestation exists only in the middle—between the two points of unmanifestation—why should one cry for the body manifested in the interim?

TEXT 38

अहो वयं धन्यतमा यदत्र
त्यक्ताः पितृभ्यां न विचिन्तयामः ।
अभक्ष्यमाणा अबला वृकादिभिः
स रक्षिता रक्षति यो हि गर्भे ॥३८॥

aho vayaṁ dhanyatamā yad atra
tyaktāḥ pitṛbhyāṁ na vicintayāmaḥ
abhakṣyamāṇā abalā vṛkādibhiḥ
sa rakṣitā rakṣati yo hi garbhe

aho—alas; *vayam*—we; *dhanya-tamāḥ*—most fortunate; *yat*—because; *atra*—at the present moment; *tyaktāḥ*—left alone, without protection; *pitṛbhyām*—by both father and mother; *na*—not; *vicintayāmaḥ*—worry; *abhakṣyamāṇāḥ*—not being eaten; *abalāḥ*—very weak; *vṛka-ādibhiḥ*—by tigers and other ferocious animals; *saḥ*—He (the Supreme Personality of Godhead); *rakṣitā*—will protect; *rakṣati*—has protected; *yaḥ*—who; *hi*—indeed; *garbhe*—within the womb.

TRANSLATION

It is wonderful that these elderly women do not have a higher sense of life than we do. Indeed, we are most fortunate, for although we are children and have been left to struggle in material life, unprotected by father and mother, and although we are very

weak, we have not been vanquished or eaten by ferocious animals. Thus we have a firm belief that the Supreme Personality of Godhead, who has given us protection even in the womb of the mother, will protect us everywhere.

PURPORT

As stated in *Bhagavad-gītā* (18.61), *īśvaraḥ sarva-bhūtānāṁ hṛd-deśe 'rjuna tiṣṭhati:* the Lord is present in the core of everyone's heart. Thus the Lord gives protection to everyone and gives the different types of bodies the living entity wants to enjoy. Everything is done by the order of the Supreme Personality of Godhead. Therefore one should not lament the birth and death of a living being, which have been arranged by the Supreme Lord. Lord Kṛṣṇa says in *Bhagavad-gītā* (15.15), *sarvasya cāhaṁ hṛdi sanniviṣṭo mattaḥ smṛtir jñānam apohanaṁ ca:* "I am seated in everyone's heart, and from Me come remembrance, knowledge and forgetfulness." One must act according to the direction of the Lord within the heart, but because the conditioned soul wants to act independently, the Lord gives him the facility to act and experience the reactions. The Lord says, *sarva-dharmān parityajya mām ekaṁ śaraṇaṁ vraja:* "Give up all other duties and simply surrender unto Me." One who does not abide by the orders of the Supreme Personality of Godhead is given the facility to enjoy this material world. Instead of restricting him, the Lord gives the conditioned soul the opportunity to enjoy so that by mature experience, after many, many births (*bahūnāṁ janmanām ante*), he will understand that surrender to the lotus feet of Vāsudeva is the only duty of all living beings.

TEXT 39

य इच्छयेशः सृजतीदमव्ययो
य एव रक्षत्यवलुम्पते च यः ।
तस्याबलाः क्रीडनमाहुरीशितु-
श्चराचरं निग्रहसङ्ग्रहे प्रभुः ॥३९॥

ya icchayeśaḥ sṛjatīdam avyayo
ya eva rakṣaty avalumpate ca yaḥ

tasyābalāḥ krīḍanam āhur īśituś
carācaraṁ nigraha-saṅgrahe prabhuḥ

yaḥ—who; *icchayā*—by His will (without being forced by anyone); *īśaḥ*—the supreme controller; *sṛjati*—creates; *idam*—this (material world); *avyayaḥ*—remaining as He is (not having lost His own existence because of having created so many material manifestations); *yaḥ*—who; *eva*—indeed; *rakṣati*—maintains; *avalumpate*—annihilates; *ca*—also; *yaḥ*—who; *tasya*—of Him; *abalāḥ*—O poor women; *krīḍanam*—the playing; *āhuḥ*—they say; *īśituḥ*—of the Supreme Personality of Godhead; *cara-acaram*—moving and not moving; *nigraha*—in destruction; *saṅgrahe*—or in protection; *prabhuḥ*—fully able.

TRANSLATION

The boy addressed the women: O weak women! Only by the will of the Supreme Personality of Godhead, who is never diminished, is the entire world created, maintained and again annihilated. This is the verdict of the Vedic knowledge. This material creation, consisting of the moving and nonmoving, is exactly like His plaything. Being the Supreme Lord, He is completely competent to destroy and protect.

PURPORT

In this regard the queens might argue, "If our husband was protected by the Supreme Personality of Godhead when in the womb, why has he not been given protection now?" To this question the answer is, *ya icchayeśaḥ sṛjatīdam avyayo ya eva rakṣaty avalumpate ca yaḥ.* One cannot argue with the activities of the Supreme Personality of Godhead. The Lord is always free, and therefore He can protect and can also annihilate. He is not our order carrier; whatever He likes He will do. Therefore He is the Supreme Lord. The Lord does not create this material world at anyone's request, and therefore He can annihilate everything merely by His will. That is His supremacy. If one argues, "Why does He act in this way?" the answer is that He can do so because He is supreme. No one can question His activities. If one argues, "What is the purpose of this sinful creation and annihilation?" the answer is that to prove His omnipotence He can do anything, and no one can question Him. If He were answerable to us concerning why He does something and why He does not, His supremacy would be curtailed.

TEXT 40

पथि च्युतं तिष्ठति दिष्टरक्षितं
गृहे स्थितं तद्विहतं विनश्यति ।
जीवत्यनाथोऽपि तदीक्षितो वने
गृहेऽभिगुप्तोऽस्य हतो न जीवति ॥४०॥

pathi cyutaṁ tiṣṭhati diṣṭa-rakṣitaṁ
gṛhe sthitaṁ tad-vihataṁ vinaśyati
jīvaty anātho 'pi tad-īkṣito vane
gṛhe 'bhigupto 'sya hato na jīvati

pathi—on the public road; *cyutam*—some possession dropped; *tiṣṭhati*—it remains; *diṣṭa-rakṣitam*—protected by destiny; *gṛhe*—at home; *sthitam*—although situated; *tat-vihatam*—struck by the will of the Supreme; *vinaśyati*—it is lost; *jīvati*—remains alive; *anāthaḥ api*—although without a protector; *tat-īkṣitaḥ*—being protected by the Lord; *vane*—in the forest; *gṛhe*—at home; *abhiguptaḥ*—well hidden and protected; *asya*—of this one; *hataḥ*—struck; *na*—not; *jīvati*—lives.

TRANSLATION

Sometimes one loses his money on a public street, where everyone can see it, and yet his money is protected by destiny and not seen by others. Thus the man who lost it gets it back. On the other hand, if the Lord does not give protection, even money maintained very securely at home is lost. If the Supreme Lord gives one protection, even though one has no protector and is in the jungle, one remains alive, whereas a person well protected at home by relatives and others sometimes dies, no one being able to protect him.

PURPORT

These are examples of the supremacy of the Lord. Our plans to protect or annihilate do not act, but whatever He thinks of doing actually happens. The examples given in this regard are practical. Everyone has had such practical experiences, and there are also many other clear examples. For instance, Prahlāda Mahārāja said that a child is certainly dependent on his father and mother, but in spite of their presence, the child is harassed in many ways. Sometimes, in spite of a supply of good medicine and an experienced physician, a patient does not survive. Therefore, since everything is dependent on the free will of the Supreme Personality of Godhead, our only duty is to surrender unto Him and seek His protection.

TEXT 41

भूतानि तैस्तैर्निजयोनिकर्मभि-
र्भवन्ति काले न भवन्ति सर्वशः ।
न तत्र हात्मा प्रकृतावपि स्थित-
स्तस्या गुणैरन्यतमो हि बध्यते ॥४१॥

bhūtāni tais tair nija-yoni-karmabhir
bhavanti kāle na bhavanti sarvaśaḥ
na tatra hātmā prakṛtāv api sthitas
tasyā guṇair anyatamo hi badhyate

bhūtāni—all the bodies of the living entities; *taiḥ taiḥ*—their own respective; *nija-yoni*—causing their own bodies; *karmabhiḥ*—by past activities; *bhavanti*—appear; *kāle*—in due course of time; *na bhavanti*—disappear; *sarvaśaḥ*—in all respects; *na*—not; *tatra*—there; *ha*—indeed; *ātmā*—the soul; *prakṛtau*—within this material world; *api*—although; *sthitaḥ*—situated; *tasyāḥ*—of her (the material energy); *guṇaiḥ*—by different modes; *anya-tamaḥ*—most different; *hi*—indeed; *badhyate*—is bound.

TRANSLATION

Every conditioned soul receives a different type of body according to his work, and when the engagement is finished the body is finished. Although the spirit soul is situated in subtle and gross material bodies in different forms of life, he is not bound by them,

for he is always understood to be completely different from the manifested body.

PURPORT

Here it is very plainly explained that God is not responsible for the living entity's accepting different types of bodies. One has to accept a body according to the laws of nature and one's own *karma.* Therefore the Vedic injunction is that a person engaged in material activities should be given directions by which he can intelligently apply his activities to the service of the Lord to become free from the material bondage of repeated birth and death (*sva-karmaṇā tam abhyarcya siddhiṁ vindati mānavaḥ*). The Lord is always ready to give directions. Indeed, His directions are elaborately given in *Bhagavad-gītā.* If we take advantage of these directions, then in spite of our being conditioned by the laws of material nature, we shall become free to attain our original constitution (*mām eva ye prapadyante māyām etāṁ taranti te*). We should have firm faith that the Lord is supreme and that if we surrender to Him, He will take charge of us and indicate how we can get out of material life and return home, back to Godhead. Without such surrender, one is obliged to accept a certain type of body according to his *karma,* sometimes as an animal, sometimes a demigod and so on. Although the body is obtained and lost in due course of time, the spirit soul does not actually mix with the body, but is subjugated by the particular modes of nature with which he is sinfully associated. Spiritual education changes one's consciousness so that one simply carries out the orders of the Supreme Lord and becomes free from the influence of the modes of material nature.

TEXT 42

इदं शरीरं पुरुषस्य मोहजं
यथा पृथग्भौतिकमीयते गृहम् ।
यथौदकैः पार्थिवतैजसैर्जनः
कालेन जातो विकृतो विनश्यति ॥४२॥

idaṁ śarīraṁ puruṣasya mohajaṁ
yathā pṛthag bhautikam īyate gṛham

yathaudakaiḥ pārthiva-taijasair janaḥ
kālena jāto vikṛto vinaśyati

idam—this; *śarīram*—body; *puruṣasya*—of the conditioned soul; *moha-jam*—born of ignorance; *yathā*—just as; *pṛthak*—separate; *bhautikam*—material; *īyate*—is seen; *gṛham*—a house; *yathā*—just as; *udakaiḥ*—with water; *pārthiva*—with earth; *taijasaiḥ*—and with fire; *janaḥ*—the conditioned soul; *kālena*—in due course of time; *jātaḥ*—born; *vikṛtaḥ*—transformed; *vinaśyati*—is vanquished.

TRANSLATION

Just as a householder, although different from the identity of his house, thinks his house to be identical with him, so the conditioned soul, due to ignorance, accepts the body to be himself, although the body is actually different from the soul. This body is obtained through a combination of portions of earth, water and fire, and when the earth, water and fire are transformed in the course of time, the body is vanquished. The soul has nothing to do with this creation and dissolution of the body.

PURPORT

We transmigrate from one body to another in bodies that are products of our illusion, but as spirit souls we always exist separately from material, conditional life. The example given here is that a house or car is always different from its owner, but because of attachment the conditioned soul thinks it to be identical with him. A car or house is actually made of material elements; as long as the material elements combine together properly, the car or house exists, and when they are disassembled the house or the car is disassembled. The spirit soul, however, always remains as he is.

TEXT 43

यथानलो दारुषु भिन्न ईयते
यथानिलो देहगतः पृथक् स्थितः ।
यथा नभः सर्वगतं न सज्जते
तथा पुमान् सर्वगुणाश्रयः परः ॥४३॥

yathānalo dāruṣu bhinna īyate
yathānilo deha-gataḥ pṛthak sthitaḥ
yathā nabhaḥ sarva-gataṁ na sajjate
tathā pumān sarva-guṇāśrayaḥ paraḥ

yathā—just as; *analaḥ*—the fire; *dāruṣu*—in wood; *bhinnaḥ*—separate; *īyate*—is perceived; *yathā*—just as; *anilaḥ*—the air; *deha-gataḥ*—within the body; *pṛthak*—separate; *sthitaḥ*—situated; *yathā*—just as; *nabhaḥ*—the sky; *sarva-gatam*—all-pervading; *na*—not; *sajjate*—mix; *tathā*—similarly; *pumān*—the living entity; *sarva-guṇa-āśrayaḥ*—although now the shelter of the modes of material nature; *paraḥ*—transcendental to material contamination.

TRANSLATION

As fire, although situated in wood, is perceived to be different from the wood, as air, although situated within the mouth and nostrils, is perceived to be separate, and as the sky, although all-pervading, never mixes with anything, so the living entity, although now encaged within the material body, of which it is the source, is separate from it.

PURPORT

In *Bhagavad-gītā* the Supreme Personality of Godhead has explained that the material energy and spiritual energy both emanate from Him. The material energy is described as *me bhinnā prakṛtir aṣṭadhā*, the eight separated energies of the Lord. But although the eight gross and subtle material energies—namely, earth, water, fire, air, ether, mind, intelligence and false ego—are stated to be *bhinnā*, separate from the Lord, actually they are not. As fire appears separate from wood and as the air flowing through the nostrils and mouth of the body appear separate from the body, so the Paramātmā, the Supreme Personality of Godhead, appears separate from the living being but is actually separate and not separate simultaneously. This is the philosophy of *acintya-bhedābheda-tattva* propounded by Śrī Caitanya Mahāprabhu. According to the reactions of *karma*, the living being appears separate from the Supreme Personality of Godhead, but actually he is very intimately related with the

Lord. Consequently, even though we now seem neglected by the Lord, He is actually always alert to our activities. Under all circumstances, therefore, we should simply depend on the supremacy of the Supreme Personality of Godhead and thus revive our intimate relationship with Him. We must depend upon the authority and control of the Supreme Personality of Godhead.

TEXT 44

सुयज्ञो नन्वयं शेते मूढा यमनुशोचथ ।
यः श्रोता योऽनुवक्तेह स न दृश्येत कर्हिचित् ॥४४॥

suyajño nanv ayaṁ śete
mūḍhā yam anuśocatha
yaḥ śrotā yo 'nuvakteha
sa na dṛśyeta karhicit

suyajñaḥ—the king named Suyajña; *nanu*—indeed; *ayam*—this; *śete*—lies; *mūḍhāḥ*—O foolish people; *yam*—whom; *anuśocatha*—you cry for; *yaḥ*—he who; *śrotā*—the hearer; *yaḥ*—he who; *anuvaktā*—the speaker; *iha*—in this world; *saḥ*—he; *na*—not; *dṛśyeta*—is visible; *karhicit*—at any time.

TRANSLATION

Yamarāja continued: O lamenters, you are all fools! The person named Suyajña, for whom you lament, is still lying before you and has not gone anywhere. Then what is the cause for your lamentation? Previously he heard you and replied to you, but now, not finding him, you are lamenting. This is contradictory behavior, for you have never actually seen the person within the body who heard you and replied. There is no need for your lamentation, for the body you have always seen is lying here.

PURPORT

This instruction by Yamarāja in the form of a boy is understandable even for a common man. A common man who considers the body the self is certainly comparable to an animal (*yasyātma-buddhiḥ kuṇape tri-dhātuke . . . sa eva go-kharaḥ*). But even a common man can understand that after death a person is gone. Although the body is still there, a dead man's relatives lament that the person has gone away, for a common man sees the body but cannot see the soul. As described in *Bhagavad-gītā*, *dehino 'smin yathā dehe:* the soul, the proprietor of the body, is within. After death, when the breath within the nostrils has stopped, one can understand that the person within the body, who was hearing and replying, has now gone. Therefore, in effect, the common man concludes that actually the spirit soul was different from the body and has now gone away. Thus even a common man, coming to his senses, can know that the real person who was within the body and was hearing and replying was never seen. For that which was never seen, what is the need of lamentation?

TEXT 45

न श्रोता नानुवक्तायं मुख्योऽप्यत्र महानसुः ।
यस्त्विहेन्द्रियवानात्मा स चान्यः प्राणदेहयोः ॥४५॥

na śrotā nānuvaktāyaṁ
mukhyo 'py atra mahān asuḥ
yas tv ihendriyavān ātmā
sa cānyaḥ prāṇa-dehayoḥ

na—not; *śrotā*—the listener; *na*—not; *anuvaktā*—the speaker; *ayam*—this; *mukhyaḥ*—chief; *api*—although; *atra*—in this body; *mahān*—the great; *asuḥ*—life air; *yaḥ*—he who; *tu*—but; *iha*—in this body; *indriya-vān*—possessing all the sense organs; *ātmā*—the soul; *saḥ*—he; *ca*—and; *anyaḥ*—different; *prāṇa-dehayoḥ*—from the life air and the material body.

TRANSLATION

In the body the most important substance is the life air, but that also is neither the listener nor the speaker. Beyond even the life air, the soul also can do nothing, for the Supersoul is actually the director, in cooperation with the individual soul. The Supersoul

conducting the activities of the body is different from the body and living force.

PURPORT

The Supreme Personality of Godhead distinctly says in *Bhagavad-gītā* (15.15), *sarvasya cāhaṁ hṛdi sanniviṣṭo mattaḥ smṛtir jñānam apohanaṁ ca:* "I am seated in everyone's heart, and from Me come remembrance, knowledge and forgetfulness." Although the *ātmā*, or soul, is present in every material body (*dehino 'smin yathā dehe*), he is not actually the chief person acting through the senses, mind and so on. The soul can merely act in cooperation with the Supersoul because it is the Supersoul who gives him directions to act or not to act (*mattaḥ smṛtir jñānam apohanaṁ ca*). One cannot act without His sanction, for the Supersoul is *upadraṣṭā* and *anumantā*, the witness and sanctioner. One who studies carefully, under the direction of a bona fide spiritual master, can understand the real knowledge that the Supreme Personality of Godhead is actually the conductor of all the activities of the individual soul, and the controller of their results as well. Although the individual soul possesses the *indriyas*, or senses, he is not actually the proprietor, for the proprietor is the Supersoul. Consequently the Supersoul is called Hṛṣīkeśa, and the individual soul is advised by the direction of the Supersoul to surrender to Him and thus be happy (*sarva-dharmān parityajya mām ekaṁ śaraṇaṁ vraja*). Thus he can become immortal and be transferred to the spiritual kingdom, where he will achieve the highest success of an eternal, blissful life of knowledge. In conclusion, the individual soul is different from the body, senses, living force and the airs within the body, and above him is the Supersoul, who gives the individual soul all facilities. The individual soul who renders everything to the Supersoul lives very happily within the body.

TEXT 46

भूतेन्द्रियमनोलिङ्गान् देहानुच्चावचान् विभुः।
भजत्युत्सृजति ह्यन्यस्तच्चापि स्वेन तेजसा ॥४६॥

bhūtendriya-mano-liṅgān
dehān uccāvacān vibhuḥ

bhajaty utsṛjati hy anyas
tac cāpi svena tejasā

bhūta—by the five material elements; *indriya*—the ten senses; *manaḥ*—and the mind; *liṅgān*—characterized; *dehān*—gross material bodies; *ucca-avacān*—high class and low class; *vibhuḥ*—the individual soul, which is the lord of the body and senses; *bhajati*—achieves; *utsṛjati*—gives up; *hi*—indeed; *anyaḥ*—being different; *tat*—that; *ca*—also; *api*—indeed; *svena*—by his own; *tejasā*—power of advanced knowledge.

TRANSLATION

The five material elements, the ten senses and the mind all combine to form the various parts of the gross and subtle bodies. The living entity comes in contact with his material bodies, whether high or low, and later gives them up by his personal prowess. This strength can be perceived in a living entity's personal power to possess different types of bodies.

PURPORT

The conditioned soul has knowledge, and if he wants to fully utilize the gross and subtle bodies for his real advancement in life, he can do so. It is therefore said here that by his high intelligence (*svena tejasā*), by the superior power of superior knowledge achieved from the right source—the spiritual master, or *ācārya*—he can give up his conditional life in a material body and return home, back to Godhead. However, if he wants to keep himself in the darkness of this material world, he can do so. The Lord confirms this as follows in *Bhagavad-gītā* (9.25):

yānti deva-vratā devān
pitṝn yānti pitṛ-vratāḥ
bhūtāni yānti bhūtejyā
yānti mad-yājino 'pi mām

"Those who worship the demigods will take birth among the demigods; those who worship ghosts and spirits will take birth among such beings;

those who worship ancestors go to the ancestors; and those who worship Me will live with Me."

The human form of body is valuable. One can use this body to go to the higher planetary systems, to Pitṛloka, or he can remain in this lower planetary system, but if one tries he can also return home, back to Godhead. This prowess is given by the Supreme Personality of Godhead as the Supersoul. Therefore the Lord says, *mattaḥ smṛtir jñānam apohanaṁ ca:* "From Me come remembrance, knowledge and forgetfulness." If one wants to receive real knowledge from the Supreme Personality of Godhead, one can become free from bondage to repeated acceptance of material bodies. If one takes to the devotional service of the Lord and surrenders unto Him, the Lord is prepared to give one directions by which to return home, back to Godhead, but if one foolishly wants to keep himself in darkness, he can continue in a life of material existence.

TEXT 47

यावल्लिङ्गान्वितो ह्यात्मा तावत् कर्म निबन्धनम् ।
ततो विपर्ययः क्लेशो मायायोगोऽनुवर्तते ॥४७॥

yāval liṅgānvito hy ātmā
tāvat karma-nibandhanam
tato viparyayaḥ kleśo
māyā-yogo 'nuvartate

yāvat—as long as; *liṅga-anvitaḥ*—covered by the subtle body; *hi*—indeed; *ātmā*—the soul; *tāvat*—that long; *karma*—of fruitive activities; *nibandhanam*—bondage; *tataḥ*—from that; *viparyayaḥ*—reversal (wrongly thinking the body to be the self); *kleśaḥ*—misery; *māyā-yogaḥ*—a strong relationship with the external, illusory energy; *anuvartate*—follows.

TRANSLATION

As long as the spirit soul is covered by the subtle body, consisting of the mind, intelligence and false ego, he is bound to the results of his fruitive activities. Because of this covering, the spirit

soul is connected with the material energy and must accordingly suffer material conditions and reversals, continually, life after life.

PURPORT

The living entity is bound by the subtle body, consisting of the mind, intelligence and false ego. At the time of death, therefore, the position of the mind becomes the cause for the next body. As confirmed in *Bhagavad-gītā* (8.6), *yaṁ yaṁ vāpi smaran bhāvaṁ tyajaty ante kalevaram:* at the time of death the mind sets the criteria for the spirit soul's being carried to another type of body. If a living being resists the dictation of the mind and engages the mind in the loving service of the Lord, the mind cannot degrade him. The duty of all human beings, therefore, is to keep the mind always engaged at the lotus feet of the Lord (*sa vai manaḥ kṛṣṇa-padāravindayoḥ*). When the mind is engaged at the lotus feet of Kṛṣṇa, the intelligence is purified, and then the intelligence gets inspiration from the Supersoul (*dadāmi buddhi-yogaṁ tam*). Thus the living entity makes progress toward liberation from material bondage. The individual living soul is subject to the laws of fruitive activity, but the Supersoul, Paramātmā, is not affected by the fruitive activities of the individual soul. As confirmed in the Vedic *Upaniṣad*, the Paramātmā and the *jīvātmā*, who are likened to two birds, are sitting in the body. The *jīvātmā* is enjoying or suffering by eating the fruits of the bodily activities, but the Paramātmā, who is free from such bondage, witnesses and sanctions the activities of the individual soul as the individual soul desires.

TEXT 48

वितथाभिनिवेशोऽयं यद् गुणेष्वर्थदृग्वचः ।
यथा मनोरथः स्वप्नः सर्वमैन्द्रियकं मृषा ॥४८॥

vitathābhiniveśo 'yaṁ
yad guṇeṣv artha-dṛg-vacaḥ
yathā manorathaḥ svapnaḥ
sarvam aindriyakaṁ mṛṣā

vitatha—fruitless; *abhiniveśaḥ*—the conception; *ayam*—this; *yat*—which; *guṇeṣu*—in the modes of material nature; *artha*—as a fact; *dṛk*-

vacaḥ—the seeing and talking of; *yathā*—just as; *manorathaḥ*—a mental concoction (daydream); *svapnaḥ*—a dream; *sarvam*—everything; *aindriyakam*—produced by the senses; *mṛṣā*—false.

TRANSLATION

It is fruitless to see and talk of the material modes of nature and their resultant so-called happiness and distress as if they were factual. When the mind wanders during the day and a man begins to think himself extremely important, or when he dreams at night and sees a beautiful woman enjoying with him, these are merely false dreams. Similarly, the happiness and distress caused by the material senses should be understood to be meaningless.

PURPORT

The happiness and distress derived from the activities of the material senses are not actual happiness and distress. Therefore *Bhagavad-gītā* speaks of happiness that is transcendental to the material conception of life (*sukham ātyantikaṁ yat tad buddhi-grāhyam atīndriyam*). When our senses are purified of material contamination, they become *atīndriya*, transcendental senses, and when the transcendental senses are engaged in the service of the master of the senses, Hṛṣīkeśa, one can derive real transcendental pleasure. Whatever distress or happiness we manufacture by mental concoction through the subtle mind has no reality, but is simply a mental concoction. One should therefore not imagine so-called happiness through mental concoction. Rather, the best course is to engage the mind in the service of the Lord, Hṛṣīkeśa, and thus feel real blissful life.

There is a Vedic statement *apāma-somam amṛtā abhūma apsarobhir vihārāma.* With reference to such a conception, one wants to go to the heavenly planets to enjoy with the young girls there and drink *soma-rasa.* Such imaginary pleasure, however, has no value. As confirmed in *Bhagavad-gītā* (7.23), *antavat tu phalaṁ teṣāṁ tad bhavaty alpa-medhasām:* "Men of small intelligence worship the demigods, and their fruits are limited and temporary." Even if by fruitive activity or worship of the demigods one is elevated to the higher planetary systems for sense enjoyment, his situation is condemned in *Bhagavad-gītā* as *antavat,* perishable. The happiness one enjoys in this way is like the pleasure of embracing a young woman in a dream; for some time it may be pleasing, but actually the basic principle is false. The mental concoctions of happiness and distress in this material world are compared to dreams because of their falseness. All thoughts of obtaining happiness by using the material senses have a false background and therefore have no meaning.

TEXT 49

अथ नित्यमनित्यं वा नेह शोचन्ति तद्विदः ।
नान्यथा शक्यते कर्तुं स्वभावः शोचतामिति ॥४९॥

atha nityam anityaṁ vā
neha śocanti tad-vidaḥ
nānyathā śakyate kartuṁ
sva-bhāvaḥ śocatām iti

atha—therefore; *nityam*—the eternal spirit soul; *anityam*—the temporary material body; *vā*—or; *na*—not; *iha*—in this world; *śocanti*—they lament for; *tat-vidaḥ*—those who are advanced in knowledge of the body and soul; *na*—not; *anyathā*—otherwise; *śakyate*—is able; *kartum*—to do; *sva-bhāvaḥ*—the nature; *śocatām*—of those prone to lamentation; *iti*—thus.

TRANSLATION

Those who have full knowledge of self-realization, who know very well that the spirit soul is eternal whereas the body is perishable, are not overwhelmed by lamentation. But persons who lack knowledge of self-realization certainly lament. Therefore it is difficult to educate a person in illusion.

PURPORT

According to the *mīmāṁsā* philosophers, everything is eternal, *nitya*, and according to the Sāṅkhya philosophers everything is *mithyā*, or *anitya*—impermanent. Nonetheless, without real knowledge of *ātmā*, the soul, such philosophers must be bewildered and must continue to lament as *śūdras*. Śrīla Śukadeva Gosvāmī therefore said to Parīkṣit Mahārāja:

śrotavyādīni rājendra
nṛṇāṁ santi sahasraśaḥ
apaśyatām ātma-tattvaṁ
gṛheṣu gṛha-medhinām

"Those who are materially engrossed, being blind to knowledge of the ultimate truth, have many subjects for hearing in human society, O Emperor." (*Bhāg.* 2.1.2) For ordinary persons engaged in material activities there are many, many subject matters to understand because such persons do not understand self-realization. One must therefore be educated in self-realization so that under any circumstances in life he will remain steady in his vows.

TEXT 50

लुब्धको विपिने कश्चित्पक्षिणां निर्मितोऽन्तकः ।
वितत्य जालं विदधे तत्र तत्र प्रलोभयन् ॥५०॥

lubdhako vipine kaścit
pakṣiṇāṁ nirmito 'ntakaḥ
vitatya jālaṁ vidadhe
tatra tatra pralobhayan

lubdhakaḥ—hunter; *vipine*—in the forest; *kaścit*—some; *pakṣiṇām*—of birds; *nirmitaḥ*—appointed; *antakaḥ*—killer; *vitatya*—spreading; *jālam*—a net; *vidadhe*—captured; *tatra tatra*—here and there; *pralobhayan*—luring with food.

TRANSLATION

There was once a hunter who lured birds with food and captured them after spreading a net. He lived as if appointed by death personified as the killer of the birds.

PURPORT

This is another incident from the histories.

TEXT 51

कुलिङ्गमिथुनं तत्र विचरत्समदृश्यत ।
तयोः कुलिङ्गी सहसा लुब्धकेन प्रलोभिता ॥५१॥

kuliṅga-mithunaṁ tatra
vicarat samadṛśyata
tayoḥ kuliṅgī sahasā
lubdhakena pralobhitā

kuliṅga-mithunam—a pair of (male and female) birds known as *kuliṅga; tatra*—there (where the hunter was hunting); *vicarat*—wandering; *samadṛśyata*—he saw; *tayoḥ*—of the pair; *kuliṅgī*—the female bird; *sahasā*—suddenly; *lubdhakena*—by the hunter; *pralobhitā*—allured.

TRANSLATION

While wandering in the forest, the hunter saw a pair of kuliṅga birds. Of the two, the female was captivated by the hunter's lure.

TEXT 52

सासज्जत सिचस्तन्त्र्यां महिष्यः कालयन्त्रिता ।
कुलिङ्गस्तां तथापन्नां निरीक्ष्य भृशदुःखितः ।
स्नेहादकल्पः कृपणः कृपणां पर्यदेवयत् ॥५२॥

sāsajjata sicas tantryāṁ
mahiṣyaḥ kāla-yantritā
kuliṅgas tāṁ tathāpannāṁ
nirīkṣya bhṛśa-duḥkhitaḥ
snehād akalpaḥ kṛpaṇaḥ
kṛpaṇāṁ paryadevayat

sā—the female bird; *asajjata*—trapped; *sicaḥ*—of the net; *tantryām*—in the rope; *mahiṣyaḥ*—O queens; *kāla-yantritā*—being forced by time; *kuliṅgaḥ*—the male *kuliṅga* bird; *tām*—her; *tathā*—in that condition; *āpannām*—captured; *nirīkṣya*—seeing; *bhṛśa-*

duḥkhitaḥ—very unhappy; *snehāt*—out of affection; *akalpaḥ*—unable to do anything; *kṛpaṇaḥ*—the poor bird; *kṛpaṇām*—the poor wife; *paryadevayat*—began to lament for.

TRANSLATION

O queens of Suyajña, the male kuliṅga bird, seeing his wife put into the greatest danger in the grip of Providence, became very unhappy. Because of affection, the poor bird, being unable to release her, began to lament for his wife.

TEXT 53

अहो अकरुणो देवः स्त्रियाकरुणया विभुः ।
कृपणं मामनुशोचन्त्या दीनया किं करिष्यति ।।५३।।

aho akaruṇo devaḥ
striyākaruṇayā vibhuḥ
kṛpaṇaṁ mām anuśocantyā
dīnayā kiṁ kariṣyati

aho—alas; *akaruṇaḥ*—most unkind; *devaḥ*—providence; *striyā*—with my wife; *ākaruṇayā*—who is fully compassionate; *vibhuḥ*—the Supreme Lord; *kṛpaṇam*—poor; *mām*—me; *anuśocantyā*—lamenting for; *dīnayā*—poor; *kim*—what; *kariṣyati*—shall do.

TRANSLATION

Alas, how merciless is Providence! My wife, unable to be helped by anyone, is in such an awkward position and lamenting for me. What will Providence gain by taking away this poor bird? What will be the profit?

TEXT 54

कामं नयतु मां देवः किमर्धेनात्मनो हि मे ।
दीनेन जीवता दुःखमनेन विधुरायुषा ।।५४।।

kāmaṁ nayatu māṁ devaḥ
kim ardhenātmano hi me

dīnena jīvatā duḥkham
anena vidhurāyuṣā

kāmam—as He likes; *nayatu*—let Him take away; *mām*—me; *devaḥ*—the Supreme Lord; *kim*—what use; *ardhena*—with half; *ātmanaḥ*—of the body; *hi*—indeed; *me*—my; *dīnena*—poor; *jīvatā*—living; *duḥkham*—in suffering; *anena*—this; *vidhura-āyuṣā*—having a lifetime full of affliction.

TRANSLATION

If unkind Providence takes away my wife, who is half my body, why should He not take me also? What is the use of my living with half of my body, bereaved by loss of my wife? What shall I gain in this way?

TEXT 55

कथं त्वजातपक्षांस्तान् मातृहीनान् बिभर्म्यहम् ।
मन्दभाग्याः प्रतीक्षन्ते नीडे मे मातरं प्रजाः ॥५५॥

kathaṁ tv ajāta-pakṣāṁs tān
mātṛ-hīnān bibharmy aham
manda-bhāgyāḥ pratīkṣante
nīḍe me mātaraṁ prajāḥ

katham—how; *tu*—but; *ajāta-pakṣān*—who have not grown wings to fly; *tān*—them; *mātṛ-hīnān*—bereft of their mother; *bibharmi*—shall maintain; *aham*—I; *manda-bhāgyāḥ*—very unfortunate; *pratīkṣante*—they await; *nīḍe*—in the nest; *me*—my; *mātaram*—their mother; *prajāḥ*—baby birds.

TRANSLATION

The unfortunate baby birds, bereft of their mother, are waiting in the nest for her to feed them. They are still very small and have not yet grown their wings. How shall I be able to maintain them?

PURPORT

The bird is lamenting for the mother of his children because the mother naturally maintains and cares for the children. Yamarāja, however, in the guise of a small boy, has already explained that although his mother left him uncared for and wandering in the forest, the tigers and other ferocious animals had not eaten him. The real fact is that if the Supreme Personality of Godhead protects one, even though one be motherless and fatherless, one can be maintained by the good will of the Lord. Otherwise, if the Supreme Lord does not give one protection, one must suffer in spite of the presence of his father and mother. Another example is that sometimes a patient dies in spite of a good physician and good medicine. Thus without the protection of the Lord one cannot live, with or without parents.

Another point in this verse is that fathers and mothers have protective feelings for their children even in bird and beast society, not to speak of human society. Kali-yuga, however, is so degraded that a father and mother even kill their children in the womb on the plea of their scientific knowledge that within the womb the child has no life. Prestigious medical practitioners give this opinion, and therefore the father and mother of this day kill their children within the womb. How degraded human society has become! Their scientific knowledge is so advanced that they think that within the egg and the embryo there is no life. Now these so-called scientists are receiving Nobel Prizes for advancing the theory of chemical evolution. But if chemical combinations are the source of life, why don't the scientists manufacture something like an egg through chemistry and put it in an incubator so that a chicken will come out? What is their answer? With their scientific knowledge they are unable to create even an egg. Such scientists are described in *Bhagavad-gītā* as *māyayāpahṛta-jñānāḥ*, fools whose real knowledge has been taken away. They are not men of knowledge, but they pose as scientists and philosophers, although their so-called theoretical knowledge cannot produce practical results.

TEXT 56

एवं कुलिङ्गं विलपन्तमारात्
प्रियावियोगातुरमश्रुकण्ठम् ।
स एव तं शाकुनिकः शरेण
विव्याध कालप्रहितो विलीनः ॥५६॥

evaṁ kuliṅgaṁ vilapantam ārāt
priyā-viyogāturam aśru-kaṇṭham
sa eva taṁ śākunikaḥ śareṇa
vivyādha kāla-prahito vilīnaḥ

evam—thus; *kuliṅgam*—the bird; *vilapantam*—while lamenting; *ārāt*—from a distance; *priyā-viyoga*—because of the loss of his wife; *āturam*—very aggrieved; *aśru-kaṇṭham*—with tears in the eyes; *saḥ*—he (that hunter); *eva*—indeed; *tam*—him (the male bird); *śākunikaḥ*—who could kill even a vulture; *śareṇa*—by an arrow; *vivyādha*—pierced; *kāla-prahitaḥ*—being moved by time; *vilīnaḥ*—hidden.

TRANSLATION

Because of the loss of his wife, the kuliṅga bird lamented with tears in his eyes. Meanwhile, following the dictations of mature time, the hunter, who was very carefully hidden in the distance, released his arrow, which pierced the body of the kuliṅga bird and killed him.

TEXT 57

एवं यूयमपश्यन्त्य आत्मापायमबुद्धयः ।
नैनं प्राप्स्यथ शोचन्त्यः पतिं वर्षशतैरपि ॥५७॥

evaṁ yūyam apaśyantya
ātmāpāyam abuddhayaḥ
nainaṁ prāpsyatha śocantyaḥ
patiṁ varṣa-śatair api

evam—thus; *yūyam*—you; *apaśyantyaḥ*—not seeing; *ātma-apāyam*—own death; *abuddhayaḥ*—O ignorant ones; *na*—not; *enam*—him; *prāpsyatha*—you will obtain; *śocantyaḥ*—lamenting for; *patim*—your husband; *varṣa-śataiḥ*—for a hundred years; *api*—even.

TRANSLATION

Thus Yamarāja, in the guise of a small boy, told all the queens: You are all so foolish that you lament but do not see your own

death. Afflicted by a poor fund of knowledge, you do not know that even if you lament for your dead husband for hundreds of years, you will never get him back alive, and in the meantime your lives will be finished.

PURPORT

Yamarāja once asked Mahārāja Yudhiṣṭhira, "What is the most wonderful thing within this world?" Mahārāja Yudhiṣṭhira replied (*Mahābhārata, Vana-parva* 313.116):

ahany ahani bhūtāni
gacchantīha yamālayam
śeṣāḥ sthāvaram icchanti
kim āścaryam ataḥ paraṁ

Hundreds and thousands of living entities meet death at every moment, but a foolish living being nonetheless thinks himself deathless and does not prepare for death. This is the most wonderful thing in this world. Everyone has to die because everyone is fully under the control of material nature, yet everyone thinks that he is independent, that whatever he likes he can do, that he will never meet death but live forever, and so on. So-called scientists are making various plans by which living entities in the future can live forever, but while they are thus pursuing such scientific knowledge, Yamarāja, in due course of time, will take them away from their business of so-called research.

TEXT 58

श्रीहिरण्यकशिपुरुवाच
बाल एवं प्रवदति सर्वे विस्मितचेतसः ।
ज्ञातयो मेनिरे सर्वमनित्यमयथोत्थितम् ॥५८॥

śrī-hiraṇyakaśipur uvāca
bāla evaṁ pravadati
sarve vismita-cetasaḥ
jñātayo menire sarvam
anityam ayathotthitam

śrī-hiraṇyakaśipuḥ uvāca—Śrī Hiraṇyakaśipu said; *bāle*—while Yamarāja in the form of a boy; *evam*—thus; *pravadati*—was speaking very philosophically; *sarve*—all; *vismita*—struck with wonder; *cetasaḥ*—their hearts; *jñātayaḥ*—the relatives; *menire*—they thought; *sarvam*—everything material; *anityam*—temporary; *ayathā-utthitam*—arisen from temporary phenomena.

TRANSLATION

Hiraṇyakaśipu said: While Yamarāja, in the form of a small boy, was instructing all the relatives surrounding the dead body of Suyajña, everyone was struck with wonder by his philosophical words. They could understand that everything material is temporary, not continuing to exist.

PURPORT

This is confirmed in *Bhagavad-gītā* (2.18). *Antavanta ime dehā nityasyoktāḥ śarīriṇaḥ:* the body is perishable, but the soul within the body is imperishable. Therefore the duty of those advanced in knowledge in human society is to study the constitutional position of the imperishable soul and not waste the valuable time of human life in merely maintaining the body and not considering life's real responsibility. Every human being should try to understand how the spirit soul can be happy and where he can attain an eternal, blissful life of knowledge. Human beings are meant to study these subject matters, not to be absorbed in caring for the temporary body, which is sure to change. No one knows whether he will receive a human body again; there is no guarantee, for according to one's work one may get any body, from that of a demigod to that of a dog. In this regard, Śrīla Madhvācārya comments:

ahaṁ mamābhimānādi-
tva-yathottham anityakam
mahadādi yathotthaṁ ca
nityā cāpi yathotthitā

asvatantraiva prakṛtiḥ
sva-tantro nitya eva ca

yathārtha-bhūtaś ca para
eka eva janārdanaḥ

Only Janārdana, the Supreme Personality of Godhead is ever existing, but His creation, the material world, is temporary. Therefore everyone who is captivated by the material energy and absorbed in thinking "I am this body, and everything belonging to this body is mine" is in illusion. One should think only of being eternally a part of Janārdana, and one's endeavor in this material world, especially in this human form of life, should be to attain the association of Janārdana by going back home, back to Godhead.

TEXT 59

यम एतदुपाख्याय तत्रैवान्तरधीयत ।
ज्ञातयोऽहि सुयज्ञस्य चक्रुर्यत्साम्परायिकम् ॥५९॥

yama etad upākhyāya
tatraivāntaradhīyata
jñātayo hi suyajñasya
cakrur yat sāmparāyikam

yamaḥ—Yamarāja in the form of a boy; *etat*—this; *upākhyāya*—instructing; *tatra*—there; *eva*—indeed; *antaradhīyata*—disappeared; *jñātayaḥ*—the relatives; *hi*—indeed; *suyajñasya*—of King Suyajña; *cakruḥ*—performed; *yat*—which is; *sāmparāyikam*—the funeral ceremony.

TRANSLATION

After instructing all the foolish relatives of Suyajña, Yamarāja, in the form of a boy, disappeared from their vision. Then the relatives of King Suyajña performed the ritualistic funeral ceremonies.

TEXT 60

अतः शोचत मा यूयं परं चात्मानमेव वा ।
क आत्मा कः परो वात्र स्वीयः पारक्य एव वा ।
स्वपराभिनिवेशेन विनाज्ञानेन देहिनाम् ॥६०॥

ataḥ śocata mā yūyaṁ
paraṁ cātmānam eva vā
ka ātmā kaḥ paro vātra
svīyaḥ pārakya eva vā
sva-parābhiniveśena
vinājñānena dehinām

ataḥ—therefore; *śocata*—lament for; *mā*—do not; *yūyam*—all of you; *param*—another; *ca*—and; *ātmānam*—yourself; *eva*—certainly; *vā*—or; *kaḥ*—who; *ātmā*—self; *kaḥ*—who; *paraḥ*—other; *vā*—or; *atra*—in this material world; *svīyaḥ*—one's own; *pārakyaḥ*—for others; *eva*—indeed; *vā*—or; *sva-para-abhiniveśena*—consisting of absorption in the bodily concept of oneself and others; *vinā*—besides; *ajñānena*—the lack of knowledge; *dehinām*—of all the embodied living entities.

TRANSLATION

Therefore none of you should be aggrieved for the loss of the body—whether your own or those of others. Only in ignorance does one make bodily distinctions, thinking "Who am I? Who are the others? What is mine? What is for others?"

PURPORT

In this material world, the conception of self-preservation is the first law of nature. According to this conception, one should be interested in his personal safety and should then consider society, friendship, love, nationality, community and so on, which have all developed because of the bodily conception of life and a lack of knowledge of the spirit soul. This is called *ajñāna.* As long as human society is in darkness and ignorance, men will continue to make huge arrangements in the bodily conception of life. This is described by Prahlāda Mahārāja as *bharam.* In the materialistic conception, modern civilization makes enormous arrangements for huge roads, houses, mills and factories, and this is man's conception of the advancement of civilization. People do not know, however, that at any time they themselves may be kicked out of the scene and forced to accept bodies that have nothing to do with these enormous houses, palaces, roads and automobiles. Therefore when Arjuna was thinking in terms of his bodily relationships with his kinsmen, Kṛṣṇa immediately chastised him, saying, *kutas tvā kaśmalam idaṁ viṣame samupasthitam anārya-juṣṭam:* "This bodily conception of life is befitting the *anāryas*, the non-Āryans, who are not advanced in knowledge." An Āryan civilization is a civilization advanced in spiritual knowledge. Not merely by stamping oneself an Āryan does one become an Āryan. To keep oneself in the deepest darkness concerning spiritual knowledge and at the same time claim to be an Āryan is a non-Āryan position. In this connection, Śrīla Madhvācārya quotes as follows from the *Brahma-vaivarta Purāṇa:*

ka ātmā kaḥ para iti dehādy-apekṣayā

na hi dehādir ātmā syān
na ca śatrur udīritaḥ
ato daihika-vṛddhau vā
kṣaye vā kiṁ prayojanam

yas tu deha-gato jīvaḥ
sa hi nāśaṁ na gacchati
tataḥ śatru-vivṛddhau ca
sva-nāśe śocanaṁ kutaḥ

dehādi-vyatiriktau tu
jīveśau pratijānatā
ata ātma-vivṛddhis tu
vāsudeve ratiḥ sthirā
śatru-nāśas tathājñāna-
nāśo nānyaḥ kathañcana

The purport is that as long as we are in this human form of body, our duty is to understand the soul within the body. The body is not the self; we are different from the body, and therefore there is no question of friends, enemies or responsibilities in terms of the bodily conception of life. One should not be very anxious about the body's changing from childhood to boyhood, from boyhood to old age and then to apparent annihilation. Rather, one should be very seriously concerned about the soul within the body and how to release the soul from the material clutches. The living entity within the body is never annihilated; therefore one should surely know that whether one has many friends or many enemies, his friends cannot help him, and his enemies cannot do him any harm. One should know that he is a spirit soul (*ahaṁ brahmāsmi*) and that the constitutional position of the soul is unaffected by the changes of the body. In all circumstances, everyone, as a spirit soul, must be a devotee of Lord Viṣṇu and should not be concerned with bodily relationships, whether with friends or with enemies. One should know that neither we ourselves nor our enemies in the bodily conception of life are ever killed.

TEXT 61

श्रीनारद उवाच
इति दैत्यपतेर्वाक्यं दितिराकर्ण्य सस्नुषा ।
पुत्रशोकं क्षणात्त्यक्त्वा तत्त्वे चित्तमधारयत् ॥६१॥

śrī-nārada uvāca
iti daitya-pater vākyaṁ
ditir ākarṇya sasnuṣā
putra-śokaṁ kṣaṇāt tyaktvā
tattve cittam adhārayat

śrī-nāradaḥ uvāca—Śrī Nārada Muni said; *iti*—thus; *daitya-pateḥ*—of the King of the demons; *vākyam*—the speech; *ditiḥ*—Diti, the mother of Hiraṇyakaśipu and Hiraṇyākṣa; *ākarṇya*—hearing; *sa-snuṣā*—with the wife of Hiraṇyākṣa; *putra-śokam*—the great bereavement for her son, Hiraṇyākṣa; *kṣaṇāt*—immediately; *tyaktvā*—giving up; *tattve*—in the real philosophy of life; *cittam*—heart; *adhārayat*—engaged.

TRANSLATION

Śrī Nārada Muni continued: Diti, the mother of Hiraṇyakaśipu and Hiraṇyākṣa, heard the instructions of Hiraṇyakaśipu along with her daughter-in-law, Ruṣābhānu, Hiraṇyākṣa's wife. She then forgot her grief over her son's death and thus engaged her mind and attention in understanding the real philosophy of life.

PURPORT

When a relative dies one certainly becomes very much interested in philosophy, but when the funeral ceremony is over one again becomes attentive to materialism. Even Daityas, who are materialistic persons, sometimes think of philosophy when some relative meets death. The technical term for this attitude of the materialistic person is *śmaśāna-vairāgya,* or detachment in a cemetery or place of cremation. As confirmed in *Bhagavad-gītā,* four classes of men receive an understanding of spiritual life and God—*ārta* (the distressed), *jijñāsu* (the inquisitive), *arthārthī* (one who desires material gains) and *jñānī* (one who is searching for knowledge). Especially when one is very much distressed by material conditions, one becomes interested in God. Therefore Kuntīdevī said in her prayers to Kṛṣṇa that she preferred distress to a happy mood of life. In the material world, one who is happy forgets Kṛṣṇa, or God, but sometimes, if one is actually pious but in distress, he remembers Kṛṣṇa. Queen Kuntīdevī therefore preferred distress because it is an opportunity for remembering Kṛṣṇa. When Kṛṣṇa was leaving Kuntīdevī for His own country, Kuntīdevī regretfully said that she was better off in distress because Kṛṣṇa was always present, whereas now that the Pāṇḍavas were situated in their kingdom, Kṛṣṇa was going away. For a devotee, distress is an opportunity to remember the Supreme Personality of Godhead constantly.

Thus end the Bhaktivedanta purports of the Seventh Canto, Second Chapter, of the Śrīmad-Bhāgavatam, *entitled "Hiraṇyakaśipu, King of the Demons."*

CHAPTER THREE

Hiraṇyakaśipu's Plan to Become Immortal

This chapter describes how Hiraṇyakaśipu performed a severe type of austerity for material benefit, thus causing great distress throughout the universe. Even Lord Brahmā, the chief personality within this universe, became somewhat disturbed and personally went to see why Hiraṇyakaśipu was engaged in such a severe austerity.

Hiraṇyakaśipu wanted to become immortal. He wanted not to be conquered by anyone, not to be attacked by old age and disease, and not to be harassed by any opponent. Thus he wanted to become the absolute ruler of the entire universe. With this desire, he entered the valley of Mandara Mountain and began practicing a severe type of austerity and meditation. Seeing Hiraṇyakaśipu engaged in this austerity, the demigods returned to their respective homes, but while Hiraṇyakaśipu was thus engaged, a kind of fire began blazing from his head, disturbing the entire universe and its inhabitants, including the birds, beasts and demigods. When all the higher and lower planets became too hot to live on, the demigods, being disturbed, left their abodes in the higher planets and went to see Lord Brahmā, praying to him that he curtail this unnecessary heat. The demigods disclosed to Lord Brahmā Hiraṇyakaśipu's ambition to become immortal, overcoming his short duration of life, and to be the master of all the planetary systems, even Dhruvaloka.

Upon hearing about the purpose of Hiraṇyakaśipu's austere meditation, Lord Brahmā, accompanied by the great sage Bhṛgu and great personalities like Dakṣa, went to see Hiraṇyakaśipu. He then sprinkled water from his *kamaṇḍalu,* a type of waterpot, upon Hiraṇyakaśipu's head.

Hiraṇyakaśipu, the King of the Daityas, bowed down before Lord Brahmā, the creator of this universe, offering respectful obeisances again and again and offering prayers. When Lord Brahmā agreed to give him benedictions, he prayed not be killed by any living entity, not to be killed in any place, covered or uncovered, not to die in the daytime or at night, not to be killed by any weapon, on land or in the air, and not to be killed by any human being, animal, demigod or any other entity, living or nonliving. He further prayed for supremacy over the entire universe and requested the eight yogic perfections, such as *aṇimā* and *laghimā*.

TEXT 1

श्रीनारद उवाच
हिरण्यकशिपू राजन्नजेयमजरामरम् ।
आत्मानमप्रतिद्वन्द्वमेकराजं व्यधित्सत ॥ १ ॥

śrī-nārada uvāca
hiraṇyakaśipū rājann
ajeyam ajarāmaram
ātmānam apratidvandvam
eka-rājaṁ vyadhitsata

śrī-nāradaḥ uvāca—Nārada Muni said; *hiraṇyakaśipuḥ*—the demoniac king Hiraṇyakaśipu; *rājan*—O King Yudhiṣṭhira; *ajeyam*—unconquerable by any enemy; *ajara*—without old age or disease; *amaram*—immortal; *ātmānam*—himself; *apratidvandvam*—without any rival or opponent; *eka-rājam*—the one king of the universe; *vyadhitsata*—desired to become.

TRANSLATION

Nārada Muni said to Mahārāja Yudhiṣṭhira: The demoniac king Hiraṇyakaśipu wanted to be unconquerable and free from old age and dwindling of the body. He wanted to gain all the yogic perfections like aṇimā and laghimā, to be deathless, and to be the only king of the entire universe, including Brahmaloka.

PURPORT

Such are the goals of the austerities performed by demons. Hiraṇyakaśipu wanted to receive a benediction from Lord Brahmā so that in the future he would be able to conquer Lord Brahmā's abode. Similarly, another demon received a benediction from Lord Śiva but later wanted to kill Lord Śiva through that same benediction. Thus self-interested persons, by demoniac austerity, want to kill even their benedictors, whereas the Vaiṣṇava wants to remain an ever-existing servant of the Lord and never to occupy the post of the Lord. Through *sāyujya-mukti,* which is generally demanded by *asuras,* one merges into the existence of the Lord, but although one sometimes thus achieves the goal of the theory of monism, one falls down again to struggle in material existence.

TEXT 2

स तेपे मन्दरद्रोण्यां तपः परमदारुणम् ।
ऊर्ध्वबाहुर्नभोदृष्टिः पादाङ्गुष्ठाश्रितावनिः ॥ २ ॥

sa tepe mandara-droṇyāṁ
tapaḥ parama-dāruṇam
ūrdhva-bāhur nabho-dṛṣṭiḥ
pādāṅguṣṭhāśritāvaniḥ

saḥ—he (Hiraṇyakaśipu); *tepe*—performed; *mandara-droṇyām*—in a valley of Mandara Hill; *tapaḥ*—austerity; *parama*—most; *dāruṇam*—difficult; *ūrdhva*—raising; *bāhuḥ*—arms; *nabhaḥ*—toward the sky; *dṛṣṭiḥ*—his vision; *pāda-aṅguṣṭha*—with the big toes of his feet; *āśrita*—resting on; *avaniḥ*—the ground.

TRANSLATION

In the valley of Mandara Hill, Hiraṇyakaśipu began performing his austerities by standing with his toes on the ground, keeping his arms upward and looking toward the sky. This position was extremely difficult, but he accepted it as a means to attain perfection.

TEXT 3

जटादीधितिभी रेजे संवर्तार्क इवांशुभिः ।
तस्मिंस्तपस्तप्यमाने देवाः स्थानानि भेजिरे ॥ ३ ॥

jaṭā-dīdhitibhī reje
saṁvartārka ivāṁśubhiḥ
tasmiṁs tapas tapyamāne
devāḥ sthānāni bhejire

jaṭā-dīdhitibhiḥ—by the effulgence of the hair on his head; *reje*—was shining; *saṁvarta-arkaḥ*—the sun at the time of destruction; *iva*—like; *aṁśubhiḥ*—by the beams; *tasmin*—when he (Hiraṇyakaśipu); *tapaḥ*—austerities; *tapyamāne*—was engaged in; *devāḥ*—all the demigods who were wandering throughout the universe to see Hiraṇyakaśipu's demoniac activities; *sthānāni*—to their own places; *bhejire*—returned.

TRANSLATION

From the hair on Hiraṇyakaśipu's head there emanated an effulgent light as brilliant and intolerable as the rays of the sun at the time of dissolution. Seeing the performance of such austere penances, the demigods, who had been wandering throughout the planets, now returned to their respective homes.

TEXT 4

तस्य मूर्ध्नः समुद्भूतः सधूमोऽग्निस्तपोमयः ।
तीर्यगूर्ध्वमधोलोकान् प्रातपद्विष्वगीरितः ॥ ४ ॥

tasya mūrdhnaḥ samudbhūtaḥ
sadhūmo 'gnis tapomayaḥ
tīryag ūrdhvam adho lokān
prātapad viṣvag īritaḥ

tasya—his; *mūrdhnaḥ*—from the head; *samudbhūtaḥ*—generated; *sa-dhūmaḥ*—with smoke; *agniḥ*—fire; *tapaḥ-mayaḥ*—because of severe austerities; *tīryak*—sideways; *ūrdhvam*—upward; *adhaḥ*—downward; *lokān*—all the planets; *prātapat*—heated; *viṣvak*—all around; *īritaḥ*—spreading.

TRANSLATION

Because of Hiraṇyakaśipu's severe austerities, fire came from his head, and this fire and its smoke spread throughout the sky,

encompassing the upper and lower planets, which all became extremely hot.

TEXT 5

चुक्षुभुर्नद्युदन्वन्तः सद्वीपाद्रिश्चचाल भूः ।
निपेतुः सग्रहास्तारा जज्वलुश्च दिशो दश ॥ ५ ॥

cukṣubhur nady-udanvantaḥ
sadvīpādriś cacāla bhūḥ
nipetuḥ sagrahās tārā
jajvaluś ca diśo daśa

cukṣubhuḥ—became agitated; *nadī-udanvantaḥ*—the rivers and oceans; *sa-dvīpa*—with the islands; *adriḥ*—and mountains; *cacāla*—trembled; *bhūḥ*—the surface of the globe; *nipetuḥ*—fell; *sa-grahāḥ*—with the planets; *tārāḥ*—the stars; *jajvaluḥ*—blazed; *ca*—also; *diśaḥ daśa*—the ten directions.

TRANSLATION

Because of the power of his severe austerities, all the rivers and oceans were agitated, the surface of the globe, with its mountains and islands, began trembling, and the stars and planets fell. All directions were ablaze.

TEXT 6

तेन तप्ता दिवं त्यक्त्वा ब्रह्मलोकं ययुः सुराः ।
धात्रे विज्ञापयामासुर्देवदेव जगत्पते ।
दैत्येन्द्रतपसा तप्ता दिवि स्थातुं न शक्नुमः ॥ ६ ॥

tena taptā divaṁ tyaktvā
brahmalokaṁ yayuḥ surāḥ
dhātre vijñāpayām āsur
deva-deva jagat-pate
daityendra-tapasā taptā
divi sthātuṁ na śaknumaḥ

tena—by that (fire of austerity); *taptāḥ*—burned; *divam*—their residential quarters in the upper planets; *tyaktvā*—giving up; *brahma-lokam*—to the planet where Lord Brahmā lives; *yayuḥ*—went; *surāḥ*—the demigods; *dhātre*—unto the chief of this universe, Lord Brahmā; *vijñāpayām āsuḥ*—submitted; *deva-deva*—O chief of the demigods; *jagat-pate*—O master of the universe; *daitya-indra-tapasā*—by the severe austerity performed by the King of the Daityas, Hiraṇyakaśipu; *taptāḥ*—roasted; *divi*—on the heavenly planets; *sthātum*—to stay; *na*—not; *śaknumaḥ*—we are able.

TRANSLATION

Scorched and extremely disturbed because of Hiraṇyakaśipu's severe penances, all the demigods left the planets where they reside and went to the planet of Lord Brahmā, where they informed the creator as follows: O lord of the demigods, O master of the universe, because of the fire emanating from Hiraṇyakaśipu's head as a result of his severe austerities, we have become so disturbed that we could not stay in our planets but have come to you.

TEXT 7

तस्य चोपशमं भूमन् विधेहि यदि मन्यसे ।
लोका न यावन्नङ्क्ष्यन्ति बलिहारास्तवाभिभूः ॥ ७ ॥

tasya copaśamaṁ bhūman
vidhehi yadi manyase
lokā na yāvan naṅkṣyanti
bali-hārās tavābhibhūḥ

tasya—of this; *ca*—indeed; *upaśamam*—the cessation; *bhūman*—O great personality; *vidhehi*—please execute; *yadi*—if; *manyase*—you think it right; *lokāḥ*—all the inhabitants of the various planets; *na*—not; *yāvat*—as long as; *naṅkṣyanti*—will be lost; *bali-hārāḥ*—who are obedient to the worship; *tava*—of you; *abhibhūḥ*—O chief of all the universe.

TRANSLATION

O great person, chief of the universe, if you think it proper, kindly stop these disturbances, meant to destroy everything, before all your obedient subjects are annihilated.

TEXT 8

तस्यायं किल सङ्कल्पश्चरतो दुश्चरं तपः ।
श्रूयतां किं न विदितस्तवाथापि निवेदितम् ॥ ८ ॥

tasyāyaṁ kila saṅkalpaś
carato duścaraṁ tapaḥ
śrūyatāṁ kiṁ na viditas
tavāthāpi niveditam

tasya—his; *ayam*—this; *kila*—indeed; *saṅkalpaḥ*—determination; *carataḥ*—who is executing; *duścaram*—very difficult; *tapaḥ*—austerity; *śrūyatām*—let it be heard; *kim*—what; *na*—not; *viditaḥ*—known; *tava*—of you; *athāpi*—still; *niveditam*—submitted.

TRANSLATION

Hiraṇyakaśipu has undertaken a most severe type of austerity. Although his plan is not unknown to you, kindly listen as we submit his intentions.

TEXTS 9–10

सृष्ट्वा चराचरमिदं तपोयोगसमाधिना ।
अध्यास्ते सर्वधिष्ण्येभ्यः परमेष्ठी निजासनम् ॥ ९ ॥
तदहं वर्धमानेन तपोयोगसमाधिना ।
कालात्मनोश्च नित्यत्वात्साधयिष्ये तथात्मनः ॥१०॥

sṛṣṭvā carācaram idaṁ
tapo-yoga-samādhinā
adhyāste sarva-dhiṣṇyebhyaḥ
parameṣṭhī nijāsanam

tad ahaṁ vardhamānena
tapo-yoga-samādhinā
kālātmanoś ca nityatvāt
sādhayiṣye tathātmanaḥ

sṛṣṭvā—creating; *cara*—moving; *acaram*—and not moving; *idam*—this; *tapaḥ*—of austerity; *yoga*—and mystic power; *samādhinā*—by practicing the trance; *adhyāste*—is situated in; *sarva-dhiṣṇyebhyaḥ*—than all the planets, including the heavenly planets; *parameṣṭhī*—Lord Brahmā; *nija-āsanam*—his own throne; *tat*—therefore; *aham*—I; *vardhamānena*—by dint of increasing; *tapaḥ*—austerity; *yoga*—mystic powers; *samādhinā*—and trance; *kāla*—of time; *ātmanoḥ*—and of the soul; *ca*—and; *nityatvāt*—from the eternality; *sādhayiṣye*—shall achieve; *tathā*—so much; *ātmanaḥ*—for my personal self.

TRANSLATION

"The supreme person within this universe, Lord Brahmā, has gotten his exalted post by dint of severe austerities, mystic power and trance. Consequently, after creating the universe, he has become the most worshipable demigod within it. Since I am eternal and time is eternal, I shall endeavor for such austerity, mystic power and trance for many, many births, and thus I shall occupy the same post occupied by Lord Brahmā.

PURPORT

Hiraṇyakaśipu's determination was to occupy the post of Lord Brahmā, but this was impossible because Brahmā has a long duration of life. As confirmed in *Bhagavad-gītā* (8.17), *sahasra-yuga-paryantam ahar yad brahmaṇo viduḥ:* one thousand *yugas* equals one day of Brahmā. The duration of Brahmā's life is extremely great, and consequently it was impossible for Hiraṇyakaśipu to occupy that post. Nonetheless, his decision was that since the self (*ātmā*) and time are both eternal, if he could not occupy that post in one lifetime he would continue to execute austerities life after life so that sometime he would be able to do so.

TEXT 11

अन्यथेदं विधास्येऽहमयथापूर्वमोजसा ।
किमन्यैः कालनिर्धूतैः कल्पान्ते वैष्णवादिभिः ॥११॥

anyathedaṁ vidhāsye 'ham
ayathā pūrvam ojasā
kim anyaiḥ kāla-nirdhūtaiḥ
kalpānte vaiṣṇavādibhiḥ

anyathā—just the opposite; *idam*—this universe; *vidhāsye*—shall make; *aham*—I; *ayathā*—inappropriate; *pūrvam*—as it was before; *ojasā*—by dint of the power of my austerity; *kim*—what use; *anyaiḥ*—with other; *kāla-nirdhūtaiḥ*—vanquished in due course of time; *kalpa-ante*—at the end of the millennium; *vaiṣṇava-ādibhiḥ*—with planets like Dhruvaloka or Vaikuṇṭhaloka.

TRANSLATION

"By dint of my severe austerities, I shall reverse the results of pious and impious activities. I shall overturn all the established practices within this world. Even Dhruvaloka will be vanquished at the end of the millennium. Therefore, what is the use of it? I shall prefer to remain in the position of Brahmā."

PURPORT

Hiraṇyakaśipu's demoniac determination was explained to Lord Brahmā by the demigods, who informed him that Hiraṇyakaśipu wanted to overturn all the established principles. After executing severe austerities, people within this material world are promoted to the heavenly planets, but Hiraṇyakaśipu wanted them to be unhappy, suffering because of the diplomatic feelings of the demigods, even in the heavenly planets. He wanted those who were harassed in this world by material transactions to be unhappy for the same reason, even in the heavenly planets. Indeed, he wanted to introduce such harassment everywhere. One might ask how this would be possible, since the universal order has been established since time immemorial, but Hiraṇyakaśipu was proud to declare that he would be able to do everything by the power of his *tapasya.* He even wanted to make the Vaiṣṇavas' position insecure. These are some of the symptoms of asuric determination.

TEXT 12

इति शुश्रुम निर्बन्धं तपः परममास्थितः ।
विधत्स्वानन्तरं युक्तं स्वयं त्रिभुवनेश्वर ॥१२॥

iti śuśruma nirbandhaṁ
tapaḥ paramam āsthitaḥ
vidhatsvānantaraṁ yuktaṁ
svayaṁ tri-bhuvaneśvara

iti—in this way; *śuśruma*—we have heard; *nirbandham*—strong determination; *tapaḥ*—austerity; *paramam*—very severe; *āsthitaḥ*—is situated in; *vidhatsva*—please take steps; *anantaram*—as soon as possible; *yuktam*—befitting; *svayam*—yourself; *tri-bhuvana-īśvara*—O master of the three worlds.

TRANSLATION

O lord, we have heard from reliable sources that in order to obtain your post, Hiraṇyakaśipu is now engaged in severe austerity. You are the master of the three worlds. Please, without delay, take whatever steps you deem appropriate.

PURPORT

In the material world, a servant is provided for by the master but is always planning how to capture the master's post. There have been many instances of this in history. Especially in India during the Mohammedan rule, many servants, by plans and devices, took over the posts of their masters. It is learned from Caitanya literature that one big Zamindar, Subuddhi Rāya, kept a Mohammedan boy as a servant. Of course, he treated the boy as his own child, and sometimes, when the boy would steal something, the master would chastise him by striking him with a cane. There was a mark on the boy's back from this chastisement. Later, after that boy had by crooked means become Hussain Shah, Nawab of Bengal, one day his wife saw the mark on his back and inquired about it. The Nawab replied that in his childhood he had been a servant of Subuddhi Rāya, who had punished him because of some mischievous activities. Upon hearing this, the Nawab's wife immediately became agitated and requested her husband to kill Subuddhi Rāya. Nawab Hussain Shah, of course, was very grateful to Subuddhi Rāya and therefore refused to kill him, but when his wife requested him to turn Subuddhi Rāya into a Mohammedan, the Nawab agreed. Taking some water from his waterpot, he sprinkled it upon Subuddhi Rāya and declared that Subuddhi Rāya had now become a Mohammedan. The point is that this Nawab had been an ordinary menial servant of Subuddhi Rāya but was somehow or other able to occupy the supreme post of Nawab of Bengal. This is the material world. Everyone is trying to become master through various devices, although everyone is servant of his senses. Following this system, a living entity, although servant of his senses, tries to become master of the whole universe. Hiraṇyakaśipu was a typical example of this, and Brahmā was informed by the demigods of his intentions.

TEXT 13

तवासनं द्विजगवां पारमेष्ठ्यं जगत्पते ।
भवाय श्रेयसे भूत्यै क्षेमाय विजयाय च ॥१३॥

tavāsanaṁ dvija-gavāṁ
pārameṣṭhyaṁ jagat-pate
bhavāya śreyase bhūtyai
kṣemāya vijayāya ca

tava—your; *āsanam*—position on the throne; *dvija*—of the brahminical culture or the *brāhmaṇas; gavām*—of the cows; *pārameṣṭhyam*—supreme; *jagat-pate*—O master of the whole universe; *bhavāya*—for improvement; *śreyase*—for the ultimate happiness; *bhūtyai*—for increasing the opulence; *kṣemāya*—for the maintenance and good fortune; *vijayāya*—for the victory and increasing prestige; *ca*—and.

TRANSLATION

O Lord Brahmā, your position within this universe is certainly most auspicious for everyone, especially the cows and brāhmaṇas. Brahminical culture and the protection of cows can be increasingly glorified, and thus all kinds of material happiness, opulence and good fortune will automatically increase. But unfortunately, if Hiraṇyakaśipu occupies your seat, everything will be lost.

PURPORT

In this verse the words *dvija-gavāṁ pārameṣṭhyam* indicate the most exalted position of the *brāhmaṇas*, brahminical culture and the cows. In Vedic culture, the welfare of the cows and the welfare of the *brāhmaṇas* are essential. Without a proper arrangement for developing brahminical culture and protecting cows, all the affairs of administration will go to hell. Being afraid that Hiraṇyakaśipu would occupy the post of Brahmā, all the demigods were extremely disturbed. Hiraṇyakaśipu was a well-known demon, and the demigods knew that if demons and Rākṣasas were to occupy the supreme post, brahminical culture and protection of cows would come to an end. As stated in *Bhagavad-gītā* (5.29), the original proprietor of everything is Lord Kṛṣṇa (*bhoktāraṁ yajña-tapasāṁ sarva-loka-maheśvaram*). The Lord, therefore, knows particularly well how to develop the material condition of the living entities within this material world. In every universe there is one Brahmā engaged on behalf of Lord Kṛṣṇa, as confirmed in *Śrīmad-Bhāgavatam* (*tene brahma hṛdā ya ādi-kavaye*). The principal creator in each *brahmāṇḍa* is Lord Brahmā, who imparts Vedic knowledge to his disciples and sons. On every planet, the king or supreme controller must be a representative of Brahmā. Therefore, if a Rākṣasa, or demon, were situated in Brahmā's post, then the entire arrangement of the universe, especially the protection of the brahminical culture and cows, would be ruined. All the demigods anticipated this danger, and therefore they went to request Lord Brahmā to take immediate steps to thwart Hiraṇyakaśipu's plan.

In the beginning of creation, Lord Brahmā was attacked by two demons—Madhu and Kaiṭabha—but Kṛṣṇa saved him. Therefore Kṛṣṇa is addressed as *madhu-kaiṭabha-hantṛ*. Now again, Hiraṇyakaśipu was trying to replace Brahmā. The material world is so situated that even the position of Lord Brahmā, not to speak of ordinary living entities, is sometimes in danger. Nonetheless, until the time of Hiraṇyakaśipu, no one had tried to replace Lord Brahmā. Hiraṇyakaśipu, however, was such a great demon that he maintained this ambition.

The word *bhūtyai* means "for increasing opulence," and the word *śreyase* refers to ultimately returning home, back to Godhead. In spiritual advancement, one's material position improves at the same time that the path of liberation becomes clear and one is freed from material bondage. If one is situated in an opulent position in spiritual advancement, his opulence never decreases. Therefore such a spiritual benediction is called *bhūti* or *vibhūti*. Kṛṣṇa confirms this in *Bhagavad-gītā* (10.41). *Yad yad vibhūtimat sattvaṁ . . . mama tejo-'ṁśa-sambhavam:* if a devotee advances in spiritual consciousness and thus becomes materially opulent also, his position is a special gift from the Lord. Such opulence is never to be considered material. At the present, especially on this planet earth, the influence of Lord Brahmā has decreased considerably, and the representatives of Hiraṇyakaśipu—the Rākṣasas and demons—have taken charge. Therefore there is no protection of brahminical culture and cows, which are the basic prerequisites for all kinds of good fortune. This age is very dangerous because society is being managed by demons and Rākṣasas.

TEXT 14

इति विज्ञापितो देवैर्भगवानात्मभूर्नृप ।
परितो भृगुदक्षाद्यैर्ययौ दैत्येश्वराश्रमम् ॥१४॥

iti vijñāpito devair
bhagavān ātmabhūr nṛpa
parito bhṛgu-dakṣādyair
yayau daityeśvarāśramam

iti—thus; *vijñāpitaḥ*—informed; *devaiḥ*—by all the demigods; *bhagavān*—the most powerful; *ātma-bhūḥ*—Lord Brahmā, who was born from the lotus flower; *nṛpa*—O King; *paritaḥ*—being surrounded; *bhṛgu*—by Bhṛgu; *dakṣa*—Dakṣa; *ādyaiḥ*—and others; *yayau*—went;

daitya-īśvara—of Hiraṇyakaśipu, the King of the Daityas; *āśramam*—to the place of austerity.

TRANSLATION

O King, being thus informed by the demigods, the most powerful Lord Brahmā, accompanied by Bhṛgu, Dakṣa and other great sages, immediately started for the place where Hiraṇyakaśipu was performing his penances and austerities.

PURPORT

Lord Brahmā was waiting for the austerities performed by Hiraṇyakaśipu to mature so that he could go there and offer benedictions according to Hiraṇyakaśipu's desire. Now, taking the opportunity of being accompanied by all the demigods and great saintly persons, Brahmā went there to award him the benediction he desired.

TEXTS 15–16

न ददर्श प्रतिच्छन्नं वल्मीकतृणकीचकैः ।
पिपीलिकाभिराचीर्णं मेदस्त्वङ्मांसशोणितम् ॥१५॥
तपन्तं तपसा लोकान् यथाभ्रापिहितं रविम् ।
विलक्ष्य विस्मितः प्राह हसंस्तं हंसवाहनः ॥१६॥

na dadarśa praticchannaṁ
valmīka-tṛṇa-kīcakaiḥ
pipīlikābhir ācīrṇaṁ
medas-tvaṅ-māṁsa-śoṇitam

tapantaṁ tapasā lokān
yathābhrāpihitaṁ ravim
vilakṣya vismitaḥ prāha
hasaṁs taṁ haṁsa-vāhanaḥ

na—not; *dadarśa*—saw; *praticchannam*—covered; *valmīka*—by an anthill; *tṛṇa*—grass; *kīcakaiḥ*—and bamboo sticks; *pipīlikābhiḥ*—by the ants; *ācīrṇam*—eaten all around; *medaḥ*—whose fat; *tvak*—skin;

māṁsa—the flesh; *śoṇitam*—and blood; *tapantam*—heating; *tapasā*—by a severe type of penance; *lokān*—all the three worlds; *yathā*—just as; *abhra*—by clouds; *apihitam*—covered; *ravim*—the sun; *vilakṣya*—seeing; *vismitaḥ*—struck with wonder; *prāha*—said; *hasan*—smiling; *tam*—to him; *haṁsa-vāhanaḥ*—Lord Brahmā, who rides a swan airplane.

TRANSLATION

Lord Brahmā, who is carried by a swan airplane, at first could not see where Hiraṇyakaśipu was, for Hiraṇyakaśipu's body was covered by an anthill and by grass and bamboo sticks. Because Hiraṇyakaśipu had been there for a long time, the ants had devoured his skin, fat, flesh and blood. Then Lord Brahmā and the demigods spotted him, resembling a cloud-covered sun, heating all the world by his austerity. Struck with wonder, Lord Brahmā began to smile and then addressed him as follows.

PURPORT

The living entity can live merely by his own power, without the help of skin, marrow, bone, blood and so on, because it is said, *asaṅgo 'yaṁ puruṣaḥ*—the living entity has nothing to do with the material covering. Hiraṇyakaśipu performed a severe type of *tapasya,* austerity, for many long years. Indeed, it is said that he performed the *tapasya* for one hundred heavenly years. Since one day of the demigods equals six of our months, certainly this was a very long time. By nature's own way, his body had been almost consumed by earthworms, ants and other parasites, and therefore even Brahmā was at first unable to see him. Later, however, Brahmā could ascertain where Hiraṇyakaśipu was, and Brahmā was struck with wonder to see Hiraṇyakaśipu's extraordinary power to execute *tapasya.* Anyone would conclude that Hiraṇyakaśipu was dead because his body was covered in so many ways, but Lord Brahmā, the supreme living being in this universe, could understand that Hiraṇyakaśipu was alive but covered by material elements.

It is also to be noted that although Hiraṇyakaśipu performed this austerity for a long, long time, he was nonetheless known as a Daitya and Rākṣasa. It will be seen from verses to follow that even great saintly persons could not perform such a severe type of austerity. Why then was he called a Rākṣasa and Daitya? It is because whatever he did was for his own sense gratification. His son Prahlāda Mahārāja was only five years old, and so what could Prahlāda do? Yet simply by performing a little devotional service according to the instructions of Nārada Muni, Prahlāda became so dear to the Lord that the Lord came to save him, whereas Hiraṇyakaśipu, in spite of all his austerities, was killed. This is the difference between devotional service and all other methods of perfection. One who performs severe austerities for sense gratification is fearful to the entire world, whereas a devotee who performs even a slight amount of devotional service is a friend to everyone (*suhṛdaṁ sarva-bhūtānām*). Since the Lord is the well-wisher of every living entity and since a devotee assumes the qualities of the Lord, a devotee also acts for everyone's good fortune by performing devotional service. Thus although Hiraṇyakaśipu performed such a severe austerity, he remained a Daitya and a Rākṣasa, whereas Prahlāda Mahārāja, although born of the same Daitya father, became the most exalted devotee and was personally protected by the Supreme Lord. *Bhakti* is therefore called *sarvopādhi-vinirmuktam*, indicating that a devotee is freed from all material designations, and *anyābhilāṣitā-śūnyam*, situated in a transcendental position, free from all material desires.

TEXT 17

श्रीब्रह्मोवाच
उत्तिष्ठोत्तिष्ठ भद्रं ते तपःसिद्धोऽसि काश्यप ।
वरदोऽहमनुप्राप्तो व्रियतामीप्सितो वरः ॥१७॥

śrī-brahmovāca
uttiṣṭhottiṣṭha bhadraṁ te
tapaḥ-siddho 'si kāśyapa
varado 'ham anuprāpto
vriyatām īpsito varaḥ

śrī-brahmā uvāca—Lord Brahmā said; *uttiṣṭha*—please get up; *uttiṣṭha*—get up; *bhadram*—good fortune; *te*—unto you; *tapaḥ-siddhaḥ*—perfect in executing austerities; *asi*—you are; *kāśyapa*—O son of Kaśyapa; *vara-daḥ*—the giver of benediction; *aham*—I; *anuprāptaḥ*—arrived; *vriyatām*—let it be submitted; *īpsitaḥ*—desired; *varaḥ*—benediction.

TRANSLATION

Lord Brahmā said: O son of Kaśyapa Muni, please get up, please get up. All good fortune unto you. You are now perfect in the performance of your austerities, and therefore I may give you a benediction. You may now ask from me whatever you desire, and I shall try to fulfill your wish.

PURPORT

Śrīla Madhvācārya quotes from the *Skanda Purāṇa,* which says that Hiraṇyakaśipu, having become a devotee of Lord Brahmā, who is known as Hiraṇyagarbha, and having undergone a severe austerity to please him, is also known as Hiraṇyaka. Rākṣasas and demons worship various demigods, such as Lord Brahmā and Lord Śiva, just to take the post of these demigods. This we have already explained in previous verses.

TEXT 18

अद्राक्षमहमेतं ते हृत्सारं महदद्भुतम् ।
दंशभक्षितदेहस्य प्राणा ह्यस्थिषु शेरते ॥१८॥

adrākṣam aham etaṁ te
hṛt-sāraṁ mahad-adbhutam
daṁśa-bhakṣita-dehasya
prāṇā hy asthiṣu śerate

adrākṣam—have personally seen; *aham*—I; *etam*—this; *te*—your; *hṛt-sāram*—power of endurance; *mahat*—very great; *adbhutam*—wonderful; *daṁśa-bhakṣita*—eaten by worms and ants; *dehasya*—whose body; *prāṇāḥ*—the life air; *hi*—indeed; *asthiṣu*—in the bones; *śerate*—is taking shelter.

TRANSLATION

I have been very much astonished to see your endurance. In spite of being eaten and bitten by all kinds of worms and ants, you

are keeping your life air circulating within your bones. Certainly this is wonderful.

PURPORT

It appears that the soul can exist even through the bones, as shown by the personal example of Hiraṇyakaśipu. When great *yogīs* are in *samādhi*, even when their bodies are buried and their skin, marrow, blood and so on have all been eaten, if only their bones remain they can exist in a transcendental position. Very recently an archaeologist published findings indicating that Lord Christ, after being buried, was exhumed and that he then went to Kashmir. There have been many actual examples of *yogīs'* being buried in trance and exhumed alive and in good condition several hours later. A *yogī* can keep himself alive in a transcendental state even if buried not only for many days but for many years.

TEXT 19

नैतत्पूर्वर्षयश्चक्रुर्न करिष्यन्ति चापरे ।
निरम्बुर्धारयेत्प्राणान् को वै दिव्यसमाः शतम् ॥१९॥

naitat pūrvarṣayaś cakrur
na kariṣyanti cāpare
nirambur dhārayet prāṇān
ko vai divya-samāḥ śatam

na—not; *etat*—this; *pūrva-ṛṣayaḥ*—the sages before you, such as Bhṛgu; *cakruḥ*—executed; *na*—nor; *kariṣyanti*—will execute; *ca*—also; *apare*—others; *nirambuḥ*—without drinking water; *dhārayet*—can sustain; *prāṇān*—the life air; *kaḥ*—who; *vai*—indeed; *divya-samāḥ*—celestial years; *śatam*—one hundred.

TRANSLATION

Even saintly persons like Bhṛgu, born previously, could not perform such severe austerities, nor will anyone in the future be able to do so. Who within these three worlds can sustain his life without even drinking water for one hundred celestial years?

PURPORT

It appears that even if a *yogī* does not drink a drop of water, he can live for many, many years by the yogic process, though his outer body be eaten by ants and moths.

TEXT 20

व्यवसायेन तेऽनेन दुष्करेण मनस्विनाम् ।
तपोनिष्ठेन भवता जितोऽहं दितिनन्दन ॥२०॥

vyavasāyena te 'nena
duṣkareṇa manasvinām
tapo-niṣṭhena bhavatā
jito 'haṁ diti-nandana

vyavasāyena—by determination; *te*—your; *anena*—this; *duṣkareṇa*—difficult to perform; *manasvinām*—even for great sages and saintly persons; *tapaḥ-niṣṭhena*—aimed at executing austerity; *bhavatā*—by you; *jitaḥ*—conquered; *aham*—I; *diti-nandana*—O son of Diti.

TRANSLATION

My dear son of Diti, with your great determination and austerity you have done what was impossible even for great saintly persons, and thus I have certainly been conquered by you.

PURPORT

In regard to the word *jitaḥ*, Śrīla Madhva Muni gives the following quotation from the *Śabda-nirṇaya: parābhūtaṁ vaśa-sthaṁ ca jitabhid ucyate budhaiḥ.* "If one comes under someone else's control or is defeated by another, he is called *jitaḥ.*" Hiraṇyakaśipu's austerity was so great and wonderful that even Lord Brahmā agreed to be conquered by him.

TEXT 21

ततस्त आशिषः सर्वा ददाम्यसुरपुङ्गव ।
मर्तस्य ते ह्यमर्तस्य दर्शनं नाफलं मम ॥२१॥

tatas ta āśiṣaḥ sarvā
dadāmy asura-puṅgava
martasya te hy amartasya
darśanaṁ nāphalaṁ mama

tataḥ—because of this; *te*—unto you; *āśiṣaḥ*—benedictions; *sarvāḥ*—all; *dadāmi*—I shall give; *asura-puṅgava*—O best of the *asuras; martasya*—of one who is destined to die; *te*—such as you; *hi*—indeed; *amartasya*—of one who does not die; *darśanam*—the audience; *na*—not; *aphalam*—without results; *mama*—my.

TRANSLATION

O best of the asuras, for this reason I am now prepared to give you all benedictions, according to your desire. I belong to the celestial world of demigods, who do not die like human beings. Therefore, although you are subject to death, your audience with me will not go in vain.

PURPORT

It appears that human beings and *asuras* are subject to death, whereas demigods are not. The demigods who reside with Lord Brahmā in Satyaloka go to Vaikuṇṭhaloka in their present bodily constructions at the time of the dissolution. Therefore although Hiraṇyakaśipu had undergone severe austerities, Lord Brahmā predicted that he had to die; he could not become immortal or even gain equal status with the demigods. The great austerities and penances he had performed for so many years could not give him protection from death. This was foretold by Lord Brahmā.

TEXT 22

श्रीनारद उवाच
इत्युक्त्वादिभवो देवो भक्षिताङ्गं पिपीलिकैः ।
कमण्डलुजलेनौक्षद्दिव्येनामोघराधसा ॥२२॥

śrī-nārada uvāca
ity uktvādi-bhavo devo
bhakṣitāṅgaṁ pipīlikaiḥ

kamaṇḍalu-jalenaukṣad
divyenāmogha-rādhasā

śrī-nāradaḥ uvāca—Śrī Nārada Muni said; *iti*—thus; *uktvā*—saying; *ādi-bhavaḥ*—Lord Brahmā, the original living creature within this universe; *devaḥ*—the principal demigod; *bhakṣita-aṅgam*—Hiraṇyakaśipu's body, which had been almost completely eaten; *pipīlikaiḥ*—by the ants; *kamaṇḍalu*—from the special waterpot in the hands of Lord Brahmā; *jalena*—by water; *aukṣat*—sprinkled; *divyena*—which was spiritual, not ordinary; *amogha*—without fail; *rādhasā*—whose power.

TRANSLATION

Śrī Nārada Muni continued: After speaking these words to Hiraṇyakaśipu, Lord Brahmā, the original being of this universe, who is extremely powerful, sprinkled transcendental, infallible, spiritual water from his kamaṇḍalu upon Hiraṇyakaśipu's body, which had been eaten away by ants and moths. Thus he enlivened Hiraṇyakaśipu.

PURPORT

Lord Brahmā is the first created being within this universe and is empowered by the Supreme Lord to create. *Tene brahma hṛdā ya ādi-kavaye:* the *ādi-deva,* or *ādi-kavi*—the first living creature—was personally taught by the Supreme Personality of Godhead through the heart. There was no one to teach him, but since the Lord is situated within Brahmā's heart, Brahmā was educated by the Lord Himself. Lord Brahmā, being especially empowered, is infallible in doing whatever he wants. This is the meaning of the word *amogha-rādhasā.* He desired to restore Hiraṇyakaśipu's original body, and therefore, by sprinkling transcendental water from his waterpot, he immediately did so.

TEXT 23

स तत्कीचकवल्मीकात् सहओजोबलान्वितः ।
सर्वावयवसम्पन्नो वज्रसंहननो युवा ।
उत्थितस्तप्तहेमाभो विभावसुरिवैधसः ॥२३॥

sa tat kīcaka-valmīkāt
saha-ojo-balānvitaḥ
sarvāvayava-sampanno
vajra-saṁhanano yuvā
utthitas tapta-hemābho
vibhāvasur ivaidhasaḥ

saḥ—Hiraṇyakaśipu; *tat*—that; *kīcaka-valmīkāt*—from the anthill and bamboo grove; *sahaḥ*—mental strength; *ojaḥ*—strength of the senses; *bala*—and sufficient bodily strength; *anvitaḥ*—endowed with; *sarva*—all; *avayava*—the limbs of the body; *sampannaḥ*—fully restored; *vajra-saṁhananaḥ*—having a body as strong as a thunderbolt; *yuvā*—young; *utthitaḥ*—arisen; *tapta-hema-ābhaḥ*—whose bodily luster became like molten gold; *vibhāvasuḥ*—fire; *iva*—like; *edhasaḥ*—from fuel wood.

TRANSLATION

As soon as he was sprinkled with the water from Lord Brahmā's waterpot, Hiraṇyakaśipu arose, endowed with a full body with limbs so strong that they could bear the striking of a thunderbolt. With physical strength and a bodily luster resembling molten gold, he emerged from the anthill a completely young man, just as fire springs from fuel wood.

PURPORT

Hiraṇyakaśipu was revitalized, so much so that his body was quite competent to tolerate the striking of thunderbolts. He was now a young man with a strong body and a very beautiful bodily luster resembling molten gold. This is the rejuvenation that took place because of his severe austerity and penance.

TEXT 24

स निरीक्ष्याम्बरे देवं हंसवाहमुपस्थितम् ।
ननाम शिरसा भूमौ तद्दर्शनमहोत्सवः ॥२४॥

sa nirīkṣyāmbare devaṁ
haṁsa-vāham upasthitam
nanāma śirasā bhūmau
tad-darśana-mahotsavaḥ

saḥ—he (Hiraṇyakaśipu); *nirīkṣya*—seeing; *ambare*—in the sky; *devam*—the supreme demigod; *haṁsa-vāham*—who rides a swan airplane; *upasthitam*—situated before him; *nanāma*—offered obeisances; *śirasā*—with his head; *bhūmau*—on the ground; *tat-darśana*—by seeing Lord Brahmā; *mahā-utsavaḥ*—very much pleased.

TRANSLATION

Seeing Lord Brahmā present before him in the sky, carried by his swan airplane, Hiraṇyakaśipu was extremely pleased. He immediately fell flat with his head on the ground and began to express his obligation to the lord.

PURPORT

Lord Kṛṣṇa says in *Bhagavad-gītā* (9.23–24):

ye 'py anya-devatā-bhaktā
yajante śraddhayānvitāḥ
te 'pi mām eva kaunteya
yajanty avidhi-pūrvakam

ahaṁ hi sarva-yajñānāṁ
bhoktā ca prabhur eva ca
na tu mām abhijānanti
tattvenātaś cyavanti te

"Whatever a man may sacrifice to other gods, O son of Kuntī, is really meant for Me alone, but it is offered without true understanding. I am the only enjoyer and the only object of sacrifice. Those who do not recognize My true transcendental nature fall down."

In effect, Kṛṣṇa says, "Persons engaged in the worship of demigods are not very intelligent, although such worship is indirectly offered to

Me." For example, when a man pours water on the leaves and branches of a tree without pouring water on the root, he does so without sufficient knowledge or without observing regulative principles. The process of watering a tree is to pour water on the root. Similarly, the process of rendering service to different parts of the body is to supply food to the stomach. The demigods are, so to speak, different officers and directors in the government of the Supreme Lord. One has to follow the laws made by the government, not by the officers or directors. Similarly, everyone is to offer his worship to the Supreme Lord only. That will automatically satisfy the different officers and directors of the Lord. The officers and directors are engaged as representatives of the government, and to offer some bribe to the officers and directors is illegal. This is stated in *Bhagavad-gītā* as *avidhi-pūrvakam.* In other words, Kṛṣṇa does not approve the unnecessary worship of the demigods.

In *Bhagavad-gītā* it is clearly stated that there are many types of *yajña* performances recommended in the Vedic literatures, but actually all of them are meant for satisfying the Supreme Lord. *Yajña* means Viṣṇu. In the Third Chapter of *Bhagavad-gītā* it is clearly stated that one should work only for satisfying Yajña, or Viṣṇu. The perfectional form of human civilization, known as *varṇāśrama-dharma,* is specifically meant for satisfying Viṣṇu. Therefore, Kṛṣṇa says, "I am the enjoyer of all sacrifices because I am the supreme master." However, less intelligent persons, without knowing this fact, worship demigods for temporary benefit. Therefore they fall down to material existence and do not achieve the desired goal of life. If, however, anyone has any material desire to be fulfilled, he had better pray for it to the Supreme Lord (although that is not pure devotion), and he will thus achieve the desired result.

Although Hiraṇyakaśipu offered his obeisances unto Lord Brahmā, he was strongly inimical toward Lord Viṣṇu. This is the symptom of an *asura. Asuras* worship the demigods as being separate from the Lord, not knowing that all the demigods are powerful because of being servants of the Lord. If the Supreme Lord were to withdraw the powers of the demigods, the demigods would no longer be able to offer benedictions to their worshipers. The difference between a devotee and a nondevotee, or *asura,* is that a devotee knows that Lord Viṣṇu is the Supreme Personality of Godhead and that everyone derives power from Him. Without worshiping the demigods for particular powers, a devotee worships Lord Viṣṇu, knowing that if he desires a particular power he can get that power while acting as Lord Viṣṇu's devotee. Therefore in the *śāstra* (*Bhāg.* 2.3.10) it is recommended:

akāmaḥ sarva-kāmo vā
mokṣa-kāma udāra-dhīḥ
tīvreṇa bhakti-yogena
yajeta puruṣaṁ param

"A person who has broader intelligence, whether he be full of material desires, free from material desires, or desiring liberation, must by all means worship the supreme whole, the Personality of Godhead." Even if a person has material desires, instead of worshiping the demigods he should pray to the Supreme Lord so that his connection with the Supreme Lord will be established and he will be saved from becoming a demon or a nondevotee. In this regard, Śrīla Madhvācārya gives the following quotation from the *Brahma-tarka:*

eka-sthānaika-kāryatvād
viṣṇoḥ prādhānyatas tathā
jīvasya tad-adhīnatvān
na bhinnādhikṛtaṁ vacaḥ

Since Viṣṇu is the Supreme, by worshiping Viṣṇu one can fulfill all one's desires. There is no need to divert one's attention to any demigod.

TEXT 25

उत्थाय प्राञ्जलिः प्रह्व ईक्षमाणो दृशा विभुम् ।
हर्षाश्रुपुलकोद्भेदो गिरा गद्गदयागृणात् ॥२५॥

utthāya prāñjaliḥ prahva
īkṣamāṇo dṛśā vibhum
harṣāśru-pulakodbhedo
girā gadgadayāgṛṇāt

utthāya—getting up; *prāñjaliḥ*—with folded hands; *prahvaḥ*—in a humble manner; *īkṣamāṇaḥ*—seeing; *dṛśā*—with his eyes; *vibhum*—the supreme person within this universe; *harṣa*—of jubilation; *aśru*—with tears; *pulaka*—with hairs standing on the body; *udbhedaḥ*—enlivened; *girā*—by words; *gadgadayā*—faltering; *agṛṇāt*—prayed.

TRANSLATION

Then, getting up from the ground and seeing Lord Brahmā before him, the head of the Daityas was overwhelmed by jubilation. With tears in his eyes, his whole body shivering, he began praying in a humble mood, with folded hands and a faltering voice, to satisfy Lord Brahmā.

TEXTS 26–27

श्रीहिरण्यकशिपुरुवाच
कल्पान्ते कालसृष्टेन योऽन्धेन तमसावृतम् ।
अभिव्यनग् जगदिदं स्वयञ्ज्योतिः स्वरोचिषा॥२६॥
आत्मना त्रिवृता चेदं सृजत्यवति लुम्पति ।
रजःसत्त्वतमोधाम्ने पराय महते नमः ॥२७॥

śrī-hiraṇyakaśipur uvāca
kalpānte kāla-sṛṣṭena
yo 'ndhena tamasāvṛtam
abhivyanag jagad idaṁ
svayañjyotiḥ sva-rociṣā

ātmanā tri-vṛtā cedaṁ
sṛjaty avati lumpati
rajaḥ-sattva-tamo-dhāmne
parāya mahate namaḥ

śrī-hiraṇyakaśipuḥ uvāca—Hiraṇyakaśipu said; *kalpa-ante*—at the end of every day of Lord Brahmā; *kāla-sṛṣṭena*—created by the time factor; *yaḥ*—he who; *andhena*—by dense darkness; *tamasā*—by ignorance; *āvṛtam*—covered; *abhivyanak*—manifested; *jagat*—cosmic manifestation; *idam*—this; *svayam-jyotiḥ*—self-effulgent; *sva-rociṣā*—by his bodily rays; *ātmanā*—by himself; *tri-vṛtā*—conducted by the three modes of material nature; *ca*—also; *idam*—this material world; *sṛjati*—creates; *avati*—maintains; *lumpati*—annihilates; *rajaḥ*—of the mode of passion; *sattva*—the mode of goodness; *tamaḥ*—and the mode of ignorance; *dhāmne*—unto the supreme lord; *parāya*—unto the supreme; *mahate*—unto the great; *namaḥ*—my respectful obeisances.

TRANSLATION

Let me offer my respectful obeisances unto the supreme lord within this universe. At the end of each day of his life, the universe is fully covered with dense darkness by the influence of time, and then again, during his next day, that self-effulgent lord, by his own effulgence, manifests, maintains and destroys the entire cosmic manifestation through the material energy, which is invested with the three modes of material nature. He, Lord Brahmā, is the shelter of those modes of nature—sattva-guṇa, rajo-guṇa and tamo-guṇa.

PURPORT

The words *abhivyanag jagad idam* refer to he who creates this cosmic manifestation. The original creator is the Supreme Personality of Godhead, Kṛṣṇa (*janmādy asya yataḥ*); Lord Brahmā is the secondary creator. When Lord Brahmā is empowered by Lord Kṛṣṇa as the engineer to create the phenomenal world, he becomes the supremely powerful feature within this universe. The total material energy is created by Kṛṣṇa, and later, taking advantage of all that has necessarily been created, Lord Brahmā engineers the entire phenomenal universe. At the end of Lord Brahmā's day, everything up to Svargaloka is inundated with water, and the next morning, when there is darkness in the universe, Brahmā again brings the phenomenal manifestation into existence. Therefore he is described here as he who manifests this universe.

Trīn guṇān vṛṇoti: Lord Brahmā takes advantage of the three modes of material nature. *Prakṛti*, material nature, is described here as *tri-vṛtā*, the source of the three material modes. Śrīla Madhvācārya comments in this connection that *tri-vṛtā* means *prakṛtyā*. Thus Lord Kṛṣṇa is the original creator, and Lord Brahmā is the original engineer.

TEXT 28

नम आद्याय बीजाय ज्ञानविज्ञानमूर्तये ।
प्राणेन्द्रियमनोबुद्धिविकारैर्व्यक्तिमीयुषे ॥२८॥

nama ādyāya bījāya
jñāna-vijñāna-mūrtaye
prāṇendriya-mano-buddhi-
vikārair vyaktim īyuṣe

namaḥ—I offer my respectful obeisances; *ādyāya*—unto the original living creature; *bījāya*—the seed of the cosmic manifestation; *jñāna*—of knowledge; *vijñāna*—and of practical application; *mūrtaye*—unto the deity or form; *prāṇa*—of the life air; *indriya*—of the senses; *manaḥ*—of the mind; *buddhi*—of the intelligence; *vikāraiḥ*—by transformations; *vyaktim*—manifestation; *īyuṣe*—who has obtained.

TRANSLATION

I offer my obeisances to the original personality within this universe, Lord Brahmā, who is cognizant and who can apply his mind and realized intelligence in creating this cosmic manifestation. It is because of his activities that everything within the universe is visible. He is therefore the cause of all manifestations.

PURPORT

The *Vedānta-sūtra* begins by declaring that the Absolute Person is the original source of all creation (*janmādy asya yataḥ*). One may ask whether Lord Brahmā is the Supreme Absolute Person. No, the Supreme Absolute Person is Kṛṣṇa. Brahmā receives his mind, intelligence, materials and everything else from Kṛṣṇa, and then he becomes the secondary creator, the engineer of this universe. In this regard we may note that the creation does not take place accidentally, because of the explosion of a chunk. Such nonsensical theories are not accepted by Vedic students. The first created living being is Brahmā, who is endowed with perfect knowledge and intelligence by the Lord. As stated in *Śrīmad-Bhāgavatam, tene brahma hṛdā ya ādi-kavaye:* although Brahmā is the first created being, he is not independent, for he receives help from the Supreme Personality of Godhead through his heart. There is no one but Brahmā at the time of creation, and therefore he receives his intelligence directly from the Lord through the heart. This has been discussed in the beginning of *Śrīmad-Bhāgavatam.*

Lord Brahmā is described in this verse as the original cause of the cosmic manifestation, and this applies to his position in the material world. There are many, many such controllers, all of whom are created by the Supreme Lord, Viṣṇu. This is illustrated by an incident described in *Caitanya-caritāmṛta.* When the Brahmā of this particular universe was invited by Kṛṣṇa to Dvārakā, he thought that he was the only Brahmā. Therefore when Kṛṣṇa inquired from His servant which Brahmā was at the door to visit, Lord Brahmā was surprised. He replied that of course Lord Brahmā, the father of the four Kumāras, was waiting at the door. Later, Lord Brahmā asked Kṛṣṇa why He had inquired which Brahmā had come. He was then informed that there are millions of other Brahmās because there are millions of universes. Kṛṣṇa then called all the Brahmās, who immediately came to visit Him. The *catur-mukha* Brahmā, the four-headed Brahmā of this universe, thought himself a very insignificant creature in the presence of so many Brahmās with so many heads. Thus although there is a Brahmā who is the engineer of each universe, Kṛṣṇa is the original source of all of them.

TEXT 29

त्वमीशिषे जगतस्तस्थुषश्च
प्राणेन मुख्येन पतिः प्रजानाम् ।
चित्तस्य चित्तैर्मनइन्द्रियाणां
पतिर्महान् भूतगुणाशयेशः ॥२९॥

tvam īśiṣe jagatas tasthuṣaś ca
prāṇena mukhyena patiḥ prajānām
cittasya cittair mana-indriyāṇāṁ
patir mahān bhūta-guṇāśayeśaḥ

tvam—you; *īśiṣe*—actually control; *jagataḥ*—of the moving being; *tasthuṣaḥ*—of the being that is dull or stationed in one place; *ca*—and; *prāṇena*—by the living force; *mukhyena*—the origin of all activities; *patiḥ*—master; *prajānām*—of all living entities; *cittasya*—of the mind; *cittaiḥ*—by the consciousness; *manaḥ*—of the mind; *indriyāṇām*—and of the two kinds of senses (acting and knowledge-gathering); *patiḥ*—the master; *mahān*—great; *bhūta*—of the material elements; *guṇa*—and the qualities of the material elements; *āśaya*—of desires; *īśaḥ*—the supreme master.

TRANSLATION

Your Lordship, being the origin of the life of this material world, is the master and controller of the living entities, both moving and stationary, and you inspire their consciousness. You maintain the mind and the acting and knowledge-acquiring senses, and therefore you are the great controller of all the material elements and their qualities, and you are the controller of all desires.

PURPORT

In this verse it is clearly indicated that the original source of everything is life. Brahmā was instructed by the supreme life, Kṛṣṇa. Kṛṣṇa is the supreme living entity (*nityo nityānāṁ cetanaś cetanānām*), and Brahmā is also a living entity, but the original source of Brahmā is Kṛṣṇa. Therefore Kṛṣṇa says in *Bhagavad-gītā* (7.7), *mattaḥ parataraṁ nānyat kiñcid asti dhanañjaya:* "O Arjuna, there is no truth superior to Me." Kṛṣṇa is the original source of Brahmā, who is the original source of this universe. Brahmā is a representative of Kṛṣṇa, and therefore all the qualities and activities of Kṛṣṇa are also present in Lord Brahmā.

TEXT 30

त्वं सप्ततन्तून् वितनोषि तन्वा
त्रय्या चतुर्होत्रकविद्यया च ।
त्वमेक आत्मात्मवतामनादि-
रनन्तपारः कविरन्तरात्मा ॥३०॥

tvaṁ sapta-tantūn vitanoṣi tanvā
trayyā catur-hotraka-vidyayā ca
tvam eka ātmātmavatām anādir
ananta-pāraḥ kavir antarātmā

tvam—you; *sapta-tantūn*—the seven kinds of Vedic ritualistic ceremonies, beginning from the *agniṣṭoma-yajña; vitanoṣi*—spread; *tanvā*—by your body; *trayyā*—the three *Vedas; catuḥ-hotraka*—of the four kinds of Vedic priests, known as *hotā, adhvaryu, brahma* and *udgātā; vidyayā*—by the necessary knowledge; *ca*—also; *tvam*—you; *ekaḥ*—one; *ātmā*—the Supersoul; *ātma-vatām*—of all living entities; *anādiḥ*—without beginning; *ananta-pāraḥ*—without end; *kaviḥ*—the supreme inspirer; *antaḥ-ātmā*—the Supersoul within the core of the heart.

TRANSLATION

My dear lord, by your form as the Vedas personified and through knowledge relating to the activities of all the yajñic brāhmaṇas, you spread the Vedic ritualistic ceremonies of the seven kinds of sacrifices, headed by agniṣṭoma. Indeed, you inspire the yajñic brāhmaṇas to perform the rituals mentioned in the three Vedas. Being the Supreme Soul, the Supersoul of all living entities, you are beginningless, endless and omniscient, beyond the limits of time and space.

PURPORT

The Vedic ritualistic ceremonies, the knowledge thereof, and the person who agrees to perform them are inspired by the Supreme Soul. As confirmed in *Bhagavad-gītā, mattaḥ smṛtir jñānam apohanaṁ ca:* from the Lord come remembrance, knowledge and forgetfulness. The Supersoul is situated in everyone's heart (*sarvasya cāhaṁ hṛdi sanniviṣṭaḥ, īśvaraḥ sarva-bhūtānāṁ hṛd-deśe 'rjuna tiṣṭhati*), and when one is advanced in Vedic knowledge, the Supersoul gives him directions. Acting as Supersoul, the Lord gives inspiration to a suitable person to perform the Vedic ritualistic ceremonies. In this connection, four classes of priests, known as *ṛtvik,* are required. They are mentioned as *hotā, adhvaryu, brahma* and *udgātā.*

TEXT 31

त्वमेव कालोऽनिमिषो जनाना-
मायुर्लवाद्यवयवैः क्षिणोषि ।
कूटस्थ आत्मा परमेष्ठ्यजो महां-
स्त्वं जीवलोकस्य च जीव आत्मा ॥३१॥

tvam eva kālo 'nimiṣo janānām
āyur lavādy-avayavaiḥ kṣiṇoṣi
kūṭa-stha ātmā parameṣṭhy ajo mahāṁs
tvaṁ jīva-lokasya ca jīva ātmā

tvam—you; *eva*—indeed; *kālaḥ*—unlimited time; *animiṣaḥ*—unblinking; *janānām*—of all living entities; *āyuḥ*—the duration of life; *lava-ādi*—consisting of seconds, moments, minutes and hours; *avayavaiḥ*—by different parts; *kṣiṇoṣi*—reduce; *kūṭa-sthaḥ*—without being affected by anything; *ātmā*—the Supersoul; *parameṣṭhī*—the Supreme Lord; *ajaḥ*—the unborn; *mahān*—the great; *tvam*—you; *jīva-lokasya*—of this material world; *ca*—also; *jīvaḥ*—the cause of life; *ātmā*—the Supersoul.

TRANSLATION

O my lord, Your Lordship is eternally awake, seeing everything that happens. As eternal time, you reduce the duration of life for all living entities through your different parts, such as moments, seconds, minutes and hours. Nonetheless, you are unchanged, resting in one place as the Supersoul, witness and Supreme Lord, the birthless, all-pervading controller who is the cause of life for all living entities.

PURPORT

In this verse the word *kūṭa-stha* is very important. Although the Supreme Personality of Godhead is situated everywhere, He is the central unchanging point. *Īśvaraḥ sarva-bhūtānāṁ hṛd-deśe 'rjuna tiṣṭhati:* the Lord is situated in full in the core of everyone's heart. As indicated in the *Upaniṣads* by the word *ekatvam,* although there are millions and millions of living entities, the Lord is situated as the Supersoul in every one of them. Nonetheless, He is one in many. As stated in the *Brahma-saṁhitā, advaitam acyutam anādim ananta-rūpam:* He has many forms, yet they are *advaita*—one and unchanging. Since the Lord is all-pervading, He is also situated in eternal time. The living entities are described as parts and parcels of the Lord because He is the life and soul of all living entities, being situated within their hearts as the *antaryāmī,* as enunciated by the philosophy of inconceivable oneness and difference (*acintya-bhedābheda*). Since the living entities are part of God, they are one in quality with the Lord, yet they are different from Him. The Supersoul, who inspires all living entities to act, is one and changeless. There are varieties of subjects, objects and activities, yet the Lord is one.

TEXT 32

त्वत्तः परं नापरमप्यनेज-
देजच्च किञ्चिद् व्यतिरिक्तमस्ति ।
विद्याः कलास्ते तनवश्च सर्वा
हिरण्यगर्भोऽसि बृहत्त्रिपृष्ठः ॥३२॥

tvattaḥ paraṁ nāparam apy anejad
ejac ca kiñcid vyatiriktam asti
vidyāḥ kalās te tanavaś ca sarvā
hiraṇyagarbho 'si bṛhat tri-pṛṣṭhaḥ

tvattaḥ—from you; *param*—higher; *na*—not; *aparam*—lower; *api*—even; *anejat*—not moving; *ejat*—moving; *ca*—and; *kiñcit*—anything; *vyatiriktam*—separate; *asti*—there is; *vidyāḥ*—knowledge; *kalāḥ*—its parts; *te*—of you; *tanavaḥ*—features of the body; *ca*—and; *sarvāḥ*—all; *hiraṇya-garbhaḥ*—the one who keeps the universe within his abdomen; *asi*—you are; *bṛhat*—greater than the greatest; *tri-pṛṣṭhaḥ*—transcendental to the three modes of material nature.

TRANSLATION

There is nothing separate from you, whether it be better or lower, stationary or moving. The knowledge derived from the

Vedic literatures like the Upaniṣads, and from all the sub-limbs of the original Vedic knowledge, form your external body. You are Hiraṇyagarbha, the reservoir of the universe, but nonetheless, being situated as the supreme controller, you are transcendental to the material world, which consists of the three modes of material nature.

PURPORT

The word *param* means "the supreme cause," and *aparam* means "the effect." The supreme cause is the Supreme Personality of Godhead, and the effect is material nature. The living entities, both moving and nonmoving, are controlled by the Vedic instructions in art and science, and therefore they are all expansions of the external energy of the Supreme Personality of Godhead, who is the center as the Supersoul. The *brahmāṇḍas*, the universes, exist during the duration of a breath of the Supreme Lord (*yasyaika-niśvasita-kālam athāvalambya jīvanti loma-vilajā jagad-aṇḍa-nāthāḥ*). Thus they are also within the womb of the Supreme Personality of Godhead, Mahā-Viṣṇu. Nothing, therefore, is separate from the Supreme Lord. This is the philosophy of *acintya-bhedābheda-tattva.*

TEXT 33

व्यक्तं विभो स्थूलमिदं शरीरं
येनेन्द्रियप्राणमनोगुणांस्त्वम् ।
भुङ्क्षे स्थितो धामनि पारमेष्ठ्ये
अव्यक्त आत्मा पुरुषः पुराणः ॥३३॥

vyaktaṁ vibho sthūlam idaṁ śarīraṁ
yenendriya-prāṇa-mano-guṇāṁs tvam
bhuṅkṣe sthito dhāmani pārameṣṭhye
avyakta ātmā puruṣaḥ purāṇaḥ

vyaktam—manifested; *vibho*—O my lord; *sthūlam*—cosmic manifestation; *idam*—this; *śarīram*—external body; *yena*—by which; *indriya*—the senses; *prāṇa*—the life air; *manaḥ*—the mind; *guṇān*—

transcendental qualities; *tvam*—you; *bhuṅkṣe*—enjoy; *sthitaḥ*—situated; *dhāmani*—in your own abode; *pārameṣṭhye*—the supreme; *avyaktaḥ*—not manifested through ordinary knowledge; *ātmā*—the soul; *puruṣaḥ*—the supreme person; *purāṇaḥ*—the oldest.

TRANSLATION

O my lord, being changelessly situated in your own abode, you expand your universal form within this cosmic manifestation, thus appearing to taste the material world. You are Brahman, the Supersoul, the oldest, the Personality of Godhead.

PURPORT

It is said that the Absolute Truth appears in three features—namely, impersonal Brahman, localized Supersoul and ultimately the Supreme Personality of Godhead, Kṛṣṇa. The cosmic manifestation is the gross material body of the Supreme Personality of Godhead, who enjoys the taste of the material mellows by expanding His parts and parcels, the living entities, who are qualitatively one with Him. The Supreme Personality of Godhead, however, is situated in the Vaikuṇṭha planets, where He enjoys the spiritual mellows. Therefore the one Absolute Truth, Bhagavān, pervades all by His material cosmic manifestation, the spiritual Brahman effulgence, and His personal existence as the Supreme Lord.

TEXT 34

अनन्ताव्यक्तरूपेण येनेदमखिलं ततम् ।
चिदचिच्छक्तियुक्ताय तस्मै भगवते नमः ॥३४॥

anantāvyakta-rūpeṇa
yenedam akhilaṁ tatam
cid-acic-chakti-yuktāya
tasmai bhagavate namaḥ

ananta-avyakta-rūpeṇa—by the unlimited, unmanifested form; *yena*—by which; *idam*—this; *akhilam*—total aggregate; *tatam*—expanded; *cit*—with spiritual; *acit*—and material; *śakti*—potency; *yuk-*

tāya—unto he who is endowed; *tasmai*—unto him; *bhagavate*—unto the Supreme Personality of Godhead; *namaḥ*—I offer my respectful obeisances.

TRANSLATION

Let me offer my respectful obeisances unto the Supreme, who in his unlimited, unmanifested form has expanded the cosmic manifestation, the form of the totality of the universe. He possesses external and internal energies and the mixed energy called the marginal potency, which consists of all the living entities.

PURPORT

The Lord is endowed with unlimited potencies (*parāsya śaktir vividhaiva śrūyate*), which are summarized as three, namely external, internal and marginal. The external potency manifests this material world, the internal potency manifests the spiritual world, and the marginal potency manifests the living entities, who are mixtures of internal and external. The living entity, being part and parcel of Parabrahman, is actually internal potency, but because of being in contact with the material energy, he is an emanation of material and spiritual energies. The Supreme Personality of Godhead is above the material energy and is engaged in spiritual pastimes. The material energy is only an external manifestation of His pastimes.

TEXT 35

यदि दास्यस्यभिमतान् वरान्मे वरदोत्तम ।
भूतेभ्यस्त्वद्विसृष्टेभ्यो मृत्युर्मा भून्मम प्रभो ॥३५॥

yadi dāsyasy abhimatān
varān me varadottama
bhūtebhyas tvad-visṛṣṭebhyo
mṛtyur mā bhūn mama prabho

yadi—if; *dāsyasi*—you will give; *abhimatān*—the desired; *varān*—benedictions; *me*—unto me; *varada-uttama*—O best of all benedictors; *bhūtebhyaḥ*—from living entities; *tvat*—by you; *visṛṣṭebhyaḥ*—who are created; *mṛtyuḥ*—death; *mā*—not; *bhūt*—let there be; *mama*—my; *prabho*—O my lord.

TRANSLATION

O my lord, O best of the givers of benediction, if you will kindly grant me the benediction I desire, please let me not meet death from any of the living entities created by you.

PURPORT

After being created from the navel of Garbhodakaśāyī Viṣṇu, Lord Brahmā, the original created living being within the universe, created many other different types of living entities to reside in this universe. Therefore, from the beginning of creation, the living entities were born of a superior living entity. Ultimately, Kṛṣṇa is the supreme living being, the father of all others. *Ahaṁ bīja-pradaḥ pitā:* He is the seed-giving father of all living entities.

Thus far, Hiraṇyakaśipu has adored Lord Brahmā as the Supreme Personality of Godhead and has expected to become immortal by the benediction of Lord Brahmā. Now, however, having come to understand that even Lord Brahmā is not immortal because at the end of the millennium Lord Brahmā will also die, Hiraṇyakaśipu is very carefully asking him for benedictions that will be almost as good as immortality. His first proposal is that he not be killed by any of the different forms of living entities created by Lord Brahmā within this material world.

TEXT 36

नान्तर्बहिर्दिवा नक्तमन्यस्मादपि चायुधैः ।
न भूमौ नाम्बरे मृत्युर्न नरैर्न मृगैरपि ॥३६॥

nāntar bahir divā naktam
anyasmād api cāyudhaiḥ
na bhūmau nāmbare mṛtyur
na narair na mṛgair api

na—not; *antaḥ*—inside (the palace or home); *bahiḥ*—outside the home; *divā*—during the daytime; *naktam*—during the night; *anyasmāt*—from any others beyond Lord Brahmā; *api*—even; *ca*—also;

ayudhaiḥ—by any weapons used within this material world; *na*—nor; *bhūmau*—on the ground; *na*—not; *ambare*—in the sky; *mṛtyuḥ*—death; *na*—not; *naraiḥ*—by any men; *na*—nor; *mṛgaiḥ*—by any animal; *api*—also.

TRANSLATION

Grant me that I not die within any residence or outside any residence, during the daytime or at night, nor on the ground or in the sky. Grant me that my death not be brought by any being other than those created by you, nor by any weapon, nor by any human being or animal.

PURPORT

Hiraṇyakaśipu was very much afraid of Viṣṇu's becoming an animal to kill him because his brother had been killed by Viṣṇu when the Lord took the shape of a boar. He was therefore very careful to guard against all kinds of animals. But even without taking the shape of an animal, Viṣṇu could kill him by hurling His Sudarśana *cakra*, which can go anywhere without the Lord's physical presence. Therefore Hiraṇyakaśipu was careful to guard against all kinds of weapons. He guarded against all kinds of time, space and countries because he was afraid of being killed by someone else in another land. There are many other planets, higher and lower, and therefore he prayed for the benediction of not being killed by any resident of any of these planets. There are three original deities—Brahmā, Viṣṇu and Maheśvara. Hiraṇyakaśipu knew that Brahmā would not kill him, but he also wanted not to be killed by Lord Viṣṇu or Lord Śiva. Consequently, he prayed for such a benediction. Thus Hiraṇyakaśipu thought himself securely protected from any kind of death caused by any living entity within this universe. He also carefully guarded against natural death, which might take place within his house or outside of the house.

TEXTS 37–38

व्यसुभिर्वासुमद्भिर्वा सुरासुरमहोरगैः ।
अप्रतिद्वन्द्वतां युद्धे ऐकपत्यं च देहिनाम् ॥३७॥
सर्वेषां लोकपालानां महिमानं यथात्मनः ।
तपोयोगप्रभावाणां यन्न रिष्यति कर्हिचित् ॥३८॥

vyasubhir vāsumadbhir vā
surāsura-mahoragaiḥ
apratidvandvatāṁ yuddhe
aika-patyaṁ ca dehinām

sarveṣāṁ loka-pālānāṁ
mahimānaṁ yathātmanaḥ
tapo-yoga-prabhāvāṇāṁ
yan na riṣyati karhicit

vyasubhiḥ—by things that have no life; *vā*—or; *asumadbhiḥ*—by entities that have life; *vā*—or; *sura*—by the demigods; *asura*—the demons; *mahā-uragaiḥ*—by the great serpents who live on the lower planets; *apratidvandvatām*—without a rival; *yuddhe*—in battle; *aika-patyam*—supremacy; *ca*—and; *dehinām*—over those who have material bodies; *sarveṣām*—of all; *loka-pālānām*—the predominating deities of all planets; *mahimānam*—the glory; *yathā*—just as; *ātmanaḥ*—of yourself; *tapaḥ-yoga-prabhāvāṇām*—of those whose power is obtained by austerities and the practice of mystic *yoga; yat*—which; *na*—never; *riṣyati*—is destroyed; *karhicit*—at any time.

TRANSLATION

Grant me that I not meet death from any entity, living or nonliving. Grant me, further, that I not be killed by any demigod or demon or by any great snake from the lower planets. Since no one can kill you in the battlefield, you have no competitor. Therefore, grant me the benediction that I too may have no rival. Give me sole lordship over all the living entities and presiding deities, and give me all the glories obtained by that position. Furthermore, give me all the mystic powers attained by long austerities and the practice of yoga, for these cannot be lost at any time.

PURPORT

Lord Brahmā obtained his supreme position due to long austerities and penances, mystic *yoga*, meditation and so on. Hiraṇyakaśipu wanted a similar position. The ordinary powers achieved by mystic *yoga*, austerities and other processes are sometimes vanquished, but the powers obtained by the mercy of the Lord are never vanquished. Hiraṇyakaśipu, therefore, wanted a benediction that would never be vanquished.

Thus end the Bhaktivedanta purports of the Seventh Canto, Third Chapter, of the Śrīmad-Bhāgavatam, *entitled "Hiraṇyakaśipu's Plan to Become Immortal."*

CHAPTER FOUR

Hiraṇyakaśipu Terrorizes the Universe

This chapter fully describes how Hiraṇyakaśipu obtained power from Lord Brahmā and misused it by harassing all the living entities within this universe.

By severe austerities, Hiraṇyakaśipu satisfied Lord Brahmā and obtained the benedictions he desired. After he received these benedictions, his body, which had been almost entirely consumed, was revived with full beauty and a luster like gold. Nonetheless, he continued to be envious of Lord Viṣṇu, unable to forget Lord Viṣṇu's having killed his brother. Hiraṇyakaśipu conquered everyone in the ten directions and the three worlds and brought all living entities, both demigods and *asuras*, under his control. Becoming the master of all places, including the residence of Indra, whom he had driven out, he began enjoying life in great luxury and thus became mad. All the demigods but Lord Viṣṇu, Lord Brahmā and Lord Śiva came under his control and began serving him, but despite all his material power he was dissatisfied because he was always puffed up, proud of transgressing the Vedic regulations. All the *brāhmaṇas* were dissatisfied with him, and they cursed him with determination. Eventually, all the living entities within the universe, represented by the demigods and sages, prayed to the Supreme Lord for relief from Hiraṇyakaśipu's rule.

Lord Viṣṇu informed the demigods that they and the other living entities would be saved from the fearful conditions created by Hiraṇyakaśipu. Since Hiraṇyakaśipu was the oppressor of all the demigods, the followers of the *Vedas*, the cows, the *brāhmaṇas* and the religious, saintly persons, and since he was envious of the Supreme Lord, he would naturally be killed very soon. Hiraṇyakaśipu's last exploit would be to torment his own son Prahlāda, who was a *mahā-bhāgavata*, an exalted Vaiṣṇava. Then his life would end. When the demigods were thus reassured by the Supreme Personality of Godhead, everyone was satisfied, knowing that the miseries inflicted upon them by Hiraṇyakaśipu would come to an end.

Finally, Nārada Muni describes the characteristics of Prahlāda Mahārāja, the son of Hiraṇyakaśipu, and describes how his father envied his own qualified son. In this way the chapter ends.

TEXT 1

श्रीनारद उवाच
एवं वृतः शतधृतिर्हिरण्यकशिपोरथ ।
प्रादात्तत्तपसा प्रीतो वरांस्तस्य सुदुर्लभान् ॥ १ ॥

śrī-nārada uvāca
evaṁ vṛtaḥ śata-dhṛtir
hiraṇyakaśipor atha
prādāt tat-tapasā prīto
varāṁs tasya sudurlabhān

śrī-nāradaḥ uvāca—Śrī Nārada Muni said; *evam*—thus; *vṛtaḥ*—solicited; *śata-dhṛtiḥ*—Lord Brahmā; *hiraṇyakaśipoḥ*—of Hiraṇyakaśipu; *atha*—then; *prādāt*—delivered; *tat*—his; *tapasā*—by the difficult austerities; *prītaḥ*—being pleased; *varān*—benedictions; *tasya*—unto Hiraṇyakaśipu; *su-durlabhān*—very rarely obtained.

TRANSLATION

Nārada Muni continued: Lord Brahmā was very much satisfied by Hiraṇyakaśipu's austerities, which were difficult to perform. Therefore, when solicited for benedictions, he indeed granted them, although they were rarely to be achieved.

TEXT 2

श्रीब्रह्मोवाच
तातेमे दुर्लभाः पुंसां यान् वृणीषे वरान् मम ।
तथापि वितराम्यङ्ग वरान् यद्यपि दुर्लभान् ॥ २ ॥

śrī-brahmovāca
tāteme durlabhāḥ puṁsāṁ
yān vṛṇīṣe varān mama
tathāpi vitarāmy aṅga
varān yadyapi durlabhān

śrī-brahmā uvāca—Lord Brahmā said; *tāta*—O dear son; *ime*—all these; *durlabhāḥ*—very rarely obtained; *puṁsām*—by men; *yān*—those which; *vṛṇīṣe*—you ask; *varān*—benedictions; *mama*—from me; *tathāpi*—still; *vitarāmi*—I shall deliver; *aṅga*—O Hiraṇyakaśipu; *varān*—the benedictions; *yadyapi*—although; *durlabhān*—not generally available.

TRANSLATION

Lord Brahmā said: O Hiraṇyakaśipu, these benedictions for which you have asked are difficult to obtain for most men. Nonetheless, O my son, I shall grant you them although they are generally not available.

PURPORT

Material benedictions are not always exactly worthy of being called benedictions. If one possesses more and more, a benediction itself may become a curse, for just as achieving material opulence in this material world requires great strength and endeavor, maintaining it also requires great endeavor. Lord Brahmā informed Hiraṇyakaśipu that although he was ready to offer him whatever he had asked, the result of the benedictions would be very difficult for Hiraṇyakaśipu to maintain. Nonetheless, since Brahmā had promised, he wanted to grant all the benedictions asked. The word *durlabhān* indicates that one should not take benedictions one cannot enjoy peacefully.

TEXT 3

ततो जगाम भगवानमोघानुग्रहो विभुः ।
पूजितोऽसुरवर्येण स्तूयमानः प्रजेश्वरैः ॥ ३ ॥

tato jagāma bhagavān
amoghānugraho vibhuḥ
pūjito 'sura-varyeṇa
stūyamānaḥ prajeśvaraiḥ

tataḥ—thereafter; *jagāma*—departed; *bhagavān*—the most powerful, Lord Brahmā; *amogha*—without failure; *anugrahaḥ*—whose benediction; *vibhuḥ*—the Supreme within this universe; *pūjitaḥ*—being worshiped; *asura-varyeṇa*—by the most exalted demon (Hiraṇyakaśipu); *stūyamānaḥ*—being praised; *prajā-īśvaraiḥ*—by many demigods, the masters of different regions.

TRANSLATION

Then Lord Brahmā, who awards infallible benedictions, departed, being worshiped by the best of the demons, Hiraṇyakaśipu, and being praised by great sages and saintly persons.

TEXT 4

एवं लब्धवरो दैत्यो बिभ्रद्धेममयं वपुः ।
भगवत्यकरोद्द्वेषं भ्रातुर्वधमनुस्मरन् ॥ ४ ॥

evaṁ labdha-varo daityo
bibhrad dhemamayaṁ vapuḥ
bhagavaty akarod dveṣaṁ
bhrātur vadham anusmaran

evam—thus; *labdha-varaḥ*—having obtained his desired boon; *daityaḥ*—Hiraṇyakaśipu; *bibhrat*—acquiring; *hema-mayam*—possessing the luster of gold; *vapuḥ*—a body; *bhagavati*—unto Lord Viṣṇu, the Supreme Personality of Godhead; *akarot*—maintained; *dveṣam*—envy; *bhrātuḥ vadham*—the killing of his brother; *anusmaran*—always thinking of.

TRANSLATION

The demon Hiraṇyakaśipu, having thus been blessed by Lord Brahmā and having acquired a lustrous golden body, continued to

remember the death of his brother and therefore be envious of Lord Viṣṇu.

PURPORT

A demoniac person, in spite of acquiring all the opulences possible to obtain in this universe, continues to be envious of the Supreme Personality of Godhead.

TEXTS 5–7

स विजित्य दिशः सर्वा लोकांश्च त्रीन् महासुरः।
देवासुरमनुष्येन्द्रगन्धर्वगरुडोरगान् ॥ ५ ॥
सिद्धचारणविद्याध्रानृषीन् पितृपतीन् मनून् ।
यक्षरक्षःपिशाचेशान् प्रेतभूतपतीनपि ॥ ६ ॥
सर्वसत्त्वपतीञ्जित्वा वशमानीय विश्वजित् ।
जहार लोकपालानां स्थानानि सह तेजसा ॥ ७ ॥

sa vijitya diśaḥ sarvā
lokāṁś ca trīn mahāsuraḥ
devāsura-manuṣyendra-
gandharva-garuḍoragān

siddha-cāraṇa-vidyādhrān
ṛṣīn pitṛ-patīn manūn
yakṣa-rakṣaḥ-piśāceśān
preta-bhūta-patīn api

sarva-sattva-patīñ jitvā
vaśam ānīya viśva-jit
jahāra loka-pālānāṁ
sthānāni saha tejasā

saḥ—he (Hiraṇyakaśipu); *vijitya*—conquering; *diśaḥ*—the directions; *sarvāḥ*—all; *lokān*—planetary systems; *ca*—and; *trīn*—three (upper, lower and middle); *mahā-asuraḥ*—the great demon; *deva*—the demigods; *asura*—the demons; *manuṣya*—of the human beings;

indra—the kings; *gandharva*—the Gandharvas; *garuḍa*—the Garuḍas; *uragān*—the great serpents; *siddha*—the Siddhas; *cāraṇa*—the Cāraṇas; *vidyādhrān*—the Vidyādharas; *ṛṣīn*—the great sages and saintly persons; *pitṛ-patīn*—Yamarāja and the other leaders of the Pitās; *manūn*—all the different Manus; *yakṣa*—the Yakṣas; *rakṣaḥ*—the Rākṣasas; *piśāca-īśān*—the leaders of Piśācaloka; *preta*—of the Pretas; *bhūta*—and of the Bhūtas; *patīn*—the masters; *api*—also; *sarva-sattva-patīn*—the masters of all the different planets; *jitvā*—conquering; *vaśam ānīya*—bringing under control; *viśva-jit*—the conqueror of the whole universe; *jahāra*—usurped; *loka-pālānām*—of the demigods who manage the universal affairs; *sthānāni*—the places; *saha*—with; *tejasā*—all their power.

TRANSLATION

Hiraṇyakaśipu became the conqueror of the entire universe. Indeed, that great demon conquered all the planets in the three worlds—upper, middle and lower—including the planets of the human beings, the Gandharvas, the Garuḍas, the great serpents, the Siddhas, Cāraṇas and Vidyādharas, the great saints, Yamarāja, the Manus, the Yakṣas, the Rākṣasas, the Piśācas and their masters, and the masters of the ghosts and Bhūtas. He defeated the rulers of all the other planets where there are living entities and brought them under his control. Conquering the abodes of all, he seized their power and influence.

PURPORT

The word *garuḍa* in this verse indicates that there are planets of great birds like Garuḍa. Similarly, the word *uraga* indicates that there are planets of enormous serpents. Such a description of the various planets of the universe may challenge modern scientists who think that all planets but this earth are vacant. These scientists claim to have launched excursions to the moon, where they have found no living entities but only big craters full of dust and stone, although in fact the moon is so brilliant that it acts like the sun in illuminating the entire universe. Of course, it is not possible to convince modern scientists of the Vedic information about the universe. Nonetheless, we are not very much impressed by the words of scientists who say that all other planets are vacant and that only the earth is full of living entities.

TEXT 8

देवोद्यानश्रिया जुष्टमध्यास्ते स्म त्रिपिष्टपम् ।
महेन्द्रभवनं साक्षान्निर्मितं विश्वकर्मणा ।
त्रैलोक्यलक्ष्म्यायतनमध्युवासाखिलर्द्धिमत् ॥८॥

devodyāna-śriyā juṣṭam
adhyāste sma tri-piṣṭapam
mahendra-bhavanaṁ sākṣān
nirmitaṁ viśvakarmaṇā
trailokya-lakṣmy-āyatanam
adhyuvāsākhilarddhimat

deva-udyāna—of the famous garden of the demigods; *śriyā*—by the opulences; *juṣṭam*—enriched; *adhyāste sma*—remained in; *tri-piṣṭapam*—the higher planetary system, where various demigods live; *mahendra-bhavanam*—the palace of Indra, the King of heaven; *sākṣāt*—directly; *nirmitam*—constructed; *viśvakarmaṇā*—by the famous architect of the demigods, Viśvakarmā; *trailokya*—of all the three worlds; *lakṣmī-āyatanam*—the residence of the goddess of fortune; *adhyuvāsa*—lived in; *akhila-ṛddhi-mat*—possessing the opulence of the entire universe.

TRANSLATION

Hiraṇyakaśipu, who possessed all opulence, began residing in heaven, with its famous Nandana garden, which is enjoyed by the demigods. In fact, he resided in the most opulent palace of Indra, the King of heaven. The palace had been directly constructed by the demigod architect Viśvakarmā and was as beautifully made as if the goddess of fortune of the entire universe resided there.

PURPORT

From this description it appears that all the heavenly planets of the upper planetary system are thousands upon thousands of times more opulent than the lower planetary system in which we live. Viśvakarmā, the famous heavenly architect, is known as the constructor of many wonderful buildings in the upper planets, where there are not only beautiful buildings, but also many opulent gardens and parks, which are described as *nandana-devodyāna*, gardens quite fit to be enjoyed by the demigods. This description of the upper planetary system and its opulences is to be understood from authoritative scriptures like the Vedic literatures. Telescopes and the other imperfect instruments of scientists are inadequate for evaluating the upper planetary system. Although such instruments are needed because the vision of the so-called scientists is imperfect, the instruments themselves are also imperfect. Therefore the upper planets cannot be appraised by imperfect men using imperfect man-made instruments. Direct information received from the Vedic literature, however, is perfect, We therefore cannot accept the statement that there are no opulent residences on planets other than this earth.

TEXTS 9–12

यत्र विद्रुमसोपाना महामारकता भुवः ।
यत्र स्फाटिककुड्यानि वैदूर्यस्तम्भपङ्क्तयः ॥ ९ ॥
यत्र चित्रवितानानि पद्मरागासनानि च ।
पयःफेननिभाः शय्या मुक्तादामपरिच्छदाः ॥१०॥
कूजद्भिर्नूपुरैर्देव्यः शब्दयन्त्य इतस्ततः ।
रत्नस्थलीषु पश्यन्ति सुदतीः सुन्दरं मुखम् ॥११॥
तस्मिन्महेन्द्रभवने महाबलो
महामना निर्जितलोक एकराट् ।
रेमेऽभिवन्द्याङ्घ्रियुगः सुरादिभिः
प्रतापितैरूर्जितचण्डशासनः ॥१२॥

yatra vidruma-sopānā
mahā-mārakatā bhuvaḥ
yatra sphāṭika-kuḍyāni
vaidūrya-stambha-paṅktayaḥ

yatra citra-vitānāni
padmarāgāsanāni ca
payaḥ-phena-nibhāḥ śayyā
muktādāma-paricchadāḥ

kūjadbhir nūpurair devyaḥ
śabda-yantya itas tataḥ
ratna-sthalīṣu paśyanti
sudatīḥ sundaraṁ mukham

tasmin mahendra-bhavane mahā-balo
mahā-manā nirjita-loka eka-rāṭ
reme 'bhivandyāṅghri-yugaḥ surādibhiḥ
pratāpitair ūrjita-caṇḍa-śāsanaḥ

yatra—where (the residential quarters of King Indra); *vidruma-sopānāḥ*—steps made of coral; *mahā-mārakatāḥ*—emerald; *bhuvaḥ*—floors; *yatra*—where; *sphāṭika*—crystal; *kuḍyāni*—walls; *vaidūrya*—of *vaidūrya* stone; *stambha*—of pillars; *paṅktayaḥ*—lines; *yatra*—where; *citra*—wonderful; *vitānāni*—canopies; *padmarāga*—bedecked with rubies; *āsanāni*—seats; *ca*—also; *payaḥ*—of milk; *phena*—the foam; *nibhāḥ*—just like; *śayyāḥ*—beds; *muktādāma*—of pearls; *paricchadāḥ*—having borders; *kūjadbhiḥ*—jingling; *nūpuraiḥ*—with ankle bells; *devyaḥ*—celestial ladies; *śabda-yantyaḥ*—making sweet vibrations; *itaḥ tataḥ*—here and there; *ratna-sthalīṣu*—in places bedecked with jewels and gems; *paśyanti*—see; *su-datīḥ*—having nice teeth; *sundaram*—very beautiful; *mukham*—faces; *tasmin*—in that; *mahendra-bhavane*—the residential quarters of the heavenly King; *mahā-balaḥ*—the most powerful; *mahā-manāḥ*—highly thoughtful; *nirjita-lokaḥ*—having everyone under his control; *eka-rāṭ*—the powerful dictator; *reme*—enjoyed; *abhivandya*—worshiped; *aṅghri-yugaḥ*—whose two feet; *sura-ādibhiḥ*—by the demigods; *pratāpitaiḥ*—being disturbed; *ūrjita*—more than expected; *caṇḍa*—severe; *śāsanaḥ*—whose ruling.

TRANSLATION

The steps of King Indra's residence were made of coral, the floor was bedecked with invaluable emeralds, the walls were of

crystal, and the columns of vaidūrya stone. The wonderful canopies were beautifully decorated, the seats were bedecked with rubies, and the silk bedding, as white as foam, was decorated with pearls. The ladies of the palace, who were blessed with beautiful teeth and the most wonderfully beautiful faces, walked here and there in the palace, their ankle bells tinkling melodiously, and saw their own beautiful reflections in the gems. The demigods, however, being very much oppressed, had to bow down and offer obeisances at the feet of Hiraṇyakaśipu, who chastised the demigods very severely and for no reason. Thus Hiraṇyakaśipu lived in the palace and severely ruled everyone.

PURPORT

Hiraṇyakaśipu was so powerful in the heavenly planets that all the demigods except Lord Brahmā, Lord Śiva and Lord Viṣṇu were forced to engage in his service. Indeed, they were afraid of being severely punished if they disobeyed him. Śrīla Viśvanātha Cakravartī has compared Hiraṇyakaśipu to Mahārāja Vena, who was also atheistic and scornful of the ritualistic ceremonies mentioned in the *Vedas.* Yet Mahārāja Vena was afraid of some of the great sages such as Bhṛgu, whereas Hiraṇyakaśipu ruled in such a way that everyone feared him but Lord Viṣṇu, Lord Brahmā and Lord Śiva. Hiraṇyakaśipu was so alert against being burnt to ashes by the anger of great sages like Bhṛgu that by dint of austerity he surpassed their power and placed even them under his subordination. It appears that even in the higher planetary systems, to which people are promoted by pious activities, disturbances are created by *asuras* like Hiraṇyakaśipu. No one in the three worlds can live in peace and prosperity without disturbance.

TEXT 13

तमङ्ग मत्तं मधुनोरुगन्धिना
विवृत्तताम्राक्षमशेषधिष्ण्यपाः ।
उपासतोपायनपाणिभिर्विना
त्रिभिस्तपोयोगबलौजसां पदम् ॥ १३ ॥

tam aṅga mattaṁ madhunoru-gandhinā
vivṛtta-tāmrākṣam aśeṣa-dhiṣṇya-pāḥ
upāsatopāyana-pāṇibhir vinā
tribhis tapo-yoga-balaujasāṁ padam

tam—him (Hiraṇyakaśipu); *aṅga*—O dear King; *mattam*—intoxicated; *madhunā*—by wine; *uru-gandhinā*—strong-smelling; *vivṛtta*—rolling; *tāmra-akṣam*—having eyes like copper; *aśeṣa-dhiṣṇya-pāḥ*—the principal men of all the planets; *upāsata*—worshiped; *upāyana*—full with paraphernalia; *pāṇibhiḥ*—by their own hands; *vinā*—without; *tribhiḥ*—the three principal deities (Lord Viṣṇu, Lord Brahmā and Lord Śiva); *tapaḥ*—of austerity; *yoga*—mystic power; *bala*—bodily strength; *ojasām*—and power of the senses; *padam*—the abode.

TRANSLATION

O my dear King, Hiraṇyakaśipu was always drunk on strong-smelling wines and liquors, and therefore his coppery eyes were always rolling. Nonetheless, because he had powerfully executed great austerities in mystic yoga, although he was abominable, all but the three principal demigods—Lord Brahmā, Lord Śiva and Lord Viṣṇu—personally worshiped him to please him by bringing him various presentations with their own hands.

PURPORT

In the *Skanda Purāṇa* there is this description: *upāyanaṁ daduḥ sarve vinā devān hiraṇyakaḥ.* Hiraṇyakaśipu was so powerful that everyone but the three principal demigods—namely Lord Brahmā, Lord Śiva and Lord Viṣṇu—engaged in his service. Madhvācārya says, *ādityā vasavo rudrās tri-vidhā hi surā yataḥ.* There are three kinds of demigods—the Ādityas, the Vasus and the Rudras—beneath whom are the other demigods, like the Maruts and Sādhyas (*marutaś caiva viśve ca sādhyāś caiva ca tad-gatāḥ*). Therefore all the demigods are called *tri-piṣṭapa,* and the same word *tri* applies to Lord Brahmā, Lord Śiva and Lord Viṣṇu.

TEXT 14

जगुर्महेन्द्रासनमोजसा स्थितं
विश्वावसुस्तुम्बुरुरस्मदादयः ।
गन्धर्वसिद्धा ऋषयोऽस्तुवन्मुहु-
र्विद्याधराश्चाप्सरसश्च पाण्डव ॥१४॥

jagur mahendrāsanam ojasā sthitaṁ
viśvāvasus tumburur asmad-ādayaḥ
gandharva-siddhā ṛṣayo 'stuvan muhur
vidyādharāś cāpsarasaś ca pāṇḍava

jaguḥ—sung of the glories; *mahendra-āsanam*—the throne of King Indra; *ojasā*—by personal power; *sthitam*—situated on; *viśvāvasuḥ*—the chief singer of the Gandharvas; *tumburuḥ*—another Gandharva singer; *asmat-ādayaḥ*—including ourselves (Nārada and others also glorified Hiraṇyakaśipu); *gandharva*—the inhabitants of Gandharvaloka; *siddhāḥ*—the inhabitants of Siddhaloka; *ṛṣayaḥ*—the great sages and saintly persons; *astuvan*—offered prayers; *muhuḥ*—again and again; *vidyādharāḥ*—the inhabitants of Vidyādhara-loka; *ca*—and; *apsarasaḥ*—the inhabitants of Apsaroloka; *ca*—and; *pāṇḍava*—O descendant of Pāṇḍu.

TRANSLATION

O Mahārāja Yudhiṣṭhira, descendant of Pāṇḍu, by dint of his personal power, Hiraṇyakaśipu, being situated on the throne of King Indra, controlled the inhabitants of all the other planets. The two Gandharvas Viśvāvasu and Tumburu, I myself and the Vidyādharas, Apsarās and sages all offered prayers to him again and again just to glorify him.

PURPORT

The *asuras* sometimes become so powerful that they can engage even Nārada Muni and similar devotees in their service. This does not mean that Nārada was subordinate to Hiraṇyakaśipu. Sometimes, however, it so happens in this material world that great personalities, even great devotees, can also be controlled by the *asuras.*

TEXT 15

स एव वर्णाश्रमिभिः क्रतुभिर्भूरिदक्षिणैः ।
इज्यमानो हविर्भागानग्रहीत् स्वेन तेजसा ॥१५॥

sa eva varṇāśramibhiḥ
kratubhir bhūri-dakṣiṇaiḥ
ijyamāno havir-bhāgān
agrahīt svena tejasā

saḥ—he (Hiraṇyakaśipu); *eva*—indeed; *varṇa-āśramibhiḥ*—by persons who strictly followed the regulative principles of the four *varṇas* and four *āśramas; kratubhiḥ*—by ritualistic ceremonies; *bhūri*—abundant; *dakṣiṇaiḥ*—offered with gifts; *ijyamānaḥ*—being worshiped; *haviḥ-bhāgān*—the portions of the oblations; *agrahīt*—usurped; *svena*—by his own; *tejasā*—prowess.

TRANSLATION

Being worshiped by sacrifices offered with great gifts by those who strictly followed the principles of varṇa and āśrama, Hiraṇyakaśipu, instead of offering shares of the oblations to the demigods, accepted them himself.

TEXT 16

अकृष्टपच्या तस्यासीत् सप्तद्वीपवती मही ।
तथा कामदुघा गावो नानाश्चर्यपदं नभः ॥१६॥

akṛṣṭa-pacyā tasyāsīt
sapta-dvīpavatī mahī
tathā kāma-dughā gāvo
nānāścarya-padaṁ nabhaḥ

akṛṣṭa-pacyā—bearing grains without being cultivated or plowed; *tasya*—of Hiraṇyakaśipu; *āsīt*—was; *sapta-dvīpa-vatī*—consisting of seven islands; *mahī*—the earth; *tathā*—so much so; *kāma-dughāḥ*—

which can deliver as much milk as one desires; *gāvaḥ*—cows; *nānā*—various; *āścarya-padam*—wonderful things; *nabhaḥ*—the sky.

TRANSLATION

As if in fear of Hiraṇyakaśipu, the planet earth, which consists of seven islands, delivered food grains without being plowed. Thus it resembled cows like the surabhi of the spiritual world or the kāma-dughā of heaven. The earth yielded sufficient food grains, the cows supplied abundant milk, and outer space was beautifully decorated with wonderful phenomena.

TEXT 17

रत्नाकराश्च रत्नौघांस्तत्पत्न्यश्चोहुरूर्मिभिः ।
क्षारसीधुघृतक्षौद्रदधिक्षीरामृतोदकाः ॥१७॥

ratnākarāś ca ratnaughāṁs
tat-patnyaś cohur ūrmibhiḥ
kṣāra-sīdhu-ghṛta-kṣaudra-
dadhi-kṣīrāmṛtodakāḥ

ratnākarāḥ—the seas and oceans; *ca*—and; *ratna-oghān*—various kinds of gems and valuable stones; *tat-patnyaḥ*—the wives of the oceans and seas, namely the rivers; *ca*—also; *ūhuḥ*—carried; *ūrmibhiḥ*—by their waves; *kṣāra*—the salt ocean; *sīdhu*—the ocean of wine; *ghṛta*—the ocean of clarified butter; *kṣaudra*—the ocean of sugarcane juice; *dadhi*—the ocean of yogurt; *kṣīra*—the ocean of milk; *amṛta*—and the very sweet ocean; *udakāḥ*—water.

TRANSLATION

By the flowing of their waves, the various oceans of the universe, along with their tributaries, the rivers, which are compared to their wives, supplied various kinds of gems and jewels for Hiraṇyakaśipu's use. These oceans were the oceans of salt water, sugarcane juice, wine, clarified butter, milk, yogurt, and sweet water.

PURPORT

The water of the seas and oceans of this planet, of which we have experience, are salty, but other planets within the universe contain oceans of sugarcane juice, liquor, ghee, milk and sweet water. The rivers are figuratively described as wives of the oceans and seas because they glide down to the oceans and seas as tributaries, like the wives attached to their husbands. Modern scientists attempt excursions to other planets, but they have no information of how many different types of oceans and seas there are within the universe. According to their experience, the moon is full of dust, but this does not explain how it gives us soothing rays from a distance of millions of miles. As far as we are concerned, we follow the authority of Vyāsadeva and Śukadeva Gosvāmī, who have described the universal situation according to the Vedic literature. These authorities differ from modern scientists who conclude from their imperfect sensual experience that only this planet is inhabited by living beings whereas the other planets are all vacant or full of dust.

TEXT 18

शैला द्रोणीभिराक्रीडं सर्वर्तुषु गुणान् द्रुमाः ।
दधार लोकपालानामेक एव पृथग्गुणान् ॥१८॥

śailā droṇībhir ākrīḍaṁ
sarvartuṣu guṇān drumāḥ
dadhāra loka-pālānām
eka eva pṛthag guṇān

śailāḥ—the hills and mountains; *droṇībhiḥ*—with the valleys between them; *ākrīḍam*—pleasure grounds for Hiraṇyakaśipu; *sarva*—all; *ṛtuṣu*—in the seasons of the year; *guṇān*—different qualities (fruits and flowers); *drumāḥ*—the plants and trees; *dadhāra*—executed; *loka-pālānām*—of the other demigods in charge of different departments of natural activity; *ekaḥ*—alone; *eva*—indeed; *pṛthak*—different; *guṇān*—qualities.

TRANSLATION

The valleys between the mountains became fields of pleasure for Hiraṇyakaśipu, by whose influence all the trees and plants

produced fruits and flowers profusely in all seasons. The qualities of pouring water, drying and burning, which are all qualities of the three departmental heads of the universe—namely Indra, Vāyu and Agni—were all directed by Hiraṇyakaśipu alone, without assistance from the demigods.

PURPORT

It is said in the beginning of *Śrīmad-Bhāgavatam, tejo-vāri-mṛdāṁ yathā vinimayaḥ:* this material world is conducted by fire, water and earth, which combine and take shape. Here it is mentioned that the three modes of nature (*pṛthag guṇān*) act under the direction of different demigods. For example, King Indra is in charge of pouring water, the demigod Vāyu controls the air and dries up the water, whereas the demigod controlling fire burns everything. Hiraṇyakaśipu, however, by dint of his austere performance of mystic *yoga,* became so powerful that he alone took charge of everything, without assistance from the demigods.

TEXT 19

स इत्थं निर्जितककुबेकराड् विषयान् प्रियान् ।
यथोपजोषं भुञ्जानो नातृप्यदजितेन्द्रियः ॥१९॥

sa itthaṁ nirjita-kakub
eka-rāḍ viṣayān priyān
yathopajoṣaṁ bhuñjāno
nātṛpyad ajitendriyaḥ

saḥ—he (Hiraṇyakaśipu); *ittham*—thus; *nirjita*—conquered; *kakub*—all directions within the universe; *eka-rāṭ*—the one emperor of the whole universe; *viṣayān*—material sense objects; *priyān*—very pleasing; *yathā-upajoṣam*—as much as possible; *bhuñjānaḥ*—enjoying; *na*—did not; *atṛpyat*—was satisfied; *ajita-indriyaḥ*—being unable to control the senses.

TRANSLATION

In spite of achieving the power to control in all directions and in spite of enjoying all types of dear sense gratification as much as

possible, Hiraṇyakaśipu was dissatisfied because instead of controlling his senses he remained their servant.

PURPORT

This is an example of asuric life. Atheists can advance materially and create an extremely comfortable situation for the senses, but because they are controlled by the senses, they cannot be satisfied. This is the effect of modern civilization. Materialists are very much advanced in enjoying money and women, yet dissatisfaction prevails within human society because human society cannot be happy and peaceful without Kṛṣṇa consciousness. As far as material sense gratification is concerned, materialists may go on increasing their enjoyment as far as they can imagine, but because people in such a material condition are servants of their senses, they cannot be satisfied. Hiraṇyakaśipu was a vivid example of this dissatisfied state of humanity.

TEXT 20

एवमैश्वर्यमत्तस्य दृप्तस्योच्छास्त्रवर्तिनः ।
कालो महान् व्यतीयाय ब्रह्मशापमुपेयुषः ॥२०॥

evam aiśvarya-mattasya
dṛptasyocchāstra-vartinaḥ
kālo mahān vyatīyāya
brahma-śāpam upeyuṣaḥ

evam—thus; *aiśvarya-mattasya*—of one who was intoxicated by opulences; *dṛptasya*—greatly proud; *ut-śāstra-vartinaḥ*—transgressing the regulative principles mentioned in the *śāstras; kālaḥ*—duration of time; *mahān*—a great; *vyatīyāya*—passed; *brahma-śāpam*—a curse by exalted *brāhmaṇas; upeyuṣaḥ*—having obtained.

TRANSLATION

Hiraṇyakaśipu thus passed a long time being very much proud of his opulences and transgressing the laws and regulations mentioned in the authoritative śāstras. He was therefore subjected to a curse by the four Kumāras, who were great brāhmaṇas.

PURPORT

There have been many instances in which demons, after achieving material opulences, have become extremely proud, so much so that they have transgressed the laws and regulations given in the authoritative *śāstras*. Hiraṇyakaśipu acted in this way. As stated in *Bhagavad-gītā* (16.23):

yaḥ śāstra-vidhim utsṛjya
vartate kāma-kārataḥ
na sa siddhim avāpnoti
na sukhaṁ na parāṁ gatim

"He who discards scriptural injunctions and acts according to his own whims attains neither perfection, nor happiness, nor the supreme destination." The word *śāstra* refers to that which controls our activities. We cannot violate or transgress the laws and regulative principles mentioned in the *śāstras*. *Bhagavad-gītā* repeatedly confirms this.

tasmāc chāstraṁ pramāṇaṁ te
kāryākārya-vyavasthitau
jñātvā śāstra-vidhānoktaṁ
karma kartum ihārhasi

"One should understand what is duty and what is not duty by the regulations of the scriptures. Knowing such rules and regulations, one should act so that he may gradually be elevated." (Bg. 16.24) One should act according to the direction of the *śāstra*, but the material energy is so powerful that as soon as one becomes materially opulent, he begins to transgress the śāstric laws. As soon as one transgresses the laws of *śāstra*, he immediately enters upon the path of destruction.

TEXT 21

तस्योग्रदण्डसंविग्नाः सर्वे लोकाः सपालकाः ।
अन्यत्रालब्धशरणाः शरणं ययुरच्युतम् ॥२१॥

tasyogra-daṇḍa-saṁvignāḥ
sarve lokāḥ sapālakāḥ
anyatrālabdha-śaraṇāḥ
śaraṇaṁ yayur acyutam

tasya—of him (Hiraṇyakaśipu); *ugra-daṇḍa*—by the very fearful chastisement; *saṁvignāḥ*—disturbed; *sarve*—all; *lokāḥ*—the planets; *sa-pālakāḥ*—with their principal rulers; *anyatra*—anywhere else; *alabdha*—not obtaining; *śaraṇāḥ*—shelter; *śaraṇam*—for shelter; *yayuḥ*—approached; *acyutam*—the Supreme Personality of Godhead.

TRANSLATION

Everyone, including the rulers of the various planets, was extremely distressed because of the severe punishment inflicted upon them by Hiraṇyakaśipu. Fearful and disturbed, unable to find any other shelter, they at last surrendered to the Supreme Personality of Godhead, Viṣṇu.

PURPORT

Lord Kṛṣṇa says in *Bhagavad-gītā* (5.29):

bhoktāraṁ yajña-tapasāṁ
sarva-loka-maheśvaram
suhṛdaṁ sarva-bhūtānāṁ
jñātvā māṁ śāntim ṛcchati

"The sages, knowing Me as the ultimate purpose of all sacrifices and austerities, the Supreme Lord of all planets and demigods and the benefactor and well-wisher of all living entities, attain peace from the pangs of material miseries." The Supreme Personality of Godhead, Kṛṣṇa, is actually the best friend of everyone. In a condition of distress or misery, one wants to seek shelter of a well-wishing friend. The well-wishing friend of the perfect order is Lord Śrī Kṛṣṇa. Therefore all the inhabitants of the various planets, being unable to find any other shelter, were obliged to seek shelter at the lotus feet of the supreme friend. If from the very beginning we seek shelter of the supreme friend, there will be no cause of danger. It is said that if a dog is swimming in the water and one wants to cross the ocean by catching hold of the dog's tail, certainly he is foolish. Similarly, if in distress one seeks shelter of a demigod, he is foolish, for his efforts will be fruitless. In all circumstances, one should seek shelter of the Supreme Personality of Godhead. Then there will be no danger under any circumstances.

TEXTS 22–23

तस्यै नमोऽस्तु काष्ठायै यत्रात्मा हरिरीश्वरः ।
यद्गत्वा न निवर्तन्ते शान्ताः संन्यासिनोऽमलाः ॥२२॥
इति ते संयतात्मानः समाहितधियोऽमलाः ।
उपतस्थुर्हृषीकेशं विनिद्रा वायुभोजनाः ॥२३॥

tasyai namo 'stu kāṣṭhāyai
yatrātmā harir īśvaraḥ
yad gatvā na nivartante
śāntāḥ sannyāsino 'malāḥ

iti te saṁyatātmānaḥ
samāhita-dhiyo 'malāḥ
upatasthur hṛṣīkeśaṁ
vinidrā vāyu-bhojanāḥ

tasyai—unto that; *namaḥ*—our respectful obeisances; *astu*—let there be; *kāṣṭhāyai*—direction; *yatra*—wherein; *ātmā*—the Supersoul; *hariḥ*—the Supreme Personality of Godhead; *īśvaraḥ*—the supreme controller; *yat*—which; *gatvā*—approaching; *na*—never; *nivartante*—return; *śāntāḥ*—peaceful; *sannyāsinaḥ*—saintly persons in the renounced order of life; *amalāḥ*—pure; *iti*—thus; *te*—they; *saṁyata-ātmānaḥ*—having controlled minds; *samāhita*—steadied; *dhiyaḥ*—intelligences; *amalāḥ*—purified; *upatasthuḥ*—worshiped; *hṛṣīkeśam*—the master of the senses; *vinidrāḥ*—without sleeping; *vāyu-bhojanāḥ*—eating only air.

TRANSLATION

"Let us offer our respectful obeisances unto that direction where the Supreme Personality of Godhead is situated, where those purified souls in the renounced order of life, the great saintly persons, go, and from which, having gone, they never return." Without sleep, fully controlling their minds, and living on only their breath, the predominating deities of the various planets began worshiping Hṛṣīkeśa with this meditation.

PURPORT

The two words *tasyai kāṣṭhāyai* are very significant. Everywhere, in every direction, in every heart and in every atom, the Supreme Personality of Godhead is situated in His features as Brahman and Paramātmā. Then what is the purpose of saying *tasyai kāṣṭhāyai*—"in that direction where Hari is situated"? During Hiraṇyakaśipu's time, his influence was everywhere, but he could not force his influence into the places where the Supreme Personality of Godhead had His pastimes. For example, on this earth there are such places as Vṛndāvana and Ayodhyā, which are called *dhāmas*. In the *dhāma*, there is no influence from Kali-yuga or any demon. If one takes shelter of such a *dhāma*, worship of the Lord becomes very easy, and resultant spiritual advancement quickly takes place. In fact, in India one may still go to Vṛndāvana and similar places to achieve the results of spiritual activities quickly.

TEXT 24

तेषामाविरभूद्वाणी अरूपा मेघनिःस्वना ।
सन्नादयन्ती ककुभः साधूनामभयङ्करी ॥२४॥

teṣām āvirabhūd vāṇī
arūpā megha-niḥsvanā
sannādayantī kakubhaḥ
sādhūnām abhayaṅkarī

teṣām—in front of all of them; *āvirabhūt*—appeared; *vāṇī*—a voice; *arūpā*—without a form; *megha-niḥsvanā*—resounding like the sound of a cloud; *sannādayantī*—causing to vibrate; *kakubhaḥ*—all directions; *sādhūnām*—of the saintly persons; *abhayaṅkarī*—driving away the fearful situation.

TRANSLATION

Then there appeared before them a transcendental sound vibration, emanating from a personality not visible to material eyes. The voice was as grave as the sound of a cloud, and it was very encouraging, driving away all fear.

TEXTS 25–26

मा भैष्ट विबुधश्रेष्ठाः सर्वेषां भद्रमस्तु वः ।
मद्दर्शनं हि भूतानां सर्वश्रेयोपपत्तये ॥२५॥
ज्ञातमेतस्य दौरात्म्यं दैतेयापसदस्य यत् ।
तस्य शान्तिं करिष्यामि कालं तावत्प्रतीक्षत ॥२६॥

mā bhaiṣṭa vibudha-śreṣṭhāḥ
sarveṣāṁ bhadram astu vaḥ
mad-darśanaṁ hi bhūtānāṁ
sarva-śreyopapattaye

jñātam etasya daurātmyaṁ
daiteyāpasadasya yat
tasya śāntiṁ kariṣyāmi
kālaṁ tāvat pratīkṣata

mā—do not; *bhaiṣṭa*—fear; *vibudha-śreṣṭhāḥ*—O best of learned persons; *sarveṣām*—of all; *bhadram*—the good fortune; *astu*—let there be; *vaḥ*—unto you; *mat-darśanam*—the seeing of Me (or offering of prayers to Me or hearing about Me, all of which are absolute); *hi*—indeed; *bhūtānām*—of all living entities; *sarva-śreya*—of all good fortune; *upapattaye*—for the attainment; *jñātam*—known; *etasya*—of this; *daurātmyam*—the nefarious activities; *daiteya-apasadasya*—of the great demon, Hiraṇyakaśipu; *yat*—which; *tasya*—of this; *śāntim*—cessation; *kariṣyāmi*—I shall make; *kālam*—time; *tāvat*—until that; *pratīkṣata*—just wait.

TRANSLATION

The voice of the Lord vibrated as follows: O best of learned persons, do not fear! I wish all good fortune to you. Become My devotees by hearing and chanting about Me and offering Me prayers, for these are certainly meant to award benedictions to all living entities. I know all about the activities of Hiraṇyakaśipu and shall surely stop them very soon. Please wait patiently until that time.

PURPORT

Sometimes people are very much eager to see God. In considering the word *mad-darśanam,* "seeing Me," which is mentioned in this verse, one should note that in *Bhagavad-gītā* the Lord says, *bhaktyā mām abhijānāti.* In other words, the ability to understand the Supreme Personality of Godhead or to see Him or talk with Him depends on one's advancement in devotional service, which is called *bhakti.* In *bhakti* there are nine different activities: *śravaṇaṁ kīrtanaṁ viṣṇoḥ smaraṇaṁ pāda-sevanam/ arcanaṁ vandanaṁ dāsyaṁ sakhyam ātma-nivedanam.* Because all these devotional activities are absolute, there is no fundamental difference between worshiping the Deity in the temple, seeing Him and chanting His glories. Indeed, all of these are ways of seeing Him, for everything done in devotional service is a means of direct contact with the Lord. The vibration of the Lord's voice appeared in the presence of all the devotees, and although the person vibrating the sound was unseen to them, they were meeting or seeing the Lord because they were offering prayers and because the vibration of the Lord was present. Contrary to the laws of the material world, there is no difference between seeing the Lord, offering prayers and hearing the transcendental vibration. Pure devotees, therefore, are fully satisfied by glorifying the Lord. Such glorification is called *kīrtana.* Performing *kīrtana* and hearing the vibration of the sound Hare Kṛṣṇa is actually seeing the Supreme Personality of Godhead directly. One must realize this position, and then one will be able to understand the absolute nature of the Lord's activities.

TEXT 27

यदा देवेषु वेदेषु गोषु विप्रेषु साधुषु ।
धर्मे मयि च विद्वेषः स वा आशु विनश्यति ॥२७॥

yadā deveṣu vedeṣu
goṣu vipreṣu sādhuṣu
dharme mayi ca vidveṣaḥ
sa vā āśu vinaśyati

yadā—when; *deveṣu*—unto the demigods; *vedeṣu*—unto the Vedic scriptures; *goṣu*—unto the cows; *vipreṣu*—unto the *brāhmaṇas; sādhuṣu*—unto the saintly persons; *dharme*—unto religious principles; *mayi*—unto Me, the Supreme Personality of Godhead; *ca*—and; *vidveṣaḥ*—envious; *saḥ*—such a person; *vai*—indeed; *āśu*—very soon; *vinaśyati*—is vanquished.

TRANSLATION

When one is envious of the demigods, who represent the Supreme Personality of Godhead, of the Vedas, which give all knowledge, of the cows, brāhmaṇas, Vaiṣṇavas and religious principles, and ultimately of Me, the Supreme Personality of Godhead, he and his civilization will be vanquished without delay.

TEXT 28

निर्वैराय प्रशान्ताय स्वसुताय महात्मने ।
प्रह्लादाय यदा द्रुह्येद्धनिष्येऽपि वरोर्जितम् ॥२८॥

nirvairāya praśāntāya
sva-sutāya mahātmane
prahrādāya yadā druhyed
dhaniṣye 'pi varorjitam

nirvairāya—who is without enemies; *praśāntāya*—very sober and peaceful; *sva-sutāya*—unto his own son; *mahā-ātmane*—who is a great devotee; *prahrādāya*—Prahlāda Mahārāja; *yadā*—when; *druhyet*—will commit violence; *haniṣye*—I shall kill; *api*—although; *vara-ūrjitam*—blessed by the boons of Lord Brahmā.

TRANSLATION

When Hiraṇyakaśipu teases the great devotee Prahlāda, his own son, who is peaceful and sober and who has no enemy, I shall kill Hiraṇyakaśipu immediately, despite the benedictions of Brahmā.

PURPORT

Of all sinful activities, an offense to a pure devotee, or Vaiṣṇava, is the most severe. An offense at the lotus feet of a Vaiṣṇava is so disastrous that Śrī Caitanya Mahāprabhu has compared it to a mad elephant that enters a garden and causes great havoc by uprooting many plants and trees. If one is an offender at the lotus feet of a *brāhmaṇa* or Vaiṣṇava, his offenses uproot all his auspicious activities. One should therefore very carefully guard against committing *vaiṣṇava-aparādha,* or offenses at the lotus feet of a Vaiṣṇava. Here the Lord clearly says that although Hiraṇyakaśipu had received benedictions from Lord Brahmā, these benedictions would be null and void as soon as he committed an offense at the lotus feet of Prahlāda Mahārāja, his own son. A Vaiṣṇava like Prahlāda Mahārāja is described herein as *nirvaira,* having no enemies. Elsewhere in *Śrīmad-Bhāgavatam* (3.25.21) it is said, *ajāta-śatravaḥ śāntāḥ sādhavaḥ sādhu-bhūṣaṇāḥ:* a devotee has no enemies, he is peaceful, he abides by the scriptures, and all his characteristics are sublime. A devotee does not create enmity with anyone, but if someone becomes his enemy, that person will be vanquished by the Supreme Personality of Godhead, despite whatever benedictions he may have received from other sources. Hiraṇyakaśipu was certainly enjoying the fruitful results of his austerities, but here the Lord says that as soon as he committed an offense at the lotus feet of Prahlāda Mahārāja he would be ruined. One's longevity, opulence, beauty, education and whatever else one may possess as a result of pious activities cannot protect one if one commits an offense at the lotus feet of a Vaiṣṇava. Despite whatever one possesses, if one offends the lotus feet of a Vaiṣṇava he will be vanquished.

TEXT 29

श्रीनारद उवाच

इत्युक्ता लोकगुरुणा तं प्रणम्य दिवौकसः ।
न्यवर्तन्त गतोद्वेगा मेनिरे चासुरं हतम् ॥२९॥

śrī-nārada uvāca
ity uktā loka-guruṇā
taṁ praṇamya divaukasaḥ
nyavartanta gatodvegā
menire cāsuraṁ hatam

śrī-nāradaḥ uvāca—the great saint Nārada Muni said; *iti*—thus; *uktāḥ*—addressed; *loka-guruṇā*—by the supreme spiritual master of everyone; *tam*—unto Him; *praṇamya*—offering obeisances; *divaukasaḥ*—all the demigods; *nyavartanta*—returned; *gata-udvegāḥ*—relieved of all anxieties; *menire*—they considered; *ca*—also; *asuram*—the demon (Hiraṇyakaśipu); *hatam*—killed.

TRANSLATION

The great saint Nārada Muni continued: When the Supreme Personality of Godhead, the spiritual master of everyone, thus reassured all the demigods living in the heavenly planets, they offered their respectful obeisances unto Him and returned, confident that the demon Hiraṇyakaśipu was now practically dead.

PURPORT

The less intelligent men who are always busy worshiping the demigods should note that when the demigods are harassed by the demons, they approach the Supreme Personality of Godhead for relief. Since the demigods resort to the Supreme Personality of Godhead, why should the worshipers of the demigods not approach the Supreme Lord for whatever benefits they desire? *Śrīmad-Bhāgavatam* (2.3.10) says:

akāmaḥ sarva-kāmo vā
mokṣa-kāma udāra-dhīḥ
tīvreṇa bhakti-yogena
yajeta puruṣaṁ param

"Whether one desires everything or nothing, or whether he desires to merge into the existence of the Lord, he is intelligent only if he worships Lord Kṛṣṇa, the Supreme Personality of Godhead, by rendering transcendental loving service." Whether one is a *karmī, jñānī* or *yogī*, if one wants a particular benediction fulfilled, even if it be material, one should approach the Supreme Lord and pray to Him, for then it will be fulfilled. There is no need to approach any demigod separately for the fulfillment of any desire.

TEXT 30

तस्य दैत्यपतेः पुत्राश्चत्वारः परमाद्भुताः ।
प्रह्रादोऽभून्महांस्तेषां गुणैर्महदुपासकः ॥३०॥

tasya daitya-pateḥ putrāś
catvāraḥ paramādbhutāḥ
prahrādo 'bhūn mahāṁs teṣāṁ
guṇair mahad-upāsakaḥ

tasya—of him (Hiraṇyakaśipu); *daitya-pateḥ*—the King of the Daityas; *putrāḥ*—sons; *catvāraḥ*—four; *parama-adbhutāḥ*—very qualified and wonderful; *prahrādaḥ*—the one named Prahlāda; *abhūt*—was; *mahān*—the greatest; *teṣām*—of all of them; *guṇaiḥ*—with transcendental qualities; *mahat-upāsakaḥ*—being an unalloyed devotee of the Supreme Personality of Godhead.

TRANSLATION

Hiraṇyakaśipu had four wonderful, well-qualified sons, of whom the one named Prahlāda was the best. Indeed, Prahlāda was a reservoir of all transcendental qualities because he was an unalloyed devotee of the Personality of Godhead.

PURPORT

yasyāsti bhaktir bhagavaty akiñcanā
sarvair guṇais tatra samāsate surāḥ

"In one who has unflinching devotional faith in Kṛṣṇa, all the good qualities of Kṛṣṇa and the demigods are consistently manifest."

(*Bhāg.* 5.18.12) Prahlāda Mahārāja is praised herein for having all good qualities because of worshiping the Supreme Personality of Godhead. Therefore, a pure devotee, who has no motives, has all good qualities, material and spiritual. If one is spiritually advanced, being a staunch, liberal devotee of the Lord, all good qualities are manifest in his body. On the other hand, *harāv abhaktasya kuto mahad-guṇāḥ:* if one is not a devotee, even if he has some materially good qualities, they have no value. That is the verdict of the *Vedas.*

TEXTS 31–32

ब्रह्मण्यः शीलसम्पन्नः सत्यसन्धो जितेन्द्रियः ।
आत्मवत्सर्वभूतानामेकप्रियसुहृत्तमः ॥३१॥
दासवत्संनतार्याङ्घ्रिः पितृवद्दीनवत्सलः ।
भ्रातृवत्सदृशे स्निग्धो गुरुष्वीश्वरभावनः ।
विद्यार्थरूपजन्माढ्यो मानस्तम्भविवर्जितः ॥३२॥

brahmaṇyaḥ śīla-sampannaḥ
satya-sandho jitendriyaḥ
ātmavat sarva-bhūtānām
eka-priya-suhṛttamaḥ

dāsavat sannatāryāṅghriḥ
pitṛvad dīna-vatsalaḥ
bhrātṛvat sadṛśe snigdho
guruṣv īśvara-bhāvanaḥ
vidyārtha-rūpa-janmāḍhyo
māna-stambha-vivarjitaḥ

brahmaṇyaḥ—cultured as a good *brāhmaṇa; śīla-sampannaḥ*—possessing all good qualities; *satya-sandhaḥ*—determined to understand the Absolute Truth; *jita-indriyaḥ*—fully controlling the senses and mind; *ātma-vat*—like the Supersoul; *sarva-bhūtānām*—of all living entities; *eka-priya*—the one beloved; *suhṛt-tamaḥ*—the best friend; *dāsa-vat*—like a menial servant; *sannata*—always obedient; *ārya-aṅghriḥ*—at the lotus feet of great persons; *pitṛ-vat*—exactly like a father; *dīna-*

vatsalaḥ—kind to the poor; *bhrātṛ-vat*—exactly like a brother; *sadṛśe*—to his equals; *snigdhaḥ*—very affectionate; *guruṣu*—unto the spiritual masters; *īśvara-bhāvanaḥ*—who considered exactly like the Supreme Personality of Godhead; *vidyā*—education; *artha*—riches; *rūpa*—beauty; *janma*—aristocracy or nobility; *āḍhyaḥ*—endowed with; *māna*—pride; *stambha*—impudence; *vivarjitaḥ*—completely free from.

TRANSLATION

[The qualities of Mahārāja Prahlāda, the son of Hiraṇyakaśipu, are described herewith.] He was completely cultured as a qualified brāhmaṇa, having very good character and being determined to understand the Absolute Truth. He had full control of his senses and mind. Like the Supersoul, he was kind to every living entity and was the best friend of everyone. To respectable persons he acted exactly like a menial servant, to the poor he was like a father, to his equals he was attached like a sympathetic brother, and he considered his teachers, spiritual masters and older Godbrothers to be as good as the Supreme Personality of Godhead. He was completely free from unnatural pride that might have arisen from his good education, riches, beauty, aristocracy and so on.

PURPORT

These are some of the qualifications of a Vaiṣṇava. A Vaiṣṇava is automatically a *brāhmaṇa* because a Vaiṣṇava has all the good qualities of a *brāhmaṇa.*

śamo damas tapaḥ śaucaṁ
kṣāntir ārjavam eva ca
jñānaṁ vijñānam āstikyaṁ
brahma-karma svabhāva-jam

"Peacefulness, self-control, austerity, purity, tolerance, honesty, wisdom, knowledge, and religiousness—these are the qualities by which the *brāhmaṇas* work." (Bg. 18.42) These qualities are manifest in the body of a Vaiṣṇava. Therefore a perfect Vaiṣṇava is also a perfect *brāhmaṇa,* as indicated here by the words *brahmaṇyaḥ śīla-sampannaḥ.* A Vaiṣṇava is always determined to understand the Absolute Truth, and to understand the Absolute Truth one needs to have full control over his senses and mind. Prahlāda Mahārāja possessed all these qualities. A Vaiṣṇava is always a well-wisher to everyone. The six Gosvāmīs, for example, are described in this way: *dhīrādhīra-jana-priyau.* They were popular with both the gentle and the ruffians. A Vaiṣṇava must be equal to everyone, regardless of one's position. *Ātmavat:* a Vaiṣṇava should be like Paramātmā. *Īśvaraḥ sarva-bhūtānāṁ hṛd-deśe 'rjuna tiṣṭhati.* Paramātmā does not hate anyone; indeed, He is in the heart of a *brāhmaṇa,* but he is also even in the heart of a pig. As the moon never refuses to distribute its pleasing rays even to the home of a *caṇḍāla,* a Vaiṣṇava never refuses to act for everyone's welfare. Therefore a Vaiṣṇava is always obedient to the spiritual master (*ārya*). The word *ārya* refers to one who is advanced in knowledge. One who is deficient in knowledge cannot be called *ārya.* At the present, however, the word *ārya* is used to refer to those who are godless. This is the unfortunate situation of Kali-yuga.

The word *guru* refers to the spiritual master who initiates his disciple into advancement in the science of Kṛṣṇa, or Kṛṣṇa consciousness, as stated by Śrīla Viśvanātha Cakravartī Ṭhākura (*śrī-bhagavan-mantropadeśake gurāv ity arthaḥ*).

TEXT 33

नोद्विग्नचित्तो व्यसनेषु निःस्पृहः
श्रुतेषु दृष्टेषु गुणेष्ववस्तुदृक् ।
दान्तेन्द्रियप्राणशरीरधीः सदा
प्रशान्तकामो रहितासुरोऽसुरः ॥३३॥

nodvigna-citto vyasaneṣu niḥspṛhaḥ
śruteṣu dṛṣṭeṣu guṇeṣv avastu-dṛk
dāntendriya-prāṇa-śarīra-dhīḥ sadā
praśānta-kāmo rahitāsuro 'suraḥ

na—not; *udvigna*—agitated; *cittaḥ*—whose consciousness; *vyasaneṣu*—in dangerous conditions; *niḥspṛhaḥ*—without desire; *śruteṣu*—in things heard of (especially elevation to heavenly planets because of pious activities); *dṛṣṭeṣu*—as well as in temporal things seen; *guṇeṣu*—the objects of sense gratification under the modes of material nature; *avastu-dṛk*—seeing as if insubstantial; *dānta*—controlling; *indriya*—the senses; *prāṇa*—the living force; *śarīra*—the body; *dhīḥ*—and intelligence; *sadā*—always; *praśānta*—quieted; *kāmaḥ*—whose material desires; *rahita*—completely devoid of; *asuraḥ*—demoniac nature; *asuraḥ*—although born in a demoniac family.

TRANSLATION

Although Prahlāda Mahārāja was born in a family of asuras, he himself was not an asura but a great devotee of Lord Viṣṇu. Unlike the other asuras, he was never envious of Vaiṣṇavas. He was not agitated when put into danger, and he was neither directly nor indirectly interested in the fruitive activities described in the Vedas. Indeed, he considered everything material to be useless, and therefore he was completely devoid of material desires. He always controlled his senses and life air, and being of steady intelligence and determination, he subdued all lusty desires.

PURPORT

From this verse we discover that a man is not qualified or disqualified simply by birth. Prahlāda Mahārāja was an *asura* by birth, yet he possessed all the qualities of a perfect *brāhmaṇa* (*brahmaṇyaḥ śīla-sampannaḥ*). Anyone can become a fully qualified *brāhmaṇa* under the direction of a spiritual master. Prahlāda Mahārāja provided a vivid example of how to think of the spiritual master and accept his directions calmly.

TEXT 34

यस्मिन्महद्गुणा राजन् गृह्यन्ते कविभिर्मुहुः ।
न तेऽधुनापिधीयन्ते यथा भगवतीश्वरे ॥३४॥

yasmin mahad-guṇā rājan
gṛhyante kavibhir muhuḥ
na te 'dhunā pidhīyante
yathā bhagavatīśvare

yasmin—in whom; *mahat-guṇāḥ*—exalted transcendental qualities; *rājan*—O King; *gṛhyante*—are glorified; *kavibhiḥ*—by persons who are thoughtful and advanced in knowledge; *muhuḥ*—always; *na*—not; *te*—these; *adhunā*—today; *pidhīyante*—are obscured; *yathā*—just as; *bhagavati*—in the Supreme Personality of Godhead; *īśvare*—the supreme controller.

TRANSLATION

O King, Prahlāda Mahārāja's good qualities are still glorified by learned saints and Vaiṣṇavas. As all good qualities are always found existing in the Supreme Personality of Godhead, they also exist forever in His devotee Prahlāda Mahārāja.

PURPORT

From authoritative scripture it is learned that Prahlāda Mahārāja still lives in Vaikuṇṭhaloka as well as within this material world on the planet Sutala. This transcendental quality of existing simultaneously in different places is another qualification of the Supreme Personality of Godhead. *Goloka eva nivasaty akhilātma-bhūtaḥ:* the Lord appears in the core of everyone's heart, yet He exists on His own planet, Goloka Vṛndāvana. A devotee acquires qualities almost the same as those of the Lord because of unalloyed devotional service. Ordinary living beings cannot be so qualified, but a devotee can be qualified like the Supreme Personality of Godhead, not in full but partially.

TEXT 35

यं साधुगाथासदसि रिपवोऽपि सुरा नृप ।
प्रतिमानं प्रकुर्वन्ति किमुतान्ये भवादृशाः ॥३५॥

yaṁ sādhu-gāthā-sadasi
ripavo 'pi surā nṛpa
pratimānaṁ prakurvanti
kim utānye bhavādṛśāḥ

yam—whom; *sādhu-gāthā-sadasi*—in an assembly where saintly persons gather or exalted characteristics are discussed; *ripavaḥ*—persons who were supposed to have been Prahlāda Mahārāja's enemies (even such a devotee as Prahlāda Mahārāja had enemies, including even his own father); *api*—even; *surāḥ*—the demigods (the demigods are enemies of the demons, and since Prahlāda Mahārāja was born in a family of demons, the demigods should have been his enemies); *nṛpa*—O King Yudhiṣṭhira; *pratimānam*—a substantial example of the best among the devotees; *prakurvanti*—they make; *kim uta*—what to speak of; *anye*—others; *bhavādṛśāḥ*—exalted personalities such as yourself.

TRANSLATION

In any assembly where there are discourses about saints and devotees, O King Yudhiṣṭhira, even the enemies of the demons, namely the demigods, what to speak of you, would cite Prahlāda Mahārāja as an example of a great devotee.

TEXT 36

गुणैरलमसंख्येयैर्माहात्म्यं तस्य सूच्यते ।
वासुदेवे भगवति यस्य नैसर्गिकी रतिः ॥३६॥

guṇair alam asaṅkhyeyair
māhātmyaṁ tasya sūcyate
vāsudeve bhagavati
yasya naisargikī ratiḥ

guṇaiḥ—with spiritual qualities; *alam*—what need; *asaṅkhyeyaiḥ*—which are innumerable; *māhātmyam*—the greatness; *tasya*—of him (Prahlāda Mahārāja); *sūcyate*—is indicated; *vāsudeve*—to Lord Kṛṣṇa, the son of Vasudeva; *bhagavati*—the Supreme Personality of Godhead; *yasya*—of whom; *naisargikī*—natural; *ratiḥ*—attachment.

TRANSLATION

Who could list the innumerable transcendental qualities of Prahlāda Mahārāja? He had unflinching faith in Vāsudeva, Lord Kṛṣṇa [the son of Vasudeva], and unalloyed devotion to Him. His attachment to Lord Kṛṣṇa was natural because of his previous

devotional service. Although his good qualities cannot be enumerated, they prove that he was a great soul [mahātmā].

PURPORT

In his prayers to the ten incarnations, Jayadeva Gosvāmī says, *keśava dhṛta-narahari-rūpa jaya jagad-īśa hare.* Prahlāda Mahārāja was a devotee of Lord Nṛsiṁha, who is Keśava, Kṛṣṇa Himself. Therefore when this verse says *vāsudeve bhagavati,* one should understand that Prahlāda Mahārāja's attachment for Nṛsiṁhadeva was attachment for Kṛṣṇa, Vāsudeva, the son of Vasudeva. Prahlāda Mahārāja, therefore, is described as a great *mahātmā.* As the Lord Himself confirms in *Bhagavad-gītā* (7.19):

bahūnāṁ janmanām ante
jñānavān māṁ prapadyate
vāsudevaḥ sarvam iti
sa mahātmā sudurlabhaḥ

"After many births and deaths, he who is actually in knowledge surrenders unto Me, knowing Me to be the cause of all causes and all that is. Such a great soul is very rare." A great devotee of Kṛṣṇa, the son of Vasudeva, is a great soul very rarely to be found. Prahlāda Mahārāja's attachment for Kṛṣṇa will be explained in the next verse. *Kṛṣṇa-graha-gṛhītātmā.* Prahlāda Mahārāja's heart was always filled with thoughts of Kṛṣṇa. Therefore Prahlāda Mahārāja is the ideal devotee in Kṛṣṇa consciousness.

TEXT 37

न्यस्तक्रीडनको बालो जडवत्तन्मनस्तया ।
कृष्णग्रहगृहीतात्मा न वेद जगदीदृशम् ॥३७॥

nyasta-krīḍanako bālo
jaḍavat tan-manastayā
kṛṣṇa-graha-gṛhītātmā
na veda jagad īdṛśam

nyasta—having given up; *krīḍanakaḥ*—all sportive activities or tendencies for childhood play; *bālaḥ*—a boy; *jaḍa-vat*—as if dull, without activities; *tat-manastayā*—by being fully absorbed in Kṛṣṇa; *kṛṣṇa-graha*—by Kṛṣṇa, who is like a strong influence (like a *graha*, or planetary influence); *gṛhīta-ātmā*—whose mind was fully attracted; *na*—not; *veda*—understood; *jagat*—the entire material world; *īdṛśam*—like this.

TRANSLATION

From the very beginning of his childhood, Prahlāda Mahārāja was uninterested in childish playthings. Indeed, he gave them up altogether and remained silent and dull, being fully absorbed in Kṛṣṇa consciousness. Since his mind was always affected by Kṛṣṇa consciousness, he could not understand how the world goes on being fully absorbed in the activities of sense gratification.

PURPORT

Prahlāda Mahārāja is the vivid example of a great person fully absorbed in Kṛṣṇa consciousness. In *Caitanya-caritāmṛta* (*Madhya* 8.274) it is said:

sthāvara-jaṅgama dekhe, nā dekhe tāra mūrti
sarvatra haya nija iṣṭa-deva-sphūrti

A fully Kṛṣṇa conscious person, although situated in this material world, does not see anything but Kṛṣṇa, anywhere and everywhere. This is the sign of a *mahā-bhāgavata*. The *mahā-bhāgavata* sees Kṛṣṇa everywhere because of his attitude of pure love for Kṛṣṇa. As confirmed in the *Brahma-saṁhitā* (5.38):

premāñjana-cchurita-bhakti-vilocanena
santaḥ sadaiva hṛdayeṣu vilokayanti
yaṁ śyāmasundaram acintya-guṇa-svarūpaṁ
govindam ādi-puruṣaṁ tam ahaṁ bhajāmi

"I worship the primeval Lord, Govinda, who is always seen by the devotee whose eyes are anointed with the pulp of love. He is seen in His eternal form of Śyāmasundara, situated within the heart of the devotee." An exalted devotee, or *mahātmā*, who is rarely to be seen, remains fully conscious of Kṛṣṇa and constantly sees the Lord within the core of his heart. It is sometimes said that when one is influenced by evil stars like Saturn, Rāhu or Ketu, he cannot make advancement in any prospective activity. In just the opposite way, Prahlāda Mahārāja was influenced by Kṛṣṇa, the supreme planet, and thus he could not think of the material world and live without Kṛṣṇa consciousness. That is the sign of a *mahā-bhāgavata.* Even if one is an enemy of Kṛṣṇa, a *mahā-bhāgavata* sees him to be also engaged in Kṛṣṇa's service. Another crude example is that everything appears yellow to the jaundiced eye. Similarly, to a *mahā-bhāgavata,* everyone but himself appears to be engaged in Kṛṣṇa's service.

Prahlāda Mahārāja is the approved *mahā-bhāgavata,* the supreme devotee. In the previous verse it was stated that he had natural attachment (*naisargikī ratiḥ*). The symptoms of such natural attachment for Kṛṣṇa are described in this verse. Although Prahlāda Mahārāja was only a boy, he had no interest in playing. As stated in *Śrīmad-Bhāgavatam* (11.2.42), *viraktir anyatra ca:* the symptom of perfect Kṛṣṇa consciousness is that one loses interest in all material activities. For a small boy to give up playing is impossible, but Prahlāda Mahārāja, being situated in first-class devotional service, was always absorbed in a trance of Kṛṣṇa consciousness. Just as a materialistic person is always absorbed in thoughts of material gain, a *mahā-bhāgavata* like Prahlāda Mahārāja is always absorbed in thoughts of Kṛṣṇa.

TEXT 38

आसीनः पर्यटन्नश्नन् शयानः प्रपिबन् ब्रुवन् ।
नानुसन्धत्त एतानि गोविन्दपरिरम्भितः ॥३८॥

āsīnaḥ paryaṭann aśnan
śayānaḥ prapiban bruvan
nānusandhatta etāni
govinda-parirambhitaḥ

āsīnaḥ—while sitting; *paryaṭan*—while walking; *aśnan*—while eating; *śayānaḥ*—while lying down; *prapiban*—while drinking; *bruvan*—while talking; *na*—not; *anusandhatte*—knew; *etāni*—all these activities; *govinda*—by the Supreme Personality of Godhead, who enlivens the senses; *parirambhitaḥ*—being embraced.

TRANSLATION

Prahlāda Mahārāja was always absorbed in thought of Kṛṣṇa. Thus, being always embraced by the Lord, he did not know how his bodily necessities, such as sitting, walking, eating, lying down, drinking and talking, were being automatically performed.

PURPORT

A small child, while being cared for by his mother, does not know how the needs of the body for eating, sleeping, lying down, passing water and evacuating are being fulfilled. He is simply satisfied to be on the lap of his mother. Similarly, Prahlāda Mahārāja was exactly like a small child, being cared for by Govinda. The necessary activities of his body were performed without his knowledge. As a father and mother care for their child, Govinda cared for Prahlāda Mahārāja, who remained always absorbed in thoughts of Govinda. This is Kṛṣṇa consciousness. Prahlāda Mahārāja is the vivid example of perfection in Kṛṣṇa consciousness.

TEXT 39

क्वचिद्रुदति वैकुण्ठचिन्ताशबलचेतनः ।
क्वचिद्धसति तच्चिन्ताह्लाद उद्गायति क्वचित् ॥३९॥

kvacid rudati vaikuṇṭha-
cintā-śabala-cetanaḥ
kvacid dhasati tac-cintā-
hlāda udgāyati kvacit

kvacit—sometimes; *rudati*—cries; *vaikuṇṭha-cintā*—by thoughts of Kṛṣṇa; *śabala-cetanaḥ*—whose mind was bewildered; *kvacit*—sometimes; *hasati*—laughs; *tat-cintā*—by thoughts of Him; *āhlādaḥ*—being jubilant; *udgāyati*—chants very loudly; *kvacit*—sometimes.

TRANSLATION

Because of advancement in Kṛṣṇa consciousness, he sometimes cried, sometimes laughed, sometimes expressed jubilation and sometimes sang loudly.

PURPORT

This verse further clarifies the comparison of a devotee to a child. If a mother leaves her small child in his bed or cradle and goes away to attend to some family duties, the child immediately understands that his mother has gone away, and therefore he cries. But as soon as the mother returns and cares for the child, the child laughs and becomes jubilant. Similarly, Prahlāda Mahārāja, being always absorbed in thoughts of Kṛṣṇa, sometimes felt separation, thinking, "Where is Kṛṣṇa?" This is explained by Śrī Caitanya Mahāprabhu. *Śūnyāyitaṁ jagat sarvaṁ govinda-viraheṇa me.* When an exalted devotee feels that Kṛṣṇa is invisible, having gone away, he cries in separation, and sometimes, when he sees that Kṛṣṇa has returned to care for him, he laughs, just as a child sometimes laughs upon understanding that his mother is taking care of him. These symptoms are called *bhāva.* In *The Nectar of Devotion,* various *bhāvas,* ecstatic conditions of a devotee, are fully described. These *bhāvas* are visible in the activities of a perfect devotee.

TEXT 40

नदति क्वचिदुत्कण्ठो विलज्जो नृत्यति क्वचित् ।
क्वचित्तद्भावनायुक्तस्तन्मयोऽनुचकार ह ॥४०॥

nadati kvacid utkaṇṭho
vilajjo nṛtyati kvacit
kvacit tad-bhāvanā-yuktas
tanmayo 'nucakāra ha

nadati—exclaims loudly (addressing the Lord, "O Kṛṣṇa"); *kvacit*—sometimes; *utkaṇṭhaḥ*—being anxious; *vilajjaḥ*—without shame; *nṛtyati*—he dances; *kvacit*—sometimes; *kvacit*—sometimes; *tat-bhāvanā*—with thoughts of Kṛṣṇa; *yuktaḥ*—being absorbed; *tat-mayaḥ*—thinking as if he had become Kṛṣṇa; *anucakāra*—imitated; *ha*—indeed.

TRANSLATION

Sometimes, upon seeing the Supreme Personality of Godhead, Prahlāda Mahārāja would loudly call in full anxiety. He sometimes lost his shyness in jubilation and began dancing in ecstasy, and sometimes, being fully absorbed in thoughts of Kṛṣṇa, he felt oneness and imitated the pastimes of the Lord.

PURPORT

Prahlāda Mahārāja sometimes felt that the Lord was far away from him and therefore called Him loudly. When he saw that the Lord was before him, he was fully jubilant. Sometimes, thinking himself one with the Supreme, he imitated the Lord's pastimes, and in separation from the Lord he would sometimes show symptoms of madness. These feelings of a devotee would not be appreciated by impersonalists. One must go further and further into spiritual understanding. The first realization is impersonal Brahman, but one must go still further to realize Paramātmā and eventually the Supreme Personality of Godhead, who is worshiped by the transcendental feelings of a devotee in a relationship of *śānta, dāsya, sakhya, vātsalya* or *mādhurya*. Here the feelings of Prahlāda Mahārāja were in the mellow of *vātsalya*, filial love and affection. As a child cries when left by his mother, when Prahlāda Mahārāja felt that the Lord was away from him he began to cry (*nadati*). Again, a devotee like Prahlāda sometimes sees that the Lord is coming from a long distance to pacify him, like a mother responding to a child, saying, "My dear child, do not cry. I am coming." Then the devotee, without being ashamed due to his surroundings and circumstances, begins to dance, thinking, "Here is my Lord! My Lord is coming!" Thus the devotee, in full ecstasy, sometimes imitates the pastimes of the Lord, just as the cowherd boys used to imitate the behavior of the jungle animals. However, he does not actually become the Lord. Prahlāda Mahārāja achieved the spiritual ecstasies described herein by his advancement in spiritual understanding.

TEXT 41

क्वचिदुत्पुलकस्तूष्णीमास्ते संस्पर्शनिर्वृतः ।
अस्पन्दप्रणयानन्दसलिलामीलितेक्षणः ॥४१॥

kvacid utpulakas tūṣṇīm
āste saṁsparśa-nirvṛtaḥ
aspanda-praṇayānanda-
salilāmīliteksaṇaḥ

kvacit—sometimes; *utpulakaḥ*—with the hairs of his body standing on end; *tūṣṇīm*—completely silent; *āste*—remains; *saṁsparśa-nirvṛtaḥ*—feeling great joy by contact with the Lord; *aspanda*—steady; *praṇaya-ānanda*—due to transcendental bliss from a relationship of love; *salila*—filled with tears; *āmīlita*—half-closed; *īkṣaṇaḥ*—whose eyes.

TRANSLATION

Sometimes, feeling the touch of the Lord's lotus hands, he became spiritually jubilant and remained silent, his hairs standing on end and tears gliding down from his half-closed eyes because of his love for the Lord.

PURPORT

When a devotee feels separation from the Lord, he becomes eager to see where the Lord is, and sometimes when he feels pangs of separation, tears flow incessantly from his half-closed eyes. As stated by Śrī Caitanya Mahāprabhu in His *Śikṣāṣṭaka, yugāyitaṁ nimeṣeṇa cakṣuṣā prāvṛṣāyitam.* The words *cakṣuṣā prāvṛṣāyitam* refer to tears falling incessantly from the devotee's eyes. These symptoms, which appear in pure devotional ecstasy, were visible in the body of Prahlāda Mahārāja.

TEXT 42

स उत्तमश्लोकपदारविन्दयो-
र्निषेवयाकिञ्चनसङ्गलब्धया ।
तन्वन् परां निर्वृतिमात्मनो मुहु-
र्दुःसङ्गदीनस्य मनःशमं व्यधात् ॥४२॥

sa uttama-śloka-padāravindayor
niṣevayākiñcana-saṅga-labdhayā
tanvan parāṁ nirvṛtim ātmano muhur
duḥsaṅga-dīnasya manaḥ śamaṁ vyadhāt

saḥ—he (Prahlāda Mahārāja); *uttama-śloka-pada-aravindayoḥ*—to the lotus feet of the Supreme Personality of Godhead, who is worshiped by transcendental prayers; *niṣevayā*—by constant service; *akiñcana*—of devotees who have nothing to do with the material world; *saṅga*—in the association; *labdhayā*—obtained; *tanvan*—expanding; *parām*—highest; *nirvṛtim*—bliss; *ātmanaḥ*—of the spirit soul; *muhuḥ*—constantly; *duḥsaṅga-dīnasya*—of a person poor in spiritual understanding due to bad association; *manaḥ*—the mind; *śamam*—peaceful; *vyadhāt*—made.

TRANSLATION

Because of his association with perfect, unalloyed devotees who had nothing to do with anything material, Prahlāda Mahārāja constantly engaged in the service of the Lord's lotus feet. By seeing his bodily features when he was in perfect ecstasy, persons very poor in spiritual understanding became purified. In other words, Prahlāda Mahārāja bestowed upon them transcendental bliss.

PURPORT

Apparently Prahlāda Mahārāja was placed in circumstances in which he was always tortured by his father. In such material conditions, one cannot have an undisturbed mind, but since *bhakti* is unconditional (*ahaituky apratihatā*), Prahlāda Mahārāja was never disturbed by the chastisements of Hiraṇyakaśipu. On the contrary, the bodily symptoms of his ecstatic love for the Supreme Personality of Godhead turned the minds of his friends, who had also been born in atheistic families. Instead of being disturbed by the torments of his father, Prahlāda influenced these friends and cleansed their minds. A devotee is never contaminated by material conditions, but persons subjected to material conditions can become spiritually advanced and blissful upon seeing the behavior of a pure devotee.

TEXT 43

तस्मिन्महाभागवते महाभागे महात्मनि ।
हिरण्यकशिपू राजन्नकरोदघमात्मजे ॥४३॥

tasmin mahā-bhāgavate
mahā-bhāge mahātmani
hiraṇyakaśipū rājann
akarod agham ātmaje

tasmin—unto him; *mahā-bhāgavate*—an exalted devotee of the Lord; *mahā-bhāge*—most fortunate; *mahā-ātmani*—whose mind was very broad; *hiraṇyakaśipuḥ*—the demon Hiraṇyakaśipu; *rājan*—O King; *akarot*—performed; *agham*—very great sin; *ātma-je*—to his own son.

TRANSLATION

My dear King Yudhiṣṭhira, the demon Hiraṇyakaśipu tormented this exalted, fortunate devotee, although Prahlāda was his own son.

PURPORT

When a demon like Hiraṇyakaśipu, despite his elevated position due to severe austerities, begins to tease a devotee, he begins falling down, and the results of his austerities dwindle. One who oppresses a pure devotee loses all the results of his austerities, penances and pious activities. Since Hiraṇyakaśipu was now inclined to chastise his most exalted devotee son, Prahlāda Mahārāja, his opulences began dwindling.

TEXT 44

श्रीयुधिष्ठिर उवाच
देवर्ष एतदिच्छामो वेदितुं तव सुव्रत ।
यदात्मजाय शुद्धाय पितादात्साधवे ह्यघम् ॥४४॥

śrī-yudhiṣṭhira uvāca
devarṣa etad icchāmo
veditum tava suvrata
yad ātmajāya śuddhāya
pitādāt sādhave hy agham

śrī-yudhiṣṭhiraḥ uvāca—Mahārāja Yudhiṣṭhira inquired; *deva-ṛṣe*—O best saintly person among the demigods; *etat*—this; *icchāmaḥ*—we wish; *veditum*—to know; *tava*—from you; *su-vrata*—having the determination for spiritual advancement; *yat*—because; *ātma-jāya*—unto his own son; *śuddhāya*—who was pure and exalted; *pitā*—the father, Hiraṇyakaśipu; *adāt*—gave; *sādhave*—a great saint; *hi*—indeed; *agham*—trouble.

TRANSLATION

Mahārāja Yudhiṣṭhira said: O best of the saints among the demigods, O best of spiritual leaders, how did Hiraṇyakaśipu give so much trouble to Prahlāda Mahārāja, the pure and exalted saint, although Prahlāda was his own son? I wish to know about this subject from you.

PURPORT

To know about the Supreme Personality of Godhead and the characteristics of His pure devotee, one must inquire from authorities like Devarṣi Nārada. One cannot inquire about transcendental subject matters from a layman. As stated in *Śrīmad-Bhāgavatam* (3.25.25), *satāṁ prasaṅgān mama vīrya-saṁvido bhavanti hṛt-karṇa-rasāyanāḥ kathāḥ:* only by association with devotees can one authoritatively understand the position of the Lord and His devotees. A devotee like Nārada Muni is addressed as *suvrata. Su* means "good," and *vrata* means "vow." Thus the word *suvrata* refers to a person who has nothing to do with the material world, which is always bad. One cannot understand anything spiritual from a materialistic scholar puffed up with academic knowledge. As stated in *Bhagavad-gītā* (18.55), *bhaktyā mām abhijānāti:* one must try to understand Kṛṣṇa by devotional service and from a devotee. Therefore Yudhiṣṭhira Mahārāja was quite right in wanting to learn further about Prahlāda Mahārāja from Śrī Nārada Muni.

TEXT 45

पुत्रान् विप्रतिकूलान् स्वान् पितरः पुत्रवत्सलाः ।
उपालभन्ते शिक्षार्थं नैवाघमपरो यथा ॥४५॥

putrān vipratikūlān svān
pitaraḥ putra-vatsalāḥ

upālabhante śikṣārthaṁ
naivāgham aparo yathā

putrān—sons; *vipratikūlān*—who act against the will of the father; *svān*—their own; *pitaraḥ*—fathers; *putra-vatsalāḥ*—being very affectionate to the children; *upālabhante*—chastise; *śikṣa-artham*—to teach them lessons; *na*—not; *eva*—indeed; *agham*—punishment; *aparaḥ*—an enemy; *yathā*—like.

TRANSLATION

A father and mother are always affectionate to their children. When the children are disobedient the parents chastise them, not due to enmity but only for the child's instruction and welfare. How did Hiraṇyakaśipu, the father of Prahlāda Mahārāja, chastise such a noble son? This is what I am eager to know.

TEXT 46

किमुतानुवशान् साधूंस्तादृशान् गुरुदेवतान् ।
एतत् कौतूहलं ब्रह्मन्नस्माकं विधम प्रभो ।
पितुः पुत्राय यद् द्वेषो मरणाय प्रयोजितः ॥४६॥

kim utānuvaśān sādhūṁs
tādṛśān guru-devatān
etat kautūhalaṁ brahmann
asmākaṁ vidhama prabho
pituḥ putrāya yad dveṣo
maraṇāya prayojitaḥ

kim uta—much less; *anuvaśān*—to obedient and perfect sons; *sādhūn*—great devotees; *tādṛśān*—of that sort; *guru-devatān*—honoring the father as the Supreme Personality of Godhead; *etat*—this; *kautūhalam*—doubt; *brahman*—O *brāhmaṇa; asmākam*—of us; *vidhama*—dissipate; *prabho*—O my lord; *pituḥ*—of the father; *putrāya*—unto the son; *yat*—which; *dveṣaḥ*—envy; *maraṇāya*—for killing; *prayojitaḥ*—applied.

TRANSLATION

Mahārāja Yudhiṣṭhira further inquired: How was it possible for a father to be so violent toward an exalted son who was obedient, well-behaved and respectful to his father? O brāhmaṇa, O master, I have never heard of such a contradiction as an affectionate father's punishing his noble son with the intention of killing him. Kindly dissipate our doubts in this regard.

PURPORT

In the history of human society, an affectionate father is rarely found to chastise a noble and devoted son. Therefore Mahārāja Yudhiṣṭhira wanted Nārada Muni to dissipate his doubt.

Thus end the Bhaktivedanta purports of the Seventh Canto, Fourth Chapter, of the Śrīmad-Bhāgavatam, *entitled, "Hiraṇyakaśipu Terrorizes the Universe."*

CHAPTER FIVE

Prahlāda Mahārāja, the Saintly Son of Hiraṇyakaśipu

Prahlāda Mahārāja did not carry out the orders of his teachers, for he was always engaged in worshiping Lord Viṣṇu. As described in this chapter, Hiraṇyakaśipu tried to kill Prahlāda Mahārāja, even by having a snake bite him and by putting him under the feet of elephants, yet he was unsuccessful.

Hiraṇyakaśipu's spiritual master, Śukrācārya, had two sons named Ṣaṇḍa and Amarka, to whom Prahlāda Mahārāja was entrusted for education. Although the teachers tried to educate the boy Prahlāda in politics, economics and other material activities, he did not care for their instructions. Instead, he continued to be a pure devotee. Prahlāda Mahārāja never liked the idea of discriminating between one's friends and enemies. Because he was spiritually inclined, he was equal toward everyone.

Once upon a time, Hiraṇyakaśipu inquired from his son what the best thing was that he had learned from his teachers. Prahlāda Mahārāja replied that a man engrossed in the material consciousness of duality, thinking, "This is mine, and that belongs to my enemy," should give up his householder life and go to the forest to worship the Supreme Lord.

When Hiraṇyakaśipu heard from his son about devotional service, he decided that this small boy had been polluted by some friend in school. Thus he advised the teachers to take care of the boy so that he would not become a Kṛṣṇa conscious devotee. However, when the teachers inquired from Prahlāda Mahārāja why he was going against their teachings, Prahlāda Mahārāja taught the teachers that the mentality of ownership is false and that he was therefore trying to become an unalloyed devotee of Lord Viṣṇu. The teachers, being very angry at this answer, chastised and threatened the boy with many fearful conditions. They taught him to the best of their ability and then brought him before his father.

Hiraṇyakaśipu affectionately took his son Prahlāda on his lap and then inquired from him what the best thing was that he had learned from his teachers. As usual, Prahlāda Mahārāja began praising the nine processes of devotional service, such as *śravaṇam* and *kīrtanam.* Thus the King of the demons, Hiraṇyakaśipu, being extremely angry, chastised the teachers, Ṣaṇḍa and Amarka, for having wrongly trained Prahlāda Mahārāja. The so-called teachers informed the King that Prahlāda Mahārāja was automatically a devotee and did not listen to their instructions. When they proved themselves innocent, Hiraṇyakaśipu inquired from Prahlāda where he had learned *viṣṇu-bhakti.* Prahlāda Mahārāja replied that those who are attached to family life do not develop Kṛṣṇa consciousness, either personally or collectively. Instead, they suffer repeated birth and death in this material world and continue simply chewing the chewed. Prahlāda explained that the duty of every man is to take shelter of a pure devotee and thus become eligible to understand Kṛṣṇa consciousness.

Enraged at this answer, Hiraṇyakaśipu threw Prahlāda Mahārāja from his lap. Since Prahlāda was so treacherous that he had become a devotee of Viṣṇu, who had killed his uncle Hiraṇyākṣa, Hiraṇyakaśipu asked his assistants to kill him. The assistants of Hiraṇyakaśipu struck Prahlāda with sharp weapons, threw him under the feet of elephants, subjected him to hellish conditions, threw him from the peak of a mountain and tried to kill him in thousands of other ways, but they were unsuccessful. Hiraṇyakaśipu therefore became increasingly afraid of his son Prahlāda Mahārāja and arrested him. The sons of Hiraṇyakaśipu's spiritual master, Śukrācārya, began teaching Prahlāda in their own way, but Prahlāda Mahārāja did not accept their instructions. While the teachers were absent from the classroom, Prahlāda Mahārāja began to preach Kṛṣṇa consciousness in the school, and by his instructions all his class friends, the sons of the demons, became devotees like him.

TEXT 1

श्रीनारद उवाच

पौरोहित्याय भगवान् वृतः काव्यः किलासुरैः ।
षण्डामर्कौ सुतौ तस्य दैत्यराजगृहान्तिके ॥ १ ॥

śrī-nārada uvāca
paurohityāya bhagavān
vṛtaḥ kāvyaḥ kilāsuraiḥ
ṣaṇḍāmarkau sutau tasya
daitya-rāja-gṛhāntike

śrī-nāradaḥ uvāca—the great saint Nārada said; *paurohityāya*—to work as priest; *bhagavān*—the most powerful; *vṛtaḥ*—chosen; *kāvyaḥ*—Śukrācārya; *kila*—indeed; *asuraiḥ*—by the demons; *ṣaṇḍa-amarkau*—Ṣaṇḍa and Amarka; *sutau*—sons; *tasya*—of him; *daitya-rāja*—of the King of the demons, Hiraṇyakaśipu; *gṛha-antike*—near the residence.

TRANSLATION

The great saint Nārada Muni said: The demons, headed by Hiraṇyakaśipu, accepted Śukrācārya as their priest for ritualistic ceremonies. Śukrācārya's two sons, Ṣaṇḍa and Amarka, lived near Hiraṇyakaśipu's palace.

PURPORT

The beginning of the life story of Prahlāda is recounted as follows. Śukrācārya became the priest of the atheists, especially Hiraṇyakaśipu, and thus his two sons, Ṣaṇḍa and Amarka, resided near Hiraṇyakaśipu's residence. Śukrācārya should not have become the priest of Hiraṇyakaśipu because Hiraṇyakaśipu and his followers were all atheists. A *brāhmaṇa* should become the priest of a person interested in the advancement of spiritual culture. The very name Śukrācārya, however, indicates a person interested in obtaining benefits for his sons and descendants, regardless of how the money comes. A real *brāhmaṇa* would not become a priest for atheistic men.

TEXT 2

तौ राज्ञा प्रापितं बालं प्रह्लादं नयकोविदम् ।
पाठयामासतुः पाठ्यानन्यांश्चासुरबालकान् ॥ २ ॥

tau rājñā prāpitaṁ bālaṁ
prahlādaṁ naya-kovidam
pāṭhayām āsatuḥ pāṭhyān
anyāṁś cāsura-bālakān

tau—those two (Ṣaṇḍa and Amarka); *rājñā*—by the King; *prāpitam*—sent; *bālam*—the boy; *prahlādam*—named Prahlāda; *naya-kovidam*—who was aware of moral principles; *pāṭhayām āsatuḥ*—instructed; *pāṭhyān*—books of material knowledge; *anyān*—other; *ca*—also; *asura-bālakān*—sons of the *asuras.*

TRANSLATION

Prahlāda Mahārāja was already educated in devotional life, but when his father sent him to those two sons of Śukrācārya to be educated, they accepted him at their school along with the other sons of the asuras.

TEXT 3

यत्तत्र गुरुणा प्रोक्तं शुश्रुवेऽनुपपाठ च ।
न साधु मनसा मेने स्वपरासद्ग्रहाश्रयम् ॥ ३ ॥

yat tatra guruṇā proktaṁ
śuśruve 'nupapāṭha ca
na sādhu manasā mene
sva-parāsad-grahāśrayam

yat—which; *tatra*—there (in the school); *guruṇā*—by the teachers; *proktam*—instructed; *śuśruve*—heard; *anupapāṭha*—recited; *ca*—and; *na*—not; *sādhu*—good; *manasā*—by the mind; *mene*—considered; *sva*—of one's own; *para*—and of others; *asat-graha*—by the bad philosophy; *āśrayam*—which was supported.

TRANSLATION

Prahlāda certainly heard and recited the topics of politics and economics taught by the teachers, but he understood that political philosophy involves considering someone a friend and someone else an enemy, and thus he did not like it.

PURPORT

Politics involves accepting one group of men as enemies and another group as friends. Everything in politics is based on this philosophy, and the entire world, especially at the present, is engrossed in it. The public is concerned with friendly countries and friendly groups or enemy countries and enemy groups, but as stated in *Bhagavad-gītā*, a learned person does not make distinctions between enemies and friends. Devotees, especially, do not create friends and enemies. A devotee sees that every living being is part and parcel of Kṛṣṇa (*mamaivāṁśo jīva-bhūtaḥ*). Therefore a devotee treats friends and enemies equally by trying to educate them both in Kṛṣṇa consciousness. Of course, atheistic men do not follow the instructions of pure devotees, but instead consider a devotee their enemy. A devotee, however, never creates a situation of friendship and enmity. Although Prahlāda Mahārāja was obliged to hear the instructions of Ṣaṇḍa and Amarka, he did not like the philosophy of friends and enemies, which forms the basis of politics. He was not interested in this philosophy.

TEXT 4

एकदासुरराट् पुत्रमङ्कमारोप्य पाण्डव ।
पप्रच्छ कथ्यतां वत्स मन्यते साधु यद्भवान् ॥ ४ ॥

ekadāsura-rāṭ putram
aṅkam āropya pāṇḍava
papraccha kathyatāṁ vatsa
manyate sādhu yad bhavān

ekadā—once upon a time; *asura-rāṭ*—the Emperor of the *asuras; putram*—his son; *aṅkam*—on the lap; *āropya*—placing; *pāṇḍava*—O Mahārāja Yudhiṣṭhira; *papraccha*—inquired; *kathyatām*—let it be told; *vatsa*—my dear son; *manyate*—considers; *sādhu*—the best; *yat*—that which; *bhavān*—your good self.

TRANSLATION

My dear King Yudhiṣṭhira, once upon a time the King of the demons, Hiraṇyakaśipu, took his son Prahlāda on his lap and very

affectionately inquired: My dear son, please let me know what you think is the best of all the subjects you have studied from your teachers.

PURPORT

Hiraṇyakaśipu did not ask his young son anything that would be very difficult for him to answer; instead, he gave the boy a chance to speak plainly about whatever he thought might be best. Prahlāda Mahārāja, of course, being a perfect devotee, knew everything and could say what the best part of life is. In the *Vedas* it is said, *yasmin vijñāte sarvam evaṁ vijñātaṁ bhavati:* if one properly understands God, he can understand any subject matter very nicely. Sometimes we have to challenge big scientists and philosophers, but by the grace of Kṛṣṇa we emerge successful. It is impossible, practically speaking, for ordinary men to challenge scientists or philosophers concerning genuine knowledge, but a devotee can challenge them because the best of everything is known to a devotee by the grace of Kṛṣṇa. As confirmed in *Bhagavad-gītā* (10.11):

teṣām evānukampārtham
aham ajñāna-jaṁ tamaḥ
nāśayāmy ātma-bhāva-stho
jñāna-dīpena bhāsvatā

Kṛṣṇa, who is situated in the core of everyone's heart as the Supersoul, dissipates all the ignorance from the heart of a devotee. As a special favor, He enlightens the devotee with all knowledge by putting before him the torch of light. Prahlāda Mahārāja, therefore, knew the best of knowledge, and when his father inquired from him, Prahlāda gave him that knowledge. Prahlāda Mahārāja was able to solve the most difficult parts of problems because of his advanced Kṛṣṇa consciousness. Therefore he replied as follows.

TEXT 5

श्रीप्रह्लाद उवाच

तत्साधु मन्येऽसुरवर्य देहिनां
सदा समुद्विग्नधियामसद्ग्रहात् ।

हित्वात्मपातं गृहमन्धकूपं
वनं गतो यद्धरिमाश्रयेत ॥ ५ ॥

śrī-prahlāda uvāca
tat sādhu manye 'sura-varya dehināṁ
sadā samudvigna-dhiyām asad-grahāt
hitvātma-pātaṁ gṛham andha-kūpaṁ
vanaṁ gato yad dharim āśrayeta

śrī-prahlādaḥ uvāca—Prahlāda Mahārāja replied; *tat*—that; *sādhu*—very good, or the best part of life; *manye*—I think; *asura-varya*—O King of the *asuras; dehinām*—of persons who have accepted the material body; *sadā*—always; *samudvigna*—full of anxieties; *dhiyām*—whose intelligence; *asat-grahāt*—because of accepting the temporary body or bodily relations as real (thinking "I am this body, and everything belonging to this body is mine"); *hitvā*—giving up; *ātma-pātam*—the place where spiritual culture or self-realization is stopped; *gṛham*—the bodily concept of life, or household life; *andha-kūpam*—which is nothing but a blind well (where there is no water but one nonetheless searches for water); *vanam*—to the forest; *gataḥ*—going; *yat*—which; *harim*—the Supreme Personality of Godhead; *āśrayeta*—may take shelter of.

TRANSLATION

Prahlāda Mahārāja replied: O best of the asuras, King of the demons, as far as I have learned from my spiritual master, any person who has accepted a temporary body and temporary household life is certainly embarrassed by anxiety because of having fallen in a dark well where there is no water but only suffering. One should give up this position and go to the forest [vana]. More clearly, one should go to Vṛndāvana, where only Kṛṣṇa consciousness is prevalent, and should thus take shelter of the Supreme Personality of Godhead.

PURPORT

Hiraṇyakaśipu thought that Prahlāda, being nothing but a small boy with no actual experience, might reply with something pleasing but nothing practical. Prahlāda Mahārāja, however, being an exalted devotee, had acquired all the qualities of education.

yasyāsti bhaktir bhagavaty akiñcanā
sarvair guṇais tatra samāsate surāḥ
harāv abhaktasya kuto mahad-guṇā
manorathenāsati dhāvato bahiḥ

"One who has unflinching devotional faith in Kṛṣṇa consistently manifests all the good qualities of Kṛṣṇa and the demigods. However, he who has no devotion to the Supreme Personality of Godhead has no good qualifications because he is engaged by mental concoction in material existence, which is the external feature of the Lord." (*Bhāg.* 5.18.12) So-called educated philosophers and scientists who are simply on the mental platform cannot distinguish between what is actually *sat,* eternal, and what is *asat,* temporary. The Vedic injunction is *asato mā jyotir gama:* everyone should give up the platform of temporary existence and approach the eternal platform. The soul is eternal, and topics concerning the eternal soul are actually knowledge. Elsewhere it is said, *apaśyatām ātma-tattvaṁ gṛheṣu gṛha-medhinām:* those who are attached to the bodily conception of life and who thus stick to life as a *gṛhastha,* or householder, on the platform of material sense enjoyment, cannot see the welfare of the eternal soul. Prahlāda Mahārāja confirmed this by saying that if one wants success in life, he should immediately understand from the right sources what his self-interest is and how he should mold his life in spiritual consciousness. One should understand himself to be part and parcel of Kṛṣṇa and thus completely take shelter of His lotus feet for guaranteed spiritual success. Everyone in the material world is in the bodily conception, struggling hard for existence, life after life. Prahlāda Mahārāja therefore recommended that to stop this material condition of repeated birth and death, one should go to the forest (*vana*).

In the *varṇāśrama* system, one first becomes a *brahmacārī,* then a *gṛhastha,* a *vānaprastha* and finally a *sannyāsī.* Going to the forest means accepting *vānaprastha* life, which is between *gṛhastha* life and *sannyāsa.* As confirmed in the *Viṣṇu Purāṇa* (3.8.9), *varṇāśramācāravatā puruṣeṇa paraḥ pumān viṣṇur ārādhyate:* by accepting the institution of *varṇa* and *āśrama,* one can very easily elevate himself to the platform of worshiping Viṣṇu, the Supreme Personality of Godhead. Otherwise, if one remains in the bodily conception, one must rot within this material world, and his life will be a failure. Society must have divisions of *brāhmaṇa*, *kṣatriya*, *vaiśya* and *śūdra*, and for spiritual advancement one must gradually develop as a *brahmacārī*, *gṛhastha*, *vānaprastha* and *sannyāsī*. Prahlāda Mahārāja recommended that his father accept *vānaprastha* life because as a *gṛhastha* he was becoming increasingly demoniac due to bodily attachment. Prahlāda recommended to his father that accepting *vānaprastha* life would be better than going deeper and deeper into *gṛham andha-kūpam*, the blind well of life as a *gṛhastha*. In our Kṛṣṇa consciousness movement we therefore invite all the elderly persons of the world to come to Vṛndāvana and stay there in retired life, making advancement in spiritual consciousness, Kṛṣṇa consciousness.

TEXT 6

श्रीनारद उवाच

श्रुत्वा पुत्रगिरो दैत्यः परपक्षसमाहिताः ।
जहास बुद्धिर्बालानां भिद्यते परबुद्धिभिः ॥ ६ ॥

śrī-nārada uvāca
śrutvā putra-giro daityaḥ
para-pakṣa-samāhitāḥ
jahāsa buddhir bālānāṁ
bhidyate para-buddhibhiḥ

śrī-nāradaḥ uvāca—Nārada Muni said; *śrutvā*—hearing; *putra-giraḥ*—the instructive words of his son; *daityaḥ*—Hiraṇyakaśipu; *para-pakṣa*—on the side of the enemy; *samāhitāḥ*—full of faith; *jahāsa*—laughed; *buddhiḥ*—the intelligence; *bālānām*—of small boys; *bhidyate*—is polluted; *para-buddhibhiḥ*—by instructions from the enemy's camp.

TRANSLATION

Nārada Muni continued: When Prahlāda Mahārāja spoke about the path of self-realization in devotional service, thus being

faithful to the camp of his father's enemies, Hiraṇyakaśipu, the King of the demons, heard Prahlāda's words and he laughingly said, "Thus is the intelligence of children spoiled by the words of the enemy."

PURPORT

Hiraṇyakaśipu, being a demon, would always consider Lord Viṣṇu and His devotees to be his enemies. Therefore the word *para-pakṣa* ("on the side of the enemy") is used here. Hiraṇyakaśipu never agreed with the words of Viṣṇu, or Kṛṣṇa. Rather, he was angered by the intelligence of a Vaiṣṇava. Lord Viṣṇu, Lord Kṛṣṇa, says, *sarva-dharmān parityajya mām ekaṁ śaraṇaṁ vraja*—"Give up all other duties and surrender unto Me"—but demons like Hiraṇyakaśipu never agree to do this. Therefore Kṛṣṇa says:

na māṁ duṣkṛtino mūḍhāḥ
prapadyante narādhamāḥ
māyayāpahṛta-jñānā
āsuraṁ bhāvam āśritāḥ

"Those miscreants who are grossly foolish, lowest among mankind, whose knowledge is stolen by illusion, and who partake of the atheistic nature of demons, do not surrender unto Me." (Bg. 7.15) The *asura-bhāva*, the atheistic nature, is directly represented by Hiraṇyakaśipu. Such persons, being *mūḍha* and *narādhama*—fools and rascals, the lowest of men—would never accept Viṣṇu as the Supreme and surrender to Him. Hiraṇyakaśipu naturally became increasingly angry that his son Prahlāda was being influenced by the camp of the enemies. He therefore asked that saintly persons like Nārada not be allowed within the residential quarters of his son, for otherwise Prahlāda would be further spoiled by Vaiṣṇava instructions.

TEXT 7

सम्यग्विधार्यतां बालो गुरुगेहे द्विजातिभिः ।
विष्णुपक्षैः प्रतिच्छन्नैर्न भिद्येतास्य धीर्यथा ॥ ७ ॥

samyag vidhāryatāṁ bālo
guru-gehe dvi-jātibhiḥ
viṣṇu-pakṣaiḥ praticchannair
na bhidyetāsya dhīr yathā

samyak—completely; *vidhāryatām*—let him be protected; *bālaḥ*—this boy of tender age; *guru-gehe*—in the *guru-kula*, the place where children are sent to be instructed by the *guru; dvi-jātibhiḥ*—by *brāhmaṇas; viṣṇu-pakṣaiḥ*—who are on the side of Viṣṇu; *praticchannaiḥ*—disguised in different dresses; *na bhidyeta*—may not be influenced; *asya*—of him; *dhīḥ*—the intelligence; *yathā*—so that.

TRANSLATION

Hiraṇyakaśipu advised his assistants: My dear demons, give complete protection to this boy at the guru-kula where he is instructed, so that his intelligence will not be further influenced by Vaiṣṇavas who may go there in disguise.

PURPORT

In our Kṛṣṇa consciousness movement, the tactic of dressing oneself like an ordinary *karmī* is necessary because everyone in the demoniac kingdom is against the Vaiṣṇava teachings. Kṛṣṇa consciousness is not at all to the liking of the demons of the present age. As soon as they see a Vaiṣṇava dressed in saffron garments with beads on his neck and *tilaka* on his forehead, they are immediately irritated. They criticize the Vaiṣṇavas by sarcastically saying Hare Kṛṣṇa, and some people also chant Hare Kṛṣṇa sincerely. In either case, since Hare Kṛṣṇa is absolute, whether one chants it jokingly or sincerely, it will have its effect. The Vaiṣṇavas are pleased when the demons chant Hare Kṛṣṇa because this shows that the Hare Kṛṣṇa movement is taking ground. The greater demons, like Hiraṇyakaśipu, are always prepared to chastise the Vaiṣṇavas, and they try to make arrangements so that Vaiṣṇavas will not come to sell their books and preach Kṛṣṇa consciousness. Thus what was done by Hiraṇyakaśipu long, long ago is still being done. That is the way of materialistic life. Demons or materialists do not at all like the advancement of Kṛṣṇa consciousness, and they try to hinder it in many ways. Yet the preachers of Kṛṣṇa consciousness must go forward—in their Vaiṣṇava dress or any other dress—for the purpose of preaching. Cāṇakya Paṇḍita says that if an honest person deals with a great cheater, it is necessary for him to become a cheater also, not for the purpose of cheating but to make his preaching successful.

TEXT 8

गृहमानीतमाहूय प्रह्रादं दैत्ययाजकाः ।
प्रशस्य श्लक्ष्णया वाचा समपृच्छन्त सामभिः॥ ८ ॥

gṛham ānītam āhūya
prahrādaṁ daitya-yājakāḥ
praśasya ślakṣṇayā vācā
samapṛcchanta sāmabhiḥ

gṛham—to the place of the teachers (Ṣaṇḍa and Amarka); *ānītam*—brought; *āhūya*—calling; *prahrādam*—Prahlāda; *daitya-yājakāḥ*—the priests of the demon Hiraṇyakaśipu; *praśasya*—by pacifying; *ślakṣṇayā*—with a very mild; *vācā*—voice; *samapṛcchanta*—they questioned; *sāmabhiḥ*—by very agreeable words.

TRANSLATION

When Hiraṇyakaśipu's servants brought the boy Prahlāda back to the guru-kula [the place where the brāhmaṇas taught the boys], the priests of the demons, Ṣaṇḍa and Amarka, pacified him. With very mild voices and affectionate words, they inquired from him as follows.

PURPORT

Ṣaṇḍa and Amarka, the priests of the demons, were eager to know from Prahlāda Mahārāja who the Vaiṣṇavas were that came to instruct him in Kṛṣṇa consciousness. Their purpose was to discover the names of these Vaiṣṇavas. In the beginning they did not threaten the boy because when threatened he might not identify the real culprits. Therefore they very mildly and peacefully inquired as follows.

TEXT 9

वत्स प्रह्राद भद्रं ते सत्यं कथय मा मृषा ।
बालानति कुतस्तुभ्यमेष बुद्धिविपर्ययः ॥ ९ ॥

vatsa prahrāda bhadraṁ te
satyaṁ kathaya mā mṛṣā
bālān ati kutas tubhyam
eṣa buddhi-viparyayaḥ

vatsa—O dear son; *prahrāda*—Prahlāda; *bhadram te*—all blessings and good fortune unto you; *satyam*—the truth; *kathaya*—speak; *mā*—do not; *mṛṣā*—a lie; *bālān ati*—passing over the other demon boys; *kutaḥ*—from where; *tubhyam*—unto you; *eṣaḥ*—this; *buddhi*—of the intelligence; *viparyayaḥ*—pollution.

TRANSLATION

Dear son Prahlāda, all peace and good fortune unto you. Kindly do not speak lies; just reply with the truth. These boys you see are not like you, for they do not speak in a deviant way. How have you learned these instructions? How has your intelligence been spoiled in this way?

PURPORT

Prahlāda Mahārāja was still a boy, and therefore his teachers thought that if they pacified the little boy he would immediately speak the truth, revealing the secret of how the Vaiṣṇavas came there to teach him lessons in devotional service. It was surprising, of course, that in the same school the other boys of the Daityas were not polluted; only Prahlāda Mahārāja was supposedly polluted by the instructions of the Vaiṣṇavas. The main duty of the teachers was to inquire who those Vaiṣṇavas were that came to teach Prahlāda and spoil his intelligence.

TEXT 10

बुद्धिभेदः परकृत उताहो ते स्वतोऽभवत् ।
भण्यतां श्रोतुकामानां गुरूणां कुलनन्दन ॥१०॥

buddhi-bhedaḥ para-kṛta
utāho te svato 'bhavat
bhaṇyatāṁ śrotu-kāmānāṁ
gurūṇāṁ kula-nandana

buddhi-bhedaḥ—pollution of the intelligence; *para-kṛtaḥ*—done by the enemies; *utāho*—or; *te*—of you; *svataḥ*—by yourself; *abhavat*—was; *bhaṇyatām*—let it be told; *śrotu-kāmānām*—to us, who are very eager to hear about it; *gurūṇām*—all your teachers; *kula-nandana*—O best of your family.

TRANSLATION

O best of your family, has this pollution of your intelligence been brought about by you or by the enemies? We are all your teachers and are very eager to hear about this. Please tell us the truth.

PURPORT

Prahlāda Mahārāja's teachers were astonished that a small boy could speak such exalted Vaiṣṇava philosophy. Therefore they inquired about the Vaiṣṇavas who stealthily taught it to him, in order that these Vaiṣṇavas might be arrested and killed in the presence of Prahlāda's father, Hiraṇyakaśipu.

TEXT 11

श्रीप्रह्राद उवाच
परः स्वश्चेत्यसद्ग्राहः पुंसां यन्मायया कृतः ।
विमोहितधियां दृष्टस्तस्मै भगवते नमः ॥११॥

śrī-prahrāda uvāca
paraḥ svaś cety asad-grāhaḥ
puṁsāṁ yan-māyayā kṛtaḥ
vimohita-dhiyāṁ dṛṣṭas
tasmai bhagavate namaḥ

śrī-prahrādaḥ uvāca—Prahlāda Mahārāja replied; *paraḥ*—an enemy; *svaḥ*—a kinsman or friend; *ca*—also; *iti*—thus; *asat-grāhaḥ*—material conception of life; *puṁsām*—of persons; *yat*—of whom; *māyayā*—by the external energy; *kṛtaḥ*—created; *vimohita*—bewildered; *dhiyām*—of those whose intelligence; *dṛṣṭaḥ*—practically experienced; *tasmai*—unto Him; *bhagavate*—the Supreme Personality of Godhead; *namaḥ*—my respectful obeisances.

TRANSLATION

Prahlāda Mahārāja replied: Let me offer my respectful obeisances unto the Supreme Personality of Godhead, whose external energy has created the distinctions of "my friend" and "my enemy" by deluding the intelligence of men. Indeed, I am now actually experiencing this, although I have previously heard of it from authoritative sources.

PURPORT

As stated in *Bhagavad-gītā* (5.18):

vidyā-vinaya-sampanne
brāhmaṇe gavi hastini
śuni caiva śvapāke ca
paṇḍitāḥ sama-darśinaḥ

"The humble sage, by virtue of true knowledge, sees with equal vision a learned and gentle *brāhmaṇa*, a cow, an elephant, a dog and a dog-eater [outcaste]." *Paṇḍitāḥ*, those who are actually learned—the equipoised, advanced devotees who have full knowledge of everything—do not see any living entity as an enemy or friend. Instead, with broader vision, they see that everyone is part of Kṛṣṇa, as confirmed by Śrī Caitanya Mahāprabhu (*jīvera 'svarūpa' haya——kṛṣṇera 'nitya-dāsa'*). Every living entity, being part of the Supreme Lord, is meant to serve the Lord, just as every part of the body is meant to serve the whole body.

As servants of the Supreme Lord, all living entities are one, but a Vaiṣṇava, because of his natural humility, addresses every other living entity as *prabhu*. A Vaiṣṇava sees other servants to be so advanced that he has much to learn from them. Thus he accepts all other devotees of the Lord as *prabhus*, masters. Although everyone is a servant of the Lord, one Vaiṣṇava servant, because of humility, sees another servant as his master. Understanding of the master begins from understanding of the spiritual master.

yasya prasādād bhagavat-prasādo
yasyāprasādān na gatiḥ kuto 'pi

"By the mercy of the spiritual master one receives the benediction of Kṛṣṇa. Without the grace of the spiritual master, one cannot make any advancement."

sākṣād-dharitvena samasta-śāstrair
uktas tathā bhāvyata eva sadbhiḥ
kintu prabhor yaḥ priya eva tasya
vande guroḥ śrī-caraṇāravindam

"The spiritual master is to be honored as much as the Supreme Lord because he is the most confidential servitor of the Lord. This is acknowledged in all revealed scriptures and followed by all authorities. Therefore I offer my respectful obeisances unto the lotus feet of such a spiritual master, who is a bona fide representative of Śrī Hari [Kṛṣṇa]." The spiritual master, the servant of God, is engaged in the most confidential service of the Lord, namely delivering all the conditioned souls from the clutches of *māyā*, in which one thinks, "This person is my enemy, and that one is my friend." Actually the Supreme Personality of Godhead is the friend of all living entities, and all living entities are eternal servants of the Supreme Lord. Oneness is possible through this understanding, not through artificially thinking that every one of us is God or equal to God. The true understanding is that God is the supreme master and that all of us are servants of the Supreme Lord and are therefore on the same platform. This had already been taught to Prahlāda Mahārāja by his spiritual master, Nārada, but Prahlāda was nonetheless surprised by how a bewildered soul thinks one person his enemy and another his friend.

As long as one adheres to the philosophy of duality, thinking one person a friend and another an enemy, he should be understood to be in the clutches of *māyā*. The Māyāvādī philosopher who thinks that all living entities are God and are therefore one is also mistaken. No one is equal to

God. The servant cannot be equal to the master. According to the Vaiṣṇava philosophy, the master is one, and the servants are also one, but the distinction between the master and servant must continue even in the liberated stage. In the conditioned stage we think that some living beings are our friends whereas others are enemies, and thus we are in duality. In the liberated stage, however, the conception is that God is the master and that all living entities, being servants of God, are one.

TEXT 12

स यदानुव्रतः पुंसां पशुबुद्धिर्विभिद्यते ।
अन्य एष तथान्योऽहमिति भेदगतासती ॥१२॥

sa yadānuvrataḥ puṁsāṁ
paśu-buddhir vibhidyate
anya eṣa tathānyo 'ham
iti bheda-gatāsatī

saḥ—that Supreme Personality of Godhead; *yadā*—when; *anuvrataḥ*—favorable or pleased; *puṁsām*—of the conditioned souls; *paśu-buddhiḥ*—the animalistic conception of life ("I am the Supreme, and everyone is God"); *vibhidyate*—is destroyed; *anyaḥ*—another; *eṣaḥ*—this; *tathā*—as well as; *anyaḥ*—another; *aham*—I; *iti*—thus; *bheda*—distinction; *gata*—having; *asatī*—which is disastrous.

TRANSLATION

When the Supreme Personality of Godhead is pleased with the living entity because of his devotional service, one becomes a paṇḍita and does not make distinctions between enemies, friends and himself. Intelligently, he then thinks, "Every one of us is an eternal servant of God, and therefore we are not different from one another."

PURPORT

When Prahlāda Mahārāja's teachers and demoniac father asked him how his intelligence had been polluted, Prahlāda Mahārāja said, "As far as I am concerned, my intelligence has not been polluted. Rather, by the grace of my spiritual master and by the grace of my Lord, Kṛṣṇa, I have now learned that no one is my enemy and no one is my friend. We are all actually eternal servants of Kṛṣṇa, but under the influence of the external energy we think that we are separately situated from the Supreme Personality of Godhead as friends and enemies of one another. This mistaken idea has now been corrected, and therefore, unlike ordinary human beings, I no longer think that I am God and that others are my friends and enemies. Now I am rightly thinking that everyone is an eternal servant of God and that our duty is to serve the supreme master, for then we shall stand on the platform of oneness as servants."

Demons think of everyone as a friend or enemy, but Vaiṣṇavas say that since everyone is a servant of the Lord, everyone is on the same platform. Therefore a Vaiṣṇava treats other living entities neither as friends nor as enemies, but instead tries to spread Kṛṣṇa consciousness, teaching everyone that we are all one as servants of the Supreme Lord but are uselessly wasting our valuable lives by creating nations, communities and other groups of friends and enemies. Everyone should come to the platform of Kṛṣṇa consciousness and thus feel oneness as a servant of the Lord. Although there are 8,400,000 species of life, a Vaiṣṇava feels this oneness. The *Īśopaniṣad* advises, *ekatvam anupaśyataḥ.* A devotee should see the Supreme Personality of Godhead to be situated in everyone's heart and should also see every living entity as an eternal servant of the Lord. This vision is called *ekatvam,* oneness. Although there is a relationship of master and servant, both master and servant are one because of their spiritual identity. This is also *ekatvam.* Thus the conception of *ekatvam* for the Vaiṣṇava is different from that of the Māyāvādī.

Hiraṇyakaśipu asked Prahlāda Mahārāja how he had become antagonistic to his family. When a family member is killed by an enemy, all the members of the family would naturally be inimical to the murderer, but Hiraṇyakaśipu saw that Prahlāda had become friendly with the murderer. Therefore he asked, "Who has created this kind of intelligence in you? Have you developed this consciousness by yourself? Since you are a small boy, someone must have induced you to think this way." Prahlāda Mahārāja wanted to reply that an attitude favorable toward Viṣṇu can develop only when the Lord is favorable (*sa yadānuvrataḥ*). As stated in *Bhagavad-gītā,* Kṛṣṇa is the friend of everyone (*suhṛdaṁ sarva-bhūtānāṁ jñātvā māṁ śāntim ṛcchati*). The Lord is never an enemy to any of the millions of living entities, but is always a friend to everyone. This is true understanding. If one thinks that the Lord is an enemy, his intelligence is *paśu-buddhi,* the intelligence of an animal. He falsely thinks, "I am different from my enemy, and my enemy is different from me. The enemy has done this, and therefore my duty is to kill him." This misconception is described in this verse as *bheda-gatāsatī.* The actual fact is that everyone is a servant of the Lord, as confirmed in *Caitanya-caritāmṛta* by Śrī Caitanya Mahāprabhu (*jīvera 'svarūpa' haya—kṛṣṇera 'nitya-dāsa'*). As servants of the Lord, we are one, and there can be no questions of enmity or friendship. If one actually understands that every one of us is a servant of the Lord, where is the question of enemy or friend?

Everyone should be friendly for the service of the Lord. Everyone should praise another's service to the Lord and not be proud of his own service. This is the way of Vaiṣṇava thinking, Vaikuṇṭha thinking. There may be rivalries and apparent competition between servants in performing service, but in the Vaikuṇṭha planets the service of another servant is appreciated, not condemned. This is Vaikuṇṭha competition. There is no question of enmity between servants. Everyone should be allowed to render service to the Lord to the best of his ability, and everyone should appreciate the service of others. Such are the activities of Vaikuṇṭha. Since everyone is a servant, everyone is on the same platform and is allowed to serve the Lord according to his ability. As confirmed in *Bhagavad-gītā* (15.15), *sarvasya cāhaṁ hṛdi sanniviṣṭo mattaḥ smṛtir jñānam apohanaṁ ca:* the Lord is situated in everyone's heart, giving dictation according to the attitude of the servant. However, the Lord gives different dictation to the nondevotees and devotees. The nondevotees challenge the authority of the Supreme Lord, and therefore the Lord dictates in such a way that the nondevotees forget the Lord's service, life after life, and are punished by the laws of nature. But when a devotee very sincerely wants to render service to the Lord, the Lord dictates in a different way. As the Lord says in *Bhagavad-gītā* (10.10):

teṣāṁ satata-yuktānāṁ
bhajatāṁ prīti-pūrvakam
dadāmi buddhi-yogaṁ taṁ
yena mām upayānti te

"To those who are constantly devoted and worship Me with love, I give the understanding by which they can come to Me." Everyone is actually a servant, not an enemy or friend, and everyone is working under different directions from the Lord, who directs each living entity according to his mentality.

TEXT 13

स एष आत्मा स्वपरेत्यबुद्धिभि-
दुरत्ययानुक्रमणो निरूप्यते ।
मुह्यन्ति यद्वर्त्मनि वेदवादिनो
ब्रह्मादयो ह्येष भिनत्ति मे मतिम् ॥१३॥

sa eṣa ātmā sva-parety abuddhibhir
duratyayānukramaṇo nirūpyate
muhyanti yad-vartmani veda-vādino
brahmādayo hy eṣa bhinatti me matim

saḥ—He; *eṣaḥ*—this; *ātmā*—Supersoul situated in everyone's heart; *sva-para*—this is my own business, and that is someone else's; *iti*—thus; *abuddhibhiḥ*—by those who have such bad intelligence; *duratyaya*—very difficult to follow; *anukramaṇaḥ*—whose devotional service; *nirūpyate*—is ascertained (by scriptures or the instructions of the spiritual master); *muhyanti*—are bewildered; *yat*—of whom; *vartmani*—on the path; *veda-vādinaḥ*—the followers of Vedic instructions; *brahma-ādayaḥ*—the demigods, beginning from Lord Brahmā; *hi*—indeed; *eṣaḥ*—this one; *bhinatti*—changes; *me*—my; *matim*—intelligence.

TRANSLATION

Persons who always think in terms of "enemy" and "friend" are unable to ascertain the Supersoul within themselves. Not to speak of them, even such exalted persons as Lord Brahmā, who are fully conversant with the Vedic literature, are sometimes bewildered in following the principles of devotional service. The same Supreme Personality of Godhead who has created this situation has certainly given me the intelligence to take the side of your so-called enemy.

PURPORT

Prahlāda Mahārāja admitted frankly, "My dear teachers, you wrongly think that Lord Viṣṇu is your enemy, but because He is favorable toward me, I understand that He is the friend of everyone. You may think that I have taken the side of your enemy, but factually He has bestowed a great favor upon me."

TEXT 14

यथा भ्राम्यत्ययो ब्रह्मन् स्वयमाकर्षसन्निधौ ।
तथा मे भिद्यते चेतश्चक्रपाणेर्यदृच्छया ॥१४॥

yathā bhrāmyaty ayo brahman
svayam ākarṣa-sannidhau
tathā me bhidyate cetaś
cakra-pāṇer yadṛcchayā

yathā—just as; *bhrāmyati*—moves; *ayaḥ*—iron; *brahman*—O *brāhmaṇas; svayam*—itself; *ākarṣa*—of a magnet; *sannidhau*—in the proximity; *tathā*—similarly; *me*—my; *bhidyate*—is changed; *cetaḥ*—consciousness; *cakra-pāṇeḥ*—of Lord Viṣṇu, who has a disc in His hand; *yadṛcchayā*—simply by the will.

TRANSLATION

O brāhmaṇas [teachers], as iron attracted by a magnetic stone moves automatically toward the magnet, my consciousness, having been changed by His will, is attracted by Lord Viṣṇu, who carries a disc in His hand. Thus I have no independence.

PURPORT

For iron to be attracted by a magnet is natural. Similarly, for all living entities to be attracted toward Kṛṣṇa is natural, and therefore the Lord's real name is Kṛṣṇa, meaning He who attracts everyone and everything. The typical examples of such attraction are found in Vṛndāvana, where everything and everyone is attracted by Kṛṣṇa. The elderly persons like Nanda Mahārāja and Yaśodādevī, the friends like Śrīdāmā, Sudāmā and the other cowherd boys, the *gopīs* like Śrīmatī Rādhārāṇī and Her associates, and even the birds, beasts, cows and calves are attracted. The flowers and fruits in the gardens are attracted, the waves of the Yamunā are attracted, and the land, sky, trees, plants, animals and all other living beings are attracted by Kṛṣṇa. This is the natural situation of everything in Vṛndāvana.

Just contrary to the affairs of Vṛndāvana is the material world, where no one is attracted by Kṛṣṇa and everyone is attracted by *māyā.* This is the difference between the spiritual and material worlds. Hiraṇyakaśipu, who was in the material world, was attracted by women and money, whereas Prahlāda Mahārāja, being in his natural position, was attracted by Kṛṣṇa. In replying to Hiraṇyakaśipu's question about why Prahlāda Mahārāja had a deviant view, Prahlāda said that his view was not deviant, for the natural position of everyone is to be attracted by Kṛṣṇa. Hiraṇyakaśipu found this view deviant, Prahlāda said, because of being unnaturally unattracted by Kṛṣṇa. Hiraṇyakaśipu therefore needed purification.

As soon as one is purified of material contamination, he is again attracted by Kṛṣṇa (*sarvopādhi-vinirmuktaṁ tat-paratvena nirmalam*). In the material world, everyone is contaminated by the dirt of sense gratification and is acting according to different designations, sometimes as a human being, sometimes a beast, sometimes a demigod or tree, and so on. One must be cleansed of all these designations. Then one will be naturally attracted to Kṛṣṇa. The *bhakti* process purifies the living entity of all unnatural attractions. When one is purified he is attracted by Kṛṣṇa and begins to serve Kṛṣṇa instead of serving *māyā.* This is his natural position. A devotee is attracted by Kṛṣṇa, whereas a nondevotee, being contaminated by the dirt of material enjoyment, is not. This is confirmed by the Lord in *Bhagavad-gītā* (7.28):

yeṣāṁ tv anta-gataṁ pāpaṁ
janānāṁ puṇya-karmaṇām
te dvandva-moha-nirmuktā
bhajante māṁ dṛḍha-vratāḥ

"Persons who have acted piously in previous lives and in this life, whose sinful actions are completely eradicated and who are freed from the duality of delusion, engage themselves in My service with determination." One must be freed from all the sinful dirt of material existence. Everyone in this material world is contaminated by material desire. Unless one is free from all material desire (*anyābhilāṣitā-śūnyam*), one cannot be attracted by Kṛṣṇa.

TEXT 15

श्रीनारद उवाच
एतावद्ब्राह्मणायोक्त्वा विरराम महामतिः ।
तं सन्निभर्त्स्य कुपितः सुदीनो राजसेवकः ॥१५॥

śrī-nārada uvāca
etāvad brāhmaṇāyoktvā
virarāma mahā-matiḥ
taṁ sannibhartsya kupitaḥ
sudīno rāja-sevakaḥ

śrī-nāradaḥ uvāca—Nārada Muni said; *etāvat*—this much; *brāhmaṇāya*—unto the *brāhmaṇas*, the sons of Śukrācārya; *uktvā*—speaking; *virarāma*—became silent; *mahā-matiḥ*—Prahlāda Mahārāja, who possessed great intelligence; *tam*—him (Prahlāda Mahārāja); *sannibhartsya*—chastising very harshly; *kupitaḥ*—being angry; *sudīnaḥ*—poor in thought, or very much aggrieved; *rāja-sevakaḥ*—the servants of King Hiraṇyakaśipu.

TRANSLATION

The great saint Nārada Muni continued: The great soul Prahlāda Mahārāja became silent after saying this to his teachers, Ṣaṇḍa and Amarka, the seminal sons of Śukrācārya. These so-called brāhmaṇas then became angry at him. Because they were servants of Hiraṇyakaśipu, they were very sorry, and to chastise Prahlāda Mahārāja they spoke as follows.

PURPORT

The word *śukra* means "semen." The sons of Śukrācārya were *brāhmaṇas* by birthright, but an actual *brāhmaṇa* is one who possesses the brahminical qualities. The *brāhmaṇas* Ṣaṇḍa and Amarka, being seminal sons of Śukrācārya, did not actually possess real brahminical qualifications, for they engaged as servants of Hiraṇyakaśipu. An actual *brāhmaṇa* is very much satisfied to see anyone, not to speak of his disciple, become a devotee of Lord Kṛṣṇa. Such *brāhmaṇas* are meant to satisfy the supreme master. A *brāhmaṇa* is strictly prohibited from becoming a servant of anyone else, for that is the business of dogs and *śūdras*. A dog must satisfy his master, but a *brāhmaṇa* does not have to satisfy anyone; he is simply meant to satisfy Kṛṣṇa (*ānukūlyena kṛṣṇānuśīlanam*). That is the real qualification of a *brāhmaṇa*. Because Ṣaṇḍa and Amarka were seminal *brāhmaṇas* and had become servants of such a master as Hiraṇyakaśipu, they unnecessarily wanted to chastise Prahlāda Mahārāja.

TEXT 16

आनीयतामरे वेत्रमस्माकमयशस्करः ।
कुलाङ्गारस्य दुर्बुद्धेश्चतुर्थोऽस्योदितो दमः ॥१६॥

ānīyatām are vetram
asmākam ayaśaskaraḥ
kulāṅgārasya durbuddheś
caturtho 'syodito damaḥ

ānīyatām—let it be brought; *are*—oh; *vetram*—the stick; *asmākam*—of us; *ayaśaskaraḥ*—who is bringing defamation; *kula-aṅgārasya*—of he who is like a cinder in the dynasty; *durbuddheḥ*—having bad intelligence; *caturthaḥ*—the fourth; *asya*—for him; *uditaḥ*—declared; *damaḥ*—punishment (the stick, *argumentum ad baculum*).

TRANSLATION

Oh, please bring me a stick! This Prahlāda is damaging our name and fame. Because of his bad intelligence, he has become like a cinder in the dynasty of the demons. Now he needs to be treated by the fourth of the four kinds of political diplomacy.

PURPORT

In political affairs, when a person disobediently agitates against the government, four principles are used to suppress him—legal orders, pacification, the offer of a post, or, finally, weapons. When there are no other arguments, he is punished. In logic, this is called *argumentum ad baculum.* When the two seminal *brāhmaṇas* Ṣaṇḍa and Amarka failed to extract from Prahlāda Mahārāja the cause for his having opinions different from those of his father, they called for a stick with which to chastise him to satisfy their master, Hiraṇyakaśipu. Because Prahlāda had become a devotee, they considered him to be contaminated by bad intelligence and to be the worst descendant in the family of demons. As it is said, where ignorance is bliss, it is folly to be wise. In a society or family in which everyone is a demon, for someone to become a Vaiṣṇava is certainly folly. Thus Prahlāda Mahārāja was charged with bad intelligence because he was among demons, including his teachers, who were supposedly *brāhmaṇas.*

The members of our Kṛṣṇa consciousness movement are in a position similar to that of Prahlāda Mahārāja. All over the world, ninety-nine percent of the people are godless demons, and therefore our preaching of Kṛṣṇa consciousness, following in the footsteps of Prahlāda Mahārāja, is always hampered by many impediments. Because of their fault of being devotees, the American boys who have sacrificed everything for preaching Kṛṣṇa consciousness are charged with being members of the CIA. Moreover, the seminal *brāhmaṇas* in India, who say that one can become a *brāhmaṇa* only if born in a *brāhmaṇa* family, charge us with ruining the Hindu system of religion. Of course, the fact is that one becomes a *brāhmaṇa* by qualification. Because we are training Europeans and Americans to become qualified and are awarding them brahminical status, we are being charged with destroying the Hindu religion. Nonetheless, confronting all kinds of difficulties, we must spread the Kṛṣṇa consciousness movement with great determination, like that of Prahlāda Mahārāja. In spite of being the son of the demon Hiraṇyakaśipu, Prahlāda never feared the chastisements of the seminal *brāhmaṇa* sons of a demoniac father.

TEXT 17

दैतेयचन्दनवने जातोऽयं कण्टकद्रुमः ।
यन्मूलोन्मूलपरशोर्विष्णोर्नालायितोऽर्भकः ॥१७॥

daiteya-candana-vane
jāto 'yaṁ kaṇṭaka-drumaḥ

yan-mūlonmūla-paraśor
viṣṇor nālāyito 'rbhakaḥ

daiteya—of the demoniac family; *candana-vane*—in the sandalwood forest; *jātaḥ*—born; *ayam*—this; *kaṇṭaka-drumaḥ*—thorn tree; *yat*—of which; *mūla*—of the roots; *unmūla*—in the cutting; *paraśoḥ*—who is like an axe; *viṣṇoḥ*—of Lord Viṣṇu; *nālāyitaḥ*—the handle; *arbhakaḥ*—boy.

TRANSLATION

This rascal Prahlāda has appeared like a thorn tree in a forest of sandalwood. To cut down sandalwood trees, an axe is needed, and the wood of the thorn tree is very suitable for the handle of such an axe. Lord Viṣṇu is the axe for cutting down the sandalwood forest of the family of demons, and this Prahlāda is the handle for that axe.

PURPORT

Thorn trees generally grow in deserted places, not in sandalwood forests, but the seminal *brāhmaṇas* Ṣaṇḍa and Amarka compared the dynasty of the Daitya Hiraṇyakaśipu to a sandalwood forest and compared Prahlāda Mahārāja to a hard, strong thorn tree that could provide the handle of an axe. They compared Lord Viṣṇu to the axe itself. An axe alone cannot cut a thorn tree; it needs a handle, which may be made of the wood of a thorn tree. Thus the thorn tree of demoniac civilization can be cut to pieces by the axe of *viṣṇu-bhakti*, devotional service to Lord Kṛṣṇa. Some of the members of the demoniac civilization, like Prahlāda Mahārāja, may become the handle for the axe, to assist Lord Viṣṇu, and thus the entire forest of demoniac civilization can be cut to pieces.

TEXT 18

इति तं विविधोपायैर्भीषयंस्तर्जनादिभिः ।
प्रह्रादं ग्राहयामास त्रिवर्गस्योपपादनम् ॥१८॥

iti taṁ vividhopāyair
bhīṣayaṁs tarjanādibhiḥ

prahrādaṁ grāhayām āsa
tri-vargasyopapādanam

iti—in this way; *tam*—him (Prahlāda Mahārāja); *vividha-upāyaiḥ*—by various means; *bhīṣayan*—threatening; *tarjana-ādibhiḥ*—by chastisement, threats, etc.; *prahrādam*—unto Prahlāda Mahārāja; *grāhayām āsa*—taught; *tri-vargasya*—the three goals of life (the paths of religion, economic development and sense gratification); *upapādanam*—scripture that presents.

TRANSLATION

Ṣaṇḍa and Amarka, the teachers of Prahlāda Mahārāja, chastised and threatened their disciple in various ways and began teaching him about the paths of religion, economic development and sense gratification. This is the way they educated him.

PURPORT

In this verse the words *prahrādaṁ grāhayām āsa* are important. The words *grāhayām āsa* literally mean that they tried to induce Prahlāda Mahārāja to accept the paths of *dharma, artha* and *kāma* (religion, economic development and sense gratification). People are generally preoccupied with these three concerns, without interest in the path of liberation. Hiraṇyakaśipu, the father of Prahlāda Mahārāja, was simply interested in gold and sense enjoyment. The word *hiraṇya* means "gold," and *kaśipu* refers to soft cushions and bedding on which people enjoy sense gratification. The word *prahlāda,* however, refers to one who is always joyful in understanding Brahman (*brahma-bhūtaḥ prasannātmā*). *Prahlāda* means *prasannātmā,* always joyful. Prahlāda was always joyful in worshiping the Lord, but in accordance with the instructions of Hiraṇyakaśipu, the teachers were interested in teaching him about material things. Materialistic persons think that the path of religion is meant for improving their material conditions. The materialist goes to a temple to worship many varieties of demigods just to receive some benediction to improve his material life. He goes to a *sādhu* or so-called *svāmī* to take advantage of an easy method for achieving material opulence. In the name of religion, the so-called *sādhus* try to satisfy the senses of the materialists by showing them shortcuts to material opulence. Sometimes they give some talisman or blessing. Sometimes they attract materialistic persons by producing gold. Then they declare themselves God, and foolish materialists are attracted to them for economic development. As a result of this process of cheating, others are reluctant to accept a religious process, and instead they advise people in general to work for material advancement. This is going on all over the world. Not only now but since time immemorial, no one is interested in *mokṣa*, liberation. There are four principles—*dharma* (religion), *artha* (economic development), *kāma* (sense gratification) and *mokṣa* (liberation). People accept religion to become materially opulent. And why should one be materially opulent? For sense gratification. Thus people prefer these three *mārgas*, the three paths of materialistic life. No one is interested in liberation, and *bhagavad-bhakti*, devotional service to the Lord, is above even liberation. Therefore the process of devotional service, Kṛṣṇa consciousness, is extremely difficult to understand. This will be explained later by Prahlāda Mahārāja. The teachers Ṣaṇḍa and Amarka tried to induce Prahlāda Mahārāja to accept the materialistic way of life, but actually their attempt was a failure.

TEXT 19

तत एनं गुरुर्ज्ञात्वा ज्ञातज्ञेयचतुष्टयम् ।
दैत्येन्द्रं दर्शयामास मातृमृष्टमलङ्कृतम् ॥१९॥

tata enaṁ gurur jñātvā
jñāta-jñeya-catuṣṭayam
daityendraṁ darśayām āsa
mātṛ-mṛṣṭam alaṅkṛtam

tataḥ—thereafter; *enam*—him (Prahlāda Mahārāja); *guruḥ*—his teachers; *jñātvā*—knowing; *jñāta*—known; *jñeya*—which are to be known; *catuṣṭayam*—the four diplomatic principles (*sāma*, the process of pacifying; *dāna*, the process of giving money in charity; *bheda*, the principle of dividing; and *daṇḍa*, the principle of punishment); *daitya-indram*—unto Hiraṇyakaśipu, the King of the Daityas; *darśayām āsa*—

presented; *mātṛ-mṛṣṭam*—being bathed by his mother; *alaṅkṛtam*—decorated with ornaments.

TRANSLATION

After some time, the teachers Ṣaṇḍa and Amarka thought that Prahlāda Mahārāja was sufficiently educated in the diplomatic affairs of pacifying public leaders, appeasing them by giving them lucrative posts, dividing and ruling over them, and punishing them in cases of disobedience. Then, one day, after Prahlāda's mother had personally washed the boy and dressed him nicely with sufficient ornaments, they presented him before his father.

PURPORT

It is essential for a student who is going to be a ruler or king to learn the four diplomatic principles. There is always rivalry between a king and his citizens. Therefore, when a citizen agitates the public against the king, the duty of the king is to call him and try to pacify him with sweet words, saying, "You are very important in the state. Why should you disturb the public with some new cause for agitation?" If the citizen is not pacified, the king should then offer him some lucrative post as a governor or minister—any post that draws a high salary—so that he may be agreeable. If the enemy still goes on agitating the public, the king should try to create dissension in the enemy's camp, but if he still continues, the king should employ *argumentum ad baculum*—severe punishment—by putting him in jail or placing him before a firing squad. The teachers appointed by Hiraṇyakaśipu taught Prahlāda Mahārāja how to be a diplomat so that he could rule over the citizens very nicely.

TEXT 20

पादयोः पतितं बालं प्रतिनन्द्याशिषासुरः ।
परिष्वज्य चिरं दोर्भ्यां परमामाप निर्वृतिम् ॥२०॥

pādayoḥ patitaṁ bālaṁ
pratinandyāśiṣāsuraḥ

pariṣvajya ciraṁ dorbhyāṁ
paramām āpa nirvṛtim

pādayoḥ—at the feet; *patitam*—fallen; *bālam*—the boy (Prahlāda Mahārāja); *pratinandya*—encouraging; *āśiṣā*—with blessings ("My dear child, may you live long and be happy" and so on); *asuraḥ*—the demon Hiraṇyakaśipu; *pariṣvajya*—embracing; *ciram*—for a long time due to affection; *dorbhyām*—with his two arms; *paramām*—great; *āpa*—obtained; *nirvṛtim*—jubilation.

TRANSLATION

When Hiraṇyakaśipu saw that his child had fallen at his feet and was offering obeisances, as an affectionate father he immediately began showering blessings upon the child and embraced him with both arms. A father naturally feels happy to embrace his son, and Hiraṇyakaśipu became very happy in this way.

TEXT 21

आरोप्याङ्कमवघ्राय मूर्धन्यश्रुकलाम्बुभिः ।
आसिञ्चन् विकसद्वक्त्रमिदमाह युधिष्ठिर ॥२१॥

āropyāṅkam avaghrāya
mūrdhany aśru-kalāmbubhiḥ
āsiñcan vikasad-vaktram
idam āha yudhiṣṭhira

āropya—placing; *aṅkam*—on the lap; *avaghrāya mūrdhani*—smelling his head; *aśru*—of tears; *kalā-ambubhiḥ*—with water from drops; *āsiñcan*—moistening; *vikasat-vaktram*—his smiling face; *idam*—this; *āha*—said; *yudhiṣṭhira*—O Mahārāja Yudhiṣṭhira.

TRANSLATION

Nārada Muni continued: My dear King Yudhiṣṭhira, Hiraṇyakaśipu seated Prahlāda Mahārāja on his lap and began smelling his head. With affectionate tears gliding down from his

eyes and moistening the child's smiling face, he spoke to his son as follows.

PURPORT

If a child or disciple falls at the feet of the father or spiritual master, the superior responds by smelling the head of the subordinate.

TEXT 22

हिरण्यकशिपुरुवाच
प्रह्रादानूच्यतां तात स्वधीतं किञ्चिदुत्तमम् ।
कालेनैतावतायुष्मन् यदशिक्षद् गुरोर्भवान् ॥२२॥

hiraṇyakaśipur uvāca
prahrādānūcyatāṁ tāta
svadhītaṁ kiñcid uttamam
kālenaitāvatāyuṣman
yad aśikṣad guror bhavān

hiraṇyakaśipuḥ uvāca—King Hiraṇyakaśipu said; *prahrāda*—my dear Prahlāda; *anūcyatām*—let it be told; *tāta*—my dear son; *svadhītam*—well learned; *kiñcit*—something; *uttamam*—very nice; *kālena etāvatā*—for so much time; *āyuṣman*—O long-lived one; *yat*—which; *aśikṣat*—has learned; *guroḥ*—from your teachers; *bhavān*—yourself.

TRANSLATION

Hiraṇyakaśipu said: My dear Prahlāda, my dear son, O long-lived one, for so much time you have heard many things from your teachers. Now please repeat to me whatever you think is the best of that knowledge.

PURPORT

In this verse, Hiraṇyakaśipu inquires from his son what he has learned from his *guru*. Prahlāda Mahārāja's *gurus* were of two kinds—

Ṣaṇḍa and Amarka, the sons of Śukrācārya in the seminal disciplic succession, were the *gurus* appointed by his father, but his other *guru* was the exalted Nārada Muni, who had instructed Prahlāda when Prahlāda was within the womb of his mother. Prahlāda Mahārāja responded to the inquiry of his father with the instructions he had received from his spiritual master, Nārada. Thus there was again a difference of opinion because Prahlāda Mahārāja wanted to relate the best thing he had learned from his spiritual master, whereas Hiraṇyakaśipu expected to hear about the politics and diplomacy Prahlāda had learned from Ṣaṇḍa and Amarka. Now the dissension between the father and son became increasingly intense as Prahlāda Mahārāja began to say what he had learned from his *guru* Nārada Muni.

TEXTS 23–24

श्रीप्रह्राद उवाच
श्रवणं कीर्तनं विष्णोः स्मरणं पादसेवनम् ।
अर्चनं वन्दनं दास्यं सख्यमात्मनिवेदनम् ॥२३॥
इति पुंसार्पिता विष्णौ भक्तिश्चेन्नवलक्षणा ।
क्रियेत भगवत्यद्धा तन्मन्येऽधीतमुत्तमम् ॥२४॥

śrī-prahrāda uvāca
śravaṇaṁ kīrtanaṁ viṣṇoḥ
smaraṇaṁ pāda-sevanam
arcanaṁ vandanaṁ dāsyaṁ
sakhyam ātma-nivedanam

iti puṁsārpitā viṣṇau
bhaktiś cen nava-lakṣaṇā
kriyeta bhagavaty addhā
tan manye 'dhītam uttamam

śrī-prahrādaḥ uvāca—Prahlāda Mahārāja said; *śravaṇam*—hearing; *kīrtanam*—chanting; *viṣṇoḥ*—of Lord Viṣṇu (not anyone else); *smaraṇam*—remembering; *pāda-sevanam*—serving the feet; *arcanam*—offering worship (with *ṣoḍaśopacāra*, the sixteen kinds of paraphernalia); *vandanam*—offering prayers; *dāsyam*—becoming the servant; *sakhyam*—becoming the best friend; *ātma-nivedanam*—surrendering everything, whatever one has; *iti*—thus; *puṁsā arpitā*—offered by the devotee; *viṣṇau*—unto Lord Viṣṇu (not to anyone else); *bhaktiḥ*—devotional service; *cet*—if; *nava-lakṣaṇā*—possessing nine different processes; *kriyeta*—one should perform; *bhagavati*—unto the Supreme Personality of Godhead; *addhā*—directly or completely; *tat*—that; *manye*—I consider; *adhītam*—learning; *uttamam*—topmost.

TRANSLATION

Prahlāda Mahārāja said: Hearing and chanting about the transcendental holy name, form, qualities, paraphernalia and pastimes of Lord Viṣṇu, remembering them, serving the lotus feet of the Lord, offering the Lord respectful worship with sixteen types of paraphernalia, offering prayers to the Lord, becoming His servant, considering the Lord one's best friend, and surrendering everything unto Him (in other words, serving Him with the body, mind and words)—these nine processes are accepted as pure devotional service. One who has dedicated his life to the service of Kṛṣṇa through these nine methods should be understood to be the most learned person, for he has acquired complete knowledge.

PURPORT

When Prahlāda Mahārāja was asked by his father to say something from whatever he had learned, he considered that what he had learned from his spiritual master was the best of all teachings whereas what he had learned about diplomacy from his material teachers, Ṣaṇḍa and Amarka, was useless. *Bhaktiḥ pareśānubhavo viraktir anyatra ca* (*Bhāg.* 11.2.42). This is the symptom of pure devotional service. A pure devotee is interested only in devotional service, not in material affairs. To execute devotional service, one should always engage in hearing and chanting about Kṛṣṇa, or Lord Viṣṇu. The process of temple worship is called *arcana.* How to perform *arcana* will be explained herein. One should have complete faith in the words of Kṛṣṇa, who says that He is the great well-wishing friend of everyone (*suhṛdaṁ sarva-bhūtānām*). A devotee considers Kṛṣṇa the only friend. This is called *sakhyam.*

Puṁsārpitā viṣṇau. The word *puṁsā* means "by all living entities." There are no distinctions permitting only a man or only a *brāhmaṇa* to offer devotional service to the Lord. Everyone can do so. As confirmed in *Bhagavad-gītā* (9.32), *striyo vaiśyās tathā śūdrās te 'pi yānti parāṁ gatim:* although women, *vaiśyas* and *śūdras* are considered less intelligent, they also can become devotees and return home, back to Godhead.

After performing sacrifices, sometimes a person engaged in fruitive activity customarily offers the results to Viṣṇu. But here it is said, *bhagavaty addhā:* one must directly offer everything to Viṣṇu. This is called *sannyāsa* (not merely *nyāsa*). A *tridaṇḍi-sannyāsī* carries three *daṇḍas,* signifying *kaya-mano-vākya*—body, mind and words. All of these should be offered to Viṣṇu, and then one can begin devotional service. Fruitive workers first perform some pious activities and then formally or officially offer the results to Viṣṇu. The real devotee, however, first offers his surrender to Kṛṣṇa with his body, mind and words and then uses his body, mind and words for the service of Kṛṣṇa as Kṛṣṇa desires.

Śrīla Bhaktisiddhānta Sarasvatī Ṭhākura gives the following explanation in his *Tathya.* The word *śravaṇa* refers to giving aural reception to the holy name and descriptions of the Lord's form, qualities, entourage and pastimes as explained in *Śrīmad-Bhāgavatam, Bhagavad-gītā* and similar authorized scriptures. After aurally receiving such messages, one should memorize these vibrations and repeat them (*kīrtanam*). *Smaraṇam* means trying to understand more and more about the Supreme Lord, and *pāda-sevanam* means engaging oneself in serving the lotus feet of the Lord according to the time and circumstances. *Arcanam* means worshiping Lord Viṣṇu as one does in the temple, and *vandanam* means offering respectful obeisances. *Man-manā bhava mad-bhakto mad-yājī māṁ namaskuru. Vandanam* means *namaskuru*—offering obeisances or offering prayers. Thinking oneself to be *nitya-kṛṣṇa-dāsa,* everlastingly a servant of Kṛṣṇa, is called *dāsyam,* and *sakhyam* means being a well-wisher of Kṛṣṇa. Kṛṣṇa wants everyone to surrender unto Him because everyone is constitutionally His servant. Therefore, as a sincere friend of Kṛṣṇa, one should preach this philosophy, requesting everyone to surrender unto Kṛṣṇa. *Ātma-nivedanam* means offering Kṛṣṇa everything, including one's body, mind, intelligence and whatever one may possess.

One's sincere endeavor to perform these nine processes of devotional service is technically called *bhakti.* The word *addhā* means "directly." One should not be like the *karmīs,* who perform pious activities and then formally offer the results to Kṛṣṇa. That is *karma-kāṇḍa.* One should not aspire for the results of his pious activities, but should dedicate oneself fully and then act piously. In other words, one should act for the satisfaction of Lord Viṣṇu, not for the satisfaction of his own senses. That is the meaning of the word *addhā,* "directly."

anyābhilāṣitā-śūnyaṁ
jñāna-karmādy-anāvṛtam
ānukūlyena kṛṣṇānu-
śīlanaṁ bhaktir uttamā

"One should render transcendental loving service to the Supreme Lord Kṛṣṇa favorably and without desire for material profit or gain through fruitive activities or philosophical speculation. That is called pure devotional service." One should simply satisfy Kṛṣṇa, without being influenced by fruitive knowledge or fruitive activity.

The *Gopāla-tāpanī Upaniṣad* says that the word *bhakti* means engagement in the devotional service of the Supreme Personality of Godhead, not of anyone else. This *Upaniṣad* describes that *bhakti* is the offering of devotional service unto the Supreme Personality of Godhead. To perform devotional service, one should be relieved of the bodily conception of life and aspirations to be happy through elevation to the higher planetary systems. In other words, work performed simply for the satisfaction of the Supreme Lord, without any desire for material benefits, is called *bhakti. Bhakti* is also called *niṣkarma,* or freedom from the results of fruitive activity. *Bhakti* and *niṣkarma* are on the same platform, although devotional service and fruitive activity appear almost the same.

The nine different processes enunciated by Prahlāda Mahārāja, who learned them from Nārada Muni, may not all be required for the execution of devotional service; if a devotee performs only one of these nine without deviation, he can attain the mercy of the Supreme Personality of Godhead. Sometimes it is found that when one performs one of the processes, other processes are mixed with it. That is not improper for a devotee. When a devotee executes any one of the nine processes (*nava-*

lakṣaṇā), this is sufficient; the other eight processes are included. Now let us discuss these nine different processes.

(1) *Śravaṇam.* Hearing of the holy name of the Lord (*śravaṇam*) is the beginning of devotional service. Although any one of the nine processes is sufficient, in chronological order the hearing of the holy name of the Lord is the beginning. Indeed, it is essential. As enunciated by Lord Śrī Caitanya Mahāprabhu, *ceto-darpaṇa-mārjanam:* by chanting the holy name of the Lord, one is cleansed of the material conception of life, which is due to the dirty modes of material nature. When the dirt is cleansed from the core of one's heart, one can realize the form of the Supreme Personality of Godhead—*īśvaraḥ paramaḥ kṛṣṇaḥ sac-cid-ānanda-vigrahaḥ.* Thus by hearing the holy name of the Lord, one comes to the platform of understanding the personal form of the Lord. After realizing the Lord's form, one can realize the transcendental qualities of the Lord, and when one can understand His transcendental qualities one can understand the Lord's associates. In this way a devotee advances further and further toward complete understanding of the Lord as he awakens in realization of the Lord's holy name, transcendental form and qualities, His paraphernalia, and everything pertaining to Him. Therefore the chronological process is *śravaṇaṁ kīrtanaṁ viṣṇoḥ.* This same process of chronological understanding holds true in chanting and remembering. When the chanting of the holy name, form, qualities and paraphernalia is heard from the mouth of a pure devotee, his hearing and chanting are very pleasing. Śrīla Sanātana Gosvāmī has forbidden us to hear the chanting of an artificial devotee or nondevotee.

Hearing from the text of *Śrīmad-Bhāgavatam* is considered the most important process of hearing. *Śrīmad-Bhāgavatam* is full of transcendental chanting of the holy name, and therefore the chanting and hearing of *Śrīmad-Bhāgavatam* are transcendentally full of mellows. The transcendental holy name of the Lord may be heard and chanted accordingly to the attraction of the devotee. One may chant the holy name of Lord Kṛṣṇa, or one may chant the holy name of Lord Rāma or Nṛsiṁhadeva (*rāmādi-mūrtiṣu kalā-niyamena tiṣṭhan*). The Lord has innumerable forms and names, and devotees may meditate upon a particular form and chant the holy name according to his attraction. The best course is to hear of the holy name, form and so on from a pure devotee of the same standard as oneself. In other words, one who is attached to Kṛṣṇa should chant and hear from other pure devotees who are also attached to Lord Kṛṣṇa. The same principle applies for devotees attracted by Lord Rāma, Lord Nṛsiṁha and other forms of the Lord. Because Kṛṣṇa is the ultimate form of the Lord (*kṛṣṇas tu bhagavān svayam*), it is best to hear about Lord Kṛṣṇa's name, form and pastimes from a realized devotee who is particularly attracted by the form of Lord Kṛṣṇa. In *Śrīmad-Bhāgavatam*, great devotees like Śukadeva Gosvāmī have specifically described Lord Kṛṣṇa's holy name, form and qualities. Unless one hears about the holy name, form and qualities of the Lord, one cannot clearly understand the other processes of devotional service. Therefore Śrī Caitanya Mahāprabhu recommends that one chant the holy name of Kṛṣṇa. *Paraṁ vijayate śrī-kṛṣṇa-saṅkīrtanam.* If one is fortunate enough to hear from the mouth of realized devotees, he is very easily successful on the path of devotional service. Therefore hearing of the holy name, form and qualities of the Lord is essential.

In *Śrīmad-Bhāgavatam* (1.5.11) there is this verse:

tad-vāg-visargo janatāgha-viplavo
yasmin prati-ślokam abaddhavaty api
nāmāny anantasya yaśo-'ṅkitāni yat
śṛṇvanti gāyanti gṛṇanti sādhavaḥ

"Verses describing the name, form and qualities of Anantadeva, the unlimited Supreme Lord, are able to vanquish all the sinful reactions of the entire world. Therefore even if such verses are improperly composed, devotees hear them, describe them and accept them as bona fide and authorized." In this connection, Śrīdhara Svāmī has remarked that a pure devotee takes advantage of another pure devotee by trying to hear from him about the holy name, form and qualities of the Lord. If there is no such opportunity, he alone chants and hears the Lord's holy name.

(2) *Kīrtanam.* The hearing of the holy name has been described above. Now let us try to understand the chanting of the holy name, which is the second item in the consecutive order. It is recommended that such chanting be performed very loudly. In *Śrīmad-Bhāgavatam*, Nārada Muni says that without shame he began traveling all over the world, chanting the holy name of the Lord. Similarly, Śrī Caitanya Mahāprabhu has advised:

tṛṇād api sunīcena
taror api sahiṣṇunā
amāninā mānadena
kīrtanīyaḥ sadā hariḥ

A devotee can very peacefully chant the holy name of the Lord by behaving more humbly than the grass, being tolerant like a tree and offering respects to everyone, without expecting honor from anyone else. Such qualifications make it easier to chant the holy name of the Lord. The process of transcendental chanting can be easily performed by anyone. Even if one is physically unfit, classified lower than others, devoid of material qualifications or not at all elevated in terms of pious activities, the chanting of the holy name is beneficial. An aristocratic birth, an advanced education, beautiful bodily features, wealth and similar results of pious activities are all unnecessary for advancement in spiritual life, for one can very easily advance simply by chanting the holy name. It is understood from the authoritative source of Vedic literature that especially in this age, Kali-yuga, people are generally short-living, extremely bad in their habits, and inclined to accept methods of devotional service that are not bona fide. Moreover, they are always disturbed by material conditions, and they are mostly unfortunate. Under the circumstances, the performance of other processes, such as *yajña, dāna, tapaḥ* and *kriyā*—sacrifices, charity and so on—are not at all possible. Therefore it is recommended:

harer nāma harer nāma
harer nāmaiva kevalam
kalau nāsty eva nāsty eva
nāsty eva gatir anyathā

"In this age of quarrel and hypocrisy the only means of deliverance is chanting of the holy name of the Lord. There is no other way. There is no other way. There is no other way." Simply by chanting the holy name of the Lord, one advances perfectly in spiritual life. This is the best process for success in life. In other ages, the chanting of the holy name is equally powerful, but especially in this age, Kali-yuga, it is most powerful. *Kīrtanād eva kṛṣṇasya mukta-saṅgaḥ paraṁ vrajet:* simply by chanting the holy name of Kṛṣṇa, one is liberated and returns home, back to Godhead. Therefore, even if one is able to perform other processes of devotional service, one must adopt the chanting of the holy name as the principal method of advancing in spiritual life. *Yajñaiḥ saṅkīrtana-prāyair yajanti hi sumedhasaḥ:* those who are very sharp in their intelligence should adopt this process of chanting the holy names of the Lord. One should not, however, manufacture different types of chanting. One should adhere seriously to the chanting of the holy name as recommended in the scriptures: Hare Kṛṣṇa, Hare Kṛṣṇa, Kṛṣṇa Kṛṣṇa, Hare Hare/ Hare Rāma, Hare Rāma, Rāma Rāma, Hare Hare.

While chanting the holy name of the Lord, one should be careful to avoid ten offenses. From Sanat-kumāra it is understood that even if a person is a severe offender in many ways, he is freed from offensive life if he takes shelter of the Lord's holy name. Indeed, even if a human being is no better than a two-legged animal, he will be liberated if he takes shelter of the holy name of the Lord. One should therefore be very careful not to commit offenses at the lotus feet of the Lord's holy name. The offenses are described as follows: (*a*) to blaspheme a devotee, especially a devotee engaged in broadcasting the glories of the holy name, (*b*) to consider the name of Lord Śiva or any other demigod to be equally as powerful as the holy name of the Supreme Personality of Godhead (no one is equal to the Supreme Personality of Godhead, nor is anyone superior to Him), (*c*) to disobey the instructions of the spiritual master, (*d*) to blaspheme the Vedic literatures and literatures compiled in pursuance of the Vedic literatures, (*e*) to comment that the glories of the holy name of the Lord are exaggerated, (*f*) to interpret the holy name in a deviant way, (*g*) to commit sinful activities on the strength of chanting the holy name, (*h*) to compare the chanting of the holy name to pious activities, (*i*) to instruct the glories of the holy name to a person who has no understanding of the chanting of the holy name, (*j*) not to awaken in transcendental attachment for the chanting of the holy name, even after hearing all these scriptural injunctions.

There is no way to atone for any of these offenses. It is therefore recommended that an offender at the feet of the holy name continue to chant the holy name twenty-four hours a day. Constant chanting of the holy name will make one free of offenses, and then he will gradually be elevated to the transcendental platform on which he can chant the pure holy name and thus become a lover of the Supreme Personality of Godhead.

It is recommended that even if one commits offenses, one should continue chanting the holy name. In other words, the chanting of the holy name makes one offenseless. In the book *Nāma-kaumudī* it is recommended that if one is an offender at the lotus feet of a Vaiṣṇava, he should submit to that Vaiṣṇava and be excused; similarly, if one is an offender in chanting the holy name, he should submit to the holy name and thus be freed from his offenses. In this connection there is the following statement, spoken by Dakṣa to Lord Śiva: "I did not know the glories of your personality, and therefore I committed an offense at your lotus feet in the open assembly. You are so kind, however, that you did not accept my offense. Instead, when I was falling down because of accusing you, you saved me by your merciful glance. You are most great. Kindly excuse me and be satisfied with your own exalted qualities."

One should be very humble and meek to offer one's desires and chant prayers composed in glorification of the holy name, such as *ayi mukta-kulair upāsya mānam* and *nivṛtta-tarṣair upagīyamānād.* One should chant such prayers to become free from offenses at the lotus feet of the holy name.

(3) *Smaraṇam.* After one regularly performs the processes of hearing and chanting and after the core of one's heart is cleansed, *smaraṇam,* remembering, is recommended. In *Śrīmad-Bhāgavatam* (2.1.11) Śukadeva Gosvāmī tells King Parīkṣit:

etan nirvidyamānānām
icchatām akuto-bhayam
yogināṁ nṛpa nirṇītaṁ
harer nāmānukīrtanam

"O King, for great *yogīs* who have completely renounced all material connections, for those who desire all material enjoyment and for those who are self-satisfied by dint of transcendental knowledge, constant chanting of the holy name of the Lord is recommended." According to different relationships with the Supreme Personality of Godhead, there are varieties of *nāmānukīrtanam,* chanting of the holy name, and thus according to different relationships and mellows there are five kinds of remembering. These are as follows: (*a*) conducting research into the worship of a particular form of the Lord, (*b*) concentrating the mind on one subject and withdrawing the mind's activities of thinking, feeling and willing from all other subjects, (*c*) concentrating upon a particular form of the Lord (this is called meditation), (*d*) concentrating one's mind continuously on the form of the Lord (this is called *dhruvānusmṛti*, or perfect meditation), and (*e*) awakening a likening for concentration upon a particular form (this is called *samādhi*, or trance). Mental concentration upon particular pastimes of the Lord in particular circumstances is also called remembrance. Therefore *samādhi*, trance, can be possible in five different ways in terms of one's relationship. Specifically, the trance of devotees on the stage of neutrality is called mental concentration.

(4) *Pāda-sevanam*. According to one's taste and strength, hearing, chanting and remembrance may be followed by *pāda-sevanam*. One obtains the perfection of remembering when one constantly thinks of the lotus feet of the Lord. Being intensely attached to thinking of the Lord's lotus feet is called *pāda-sevanam*. When one is particularly adherent to the process of *pāda-sevanam*, this process gradually includes other processes, such as seeing the form of the Lord, touching the form of the Lord, circumambulating the form or temple of the Lord, visiting such places as Jagannātha Purī, Dvārakā and Mathurā to see the Lord's form, and bathing in the Ganges or Yamunā. Bathing in the Ganges and serving a pure Vaiṣṇava are also known as *tadīya-upāsanam*. This is also *pāda-sevanam*. The word *tadīya* means "in relationship with the Lord." Service to the Vaiṣṇava, Tulasī, Ganges and Yamunā are included in *pāda-sevanam*. All these processes of *pāda-sevanam* help one advance in spiritual life very quickly.

(5) *Arcanam*. After *pāda-sevanam* comes the process of *arcanam*, worship of the Deity. If one is interested in the process of *arcanam*, one must positively take shelter of a bona fide spiritual master and learn the process from him. There are many books for *arcana*, especially *Nārada-pañcarātra*. In this age, the *Pañcarātra* system is particularly recommended for *arcana*, Deity worship. There are two systems of *arcana*—the *bhāgavata* system and *pāñcarātrikī* system. In the *Śrīmad-Bhāgavatam* there is no recommendation of *pāñcarātrikī* worship because in this Kali-yuga, even without Deity worship, everything can be

perfectly performed simply through hearing, chanting, remembering and worship of the lotus feet of the Lord. Rūpa Gosvāmī states:

śrī-viṣṇoḥ śravaṇe parīkṣid abhavad vaiyāsakiḥ kīrtane
prahlādaḥ smaraṇe tad-aṅghri-bhajane lakṣmīḥ pṛthuḥ pūjane
akrūras tv abhivandane kapi-patir dāsye 'tha sakhye 'rjunaḥ
sarvasvātma-nivedane balir abhūt kṛṣṇāptir eṣāṁ param

"Parīkṣit Mahārāja attained salvation simply by hearing, and Śukadeva Gosvāmī attained salvation simply by chanting. Prahlāda Mahārāja attained salvation by remembering the Lord. The goddess of fortune, Lakṣmīdevī, attained perfection by worshiping the Lord's lotus feet. Pṛthu Mahārāja attained salvation by worshiping the Deity of the Lord. Akrūra attained salvation by offering prayers, Hanumān by rendering service, Arjuna by establishing friendship with the Lord, and Bali Mahārāja by offering everything to the service of the Lord." All these great devotees served the Lord according to a particular process, but every one of them attained salvation and became eligible to return home, back to Godhead. This is explained in *Śrīmad-Bhāgavatam.*

It is therefore recommended that initiated devotees follow the principles of *Nārada-pañcarātra* by worshiping the Deity in the temple. Especially for householder devotees who are opulent in material possessions, the path of Deity worship is strongly recommended. An opulent householder devotee who does not engage his hard-earned money in the service of the Lord is called a miser. One should not engage paid *brāhmaṇas* to worship the Deity. If one does not personally worship the Deity but engages paid servants instead, he is considered lazy, and his worship of the Deity is called artificial. An opulent householder can collect luxurious paraphernalia for Deity worship, and consequently for householder devotees the worship of the Deity is compulsory. In our Kṛṣṇa consciousness movement there are *brahmacārīs, gṛhasthas, vānaprasthas* and *sannyāsīs*, but the Deity worship in the temple should be performed especially by the householders. The *brahmacārīs* can go with the *sannyāsīs* to preach, and the *vānaprasthas* should prepare themselves for the next status of renounced life, *sannyāsa. Gṛhastha* devotees, however, are generally engaged in material activities, and therefore if they do not take to Deity worship, their falling down is positively assured. Deity worship means following the rules and regulations precisely. That will keep one steady in devotional service. Generally householders have children, and then the wives of the householders should be engaged in caring for the children, just as women acting as teachers care for the children in a nursery school.

Gṛhastha devotees must adopt the *arcana-vidhi,* or Deity worship according to the suitable arrangements and directions given by the spiritual master. Regarding those unable to take to the Deity worship in the temple, there is the following statement in the *Agni Purāṇa.* Any householder devotee circumstantially unable to worship the Deity must at least see the Deity worship, and in this way he may achieve success also. The special purpose of Deity worship is to keep oneself always pure and clean. *Gṛhastha* devotees should be actual examples of cleanliness.

Deity worship should be continued along with hearing and chanting. Therefore every *mantra* is preceded by the word *namaḥ.* In all the *mantras* there are specific potencies, of which the *gṛhastha* devotees must take advantage. There are many *mantras* preceded by the word *namaḥ,* but if one chants the holy name of the Lord, he receives the result of chanting *namaḥ* many times. By chanting the holy name of the Lord, one can reach the platform of love of Godhead. One might ask, then what is the necessity of being initiated? The answer is that even though the chanting of the holy name is sufficient to enable one to progress in spiritual life to the standard of love of Godhead, one is nonetheless susceptible to contamination because of possessing a material body. Consequently, special stress is given to the *arcana-vidhi.* One should therefore regularly take advantage of both the *bhāgavata* process and *pāñcarātrikī* process.

Deity worship has two divisions, namely pure and mixed with fruitive activities. For one who is steady, Deity worship is compulsory. Observing the various types of festivals, such as *Śrī Janmāṣṭamī, Rāma-navamī* and *Nṛsiṁha-caturdaśī,* is also included in the process of Deity worship. In other words, it is compulsory for householder devotees to observe these festivals.

Now let us discuss the offenses in Deity worship. The following are offenses: (*a*) to enter the temple with shoes or being carried on a palanquin, (*b*) not to observe the prescribed festivals, (*c*) to avoid offering obeisances in front of the Deity, (*d*) to offer prayers in an unclean state, not having washed one's hands after eating, (*e*) to offer obeisances with one hand, (*f*) to circumambulate directly in front of the Deity, (*g*) to spread one's legs before the Deity, (*h*) to sit before the Deity while holding one's ankles with one's hands, (*i*) to lie down before the Deity, (*j*) to eat before the Deity, (*k*) to speak lies before the Deity, (*l*) to address someone loudly before the Deity, (*m*) to talk nonsense before the Deity, (*n*) to cry before the Deity, (*o*) to argue before the Deity, (*p*) to chastise someone before the Deity, (*q*) to show someone favor before the Deity, (*r*) to use harsh words before the Deity, (*s*) to wear a woolen blanket before the Deity, (*t*) to blaspheme someone before the Deity, (*u*) to worship someone else before the Deity, (*v*) to use vulgar language before the Deity, (*w*) to pass air before the Deity, (*x*) to avoid very opulent worship of the Deity, even though one is able to perform it, (*y*) to eat something not offered to the Deity, (*z*) to avoid offering fresh fruits to the Deity according to the season, (*aa*) to offer food to the Deity which has already been used or from which has first been given to others (in other words, food should not be distributed to anyone else until it has been offered to the Deity), (*bb*) to sit with one's back toward the Deity, (*cc*) to offer obeisances to someone else in front of the Deity, (*dd*) not to chant proper prayers when offering obeisances to the spiritual master, (*ee*) to praise oneself before the Deity, and (*ff*) to blaspheme the demigods. In the worship of the Deity, these thirty-two offenses should be avoided.

In the *Varāha Purāṇa* the following offenses are mentioned: (*a*) to eat in the house of a rich man, (*b*) to enter the Deity's room in the dark, (*c*) to worship the Deity without following the regulative principles, (*d*) to enter the temple without vibrating any sound, (*e*) to collect food that has been seen by a dog, (*f*) to break silence while offering worship to the Deity, (*g*) to go to the toilet during the time of worshiping the Deity, (*h*) to offer incense without offering flowers, (*i*) to worship the Deity with forbidden flowers, (*j*) to begin worship without having washed one's teeth, (*k*) to begin worship after sex, (*l*) to touch a lamp, dead body or a woman during her menstrual period, or to put on red or bluish clothing, unwashed clothing, the clothing of others or soiled clothing. Other offenses are to worship the Deity after seeing a dead body, to pass air before the Deity, to show anger before the Deity, and to worship the Deity just after returning from a crematorium. After eating, one should not worship the Deity until one has digested his food, nor should one touch the Deity or engage in any Deity worship after eating safflower oil or hing. These are also offenses.

In other places, the following offenses are listed: (*a*) to be against the scriptural injunctions of the Vedic literature or to disrespect within one's heart the *Śrīmad-Bhāgavatam* while externally falsely accepting its principles, (*b*) to introduce differing *śāstras,* (*c*) to chew pan and betel before the Deity, (*d*) to keep flowers for worship on the leaf of a castor oil plant, (*e*) to worship the Deity in the afternoon, (*f*) to sit on the altar or to sit on the floor to worship the Deity (without a seat), (*g*) to touch the Deity with the left hand while bathing the Deity, (*h*) to worship the Deity with a stale or used flower, (*i*) to spit while worshiping the Deity, (*j*) to advertise one's glory while worshiping the Deity, (*k*) to apply *tilaka* to one's forehead in a curved way, (*l*) to enter the temple without having washed one's feet, (*m*) to offer the Deity food cooked by an uninitiated person, (*n*) to worship the Deity and offer *bhoga* to the Deity within the vision of an uninitiated person or non-Vaiṣṇava, (*o*) to offer worship to the Deity without worshiping Vaikuṇṭha deities like Gaṇeśa, (*p*) to worship the Deity while perspiring, (*q*) to refuse flowers offered to the Deity, (*r*) to take a vow or oath in the holy name of the Lord.

If one commits any of the above offenses, one must read at least one chapter of *Bhagavad-gītā.* This is confirmed in the *Skanda-Purāṇa, Avantī-khaṇḍa.* Similarly, there is another injunction, stating that one who reads the thousand names of Viṣṇu can be released from all offenses. In the same *Skanda-Purāṇa, Revā-khaṇḍa,* it is said that one who recites prayers to *tulasī* or sows a *tulasī* seed is also freed from all offenses. Similarly, one who worships the *śālagrāma-śilā* can also be relieved of offenses. In the *Brahmāṇḍa Purāṇa* it is said that one who worships Lord Viṣṇu, whose four hands bear a conchshell, disc, lotus flower and club, can be relieved from the above offenses. In the *Ādi-varāha Purāṇa* it is said that a worshiper who has committed offenses may fast for one day at the holy place known as Śaukarava and then bathe in the Ganges.

In the process of worshiping the Deity it is sometimes enjoined that one worship the Deity within the mind. In the *Padma Purāṇa, Uttara-khaṇḍa,* it is said, "All persons can generally worship within the mind." The *Gautamīya Tantra* states, "For a *sannyāsī* who has no home, worship of the Deity within the mind is recommended." In the *Nārada-pañcarātra* it is stated by Lord Nārāyaṇa that worship of the Deity within the mind is called *mānasa-pūjā*. One can become free from the four miseries by this method. Sometimes worship from the mind can be independently executed. According to the instruction of Āvirhotra Muni, one of the *nava-yogendras*, as mentioned in *Śrīmad-Bhāgavatam*, one may worship the Deity by chanting all the *mantras*. Eight kinds of Deities are mentioned in the *śāstra*, and the mental Deity is one of them. In this regard, the following description is given in the *Brahma-vaivarta Purāṇa*.

In the city of Pratiṣṭhāna-pura, long ago, there resided a *brāhmaṇa* who was poverty-stricken but innocent and not dissatisfied. One day he heard a discourse in an assembly of *brāhmaṇas* concerning how to worship the Deity in the temple. In that meeting, he also heard that the Deity may be worshiped within the mind. After this incident, the *brāhmaṇa*, having bathed in the Godāvarī River, began mentally worshiping the Deity. He would wash the temple within his mind, and then in his imagination he would bring water from all the sacred rivers in golden and silver waterpots. He collected all kinds of valuable paraphernalia for worship, and he worshiped the Deity very gorgeously, beginning from bathing the Deity and ending with offering *ārati*. Thus he felt great happiness. After many years had passed in this way, one day within his mind he cooked nice sweet rice with ghee to worship the Deity. He placed the sweet rice on a golden dish and offered it to Lord Kṛṣṇa, but he felt that the sweet rice was very hot, and therefore he touched it with his finger. He immediately felt that his finger had been burned by the hot sweet rice, and thus he began to lament. While the *brāhmaṇa* was in pain, Lord Viṣṇu in Vaikuṇṭha began smiling, and the goddess of fortune inquired from the Lord why He was smiling. Lord Viṣṇu then ordered His associates to bring the *brāhmaṇa* to Vaikuṇṭha. Thus the *brāhmaṇa* attained the liberation of *sāmīpya*, the facility of living near the Supreme Personality of Godhead.

(6) *Vandanam*. Although prayers are a part of Deity worship, they may be considered separately like the other items, such as hearing and chanting, and therefore separate statements are given herewith. The Lord has unlimited transcendental qualities and opulences, and one who feels influenced by the Lord's qualities in various activities offers

prayers to the Lord. In this way he becomes successful. In this connection, the following are some of the offenses to be avoided: (*a*) to offer obeisances on one hand, (*b*) to offer obeisances with one's body covered, (*c*) to show one's back to the Deity, (*d*) to offer obeisances on the left side of the Deity, (*e*) to offer obeisances very near the Deity.

(7) *Dāsyam.* There is the following statement in regard to assisting the Lord as a servant. After many, many thousands of births, when one comes to understand that he is an eternal servant of Kṛṣṇa, one can deliver others from this universe. If one simply continues to think that he is an eternal servant of Kṛṣṇa, even without performing any other process of devotional service, he can attain full success, for simply by this feeling one can perform all nine processes of devotional service.

(8) *Sakhyam.* In regard to worshiping the Lord as a friend, the *Agastya-saṁhitā* states that a devotee engaged in performing devotional service by *śravaṇam* and *kīrtanam* sometimes wants to see the Lord personally, and for this purpose he resides in the temple. Elsewhere there is this statement: "O my Lord, Supreme Personality and eternal friend, although You are full of bliss and knowledge, You have become the friend of the residents of Vṛndāvana. How fortunate are these devotees!" In this statement the word "friend" is specifically used to indicate intense love. Friendship, therefore, is better than servitude. In the stage above *dāsya-rasa,* the devotee accepts the Supreme Personality of Godhead as a friend. This is not at all astonishing, for when a devotee is pure in heart the opulence of his worship of the Deity diminishes as spontaneous love for the Personality of Godhead is manifested. In this regard, Śrīdhara Svāmī mentions Śrīdāma Vipra, who expressed to himself his feelings of obligation, thinking, "Life after life, may I be connected with Kṛṣṇa in this friendly attitude."

(9) *Ātma-nivedanam.* The word *ātma-nivedanam* refers to the stage at which one who has no motive other than to serve the Lord surrenders everything to the Lord and performs his activities only to please the Supreme Personality of Godhead. Such a devotee is like a cow that is cared for by its master. When cared for by its master, a cow is not in anxiety over its maintenance. Such a cow is always devoted to its master, and it never acts independently, but only for the master's benefit. Some devotees, therefore, consider dedication of the body to the Lord to be *ātma-nivedanam,* and as stated in the book known as *Bhakti-viveka,*

sometimes dedication of the soul to the Lord is called *ātma-nivedanam.* The best examples of *ātma-nivedanam* are found in Bali Mahārāja and Ambarīṣa Mahārāja. *Ātma-nivedanam* is also sometimes found in the behavior of Rukmiṇīdevī at Dvārakā.

TEXT 25

निशम्यैतत्सुतवचो हिरण्यकशिपुस्तदा ।
गुरुपुत्रमुवाचेदं रुषा प्रस्फुरिताधरः ॥२५॥

niśamyaitat suta-vaco
hiraṇyakaśipus tadā
guru-putram uvācedaṁ
ruṣā prasphuritādharaḥ

niśamya—hearing; *etat*—this; *suta-vacaḥ*—speech from his son; *hiraṇyakaśipuḥ*—Hiraṇyakaśipu; *tadā*—at that time; *guru-putram*—unto the son of Śukrācārya, his spiritual master; *uvāca*—spoke; *idam*—this; *ruṣā*—with anger; *prasphurita*—trembling; *adharaḥ*—whose lips.

TRANSLATION

After hearing these words of devotional service from the mouth of his son Prahlāda, Hiraṇyakaśipu was extremely angry. His lips trembling, he spoke as follows to Ṣaṇḍa, the son of his guru, Śukrācārya.

TEXT 26

ब्रह्मबन्धो किमेतत्ते विपक्षं श्रयतासता ।
असारं ग्राहितो बालो मामनादृत्य दुर्मते ॥२६॥

brahma-bandho kim etat te
vipakṣaṁ śrayatāsatā
asāraṁ grāhito bālo
mām anādṛtya durmate

brahma-bandho—O unqualified son of a *brāhmaṇa; kim etat*—what is this; *te*—by you; *vipakṣam*—the party of my enemies; *śrayatā*—taking shelter of; *asatā*—most mischievous; *asāram*—nonsense; *grāhitaḥ*—taught; *bālaḥ*—the boy; *mām*—me; *anādṛtya*—not caring for; *durmate*—O foolish teacher.

TRANSLATION

O unqualified, most heinous son of a brāhmaṇa, you have disobeyed my order and taken shelter of the party of my enemies. You have taught this poor boy about devotional service! What is this nonsense?

PURPORT

In this verse the word *asāram,* meaning, "having no substance," is significant. For a demon there is no substance in the process of devotional service, but to a devotee devotional service is the only essential factor in life. Since Hiraṇyakaśipu did not like devotional service, the essence of life, he chastised Prahlāda Mahārāja's teachers with harsh words.

TEXT 27

सन्ति ह्यसाधवो लोके दुर्मैत्राश्छद्मवेषिणः ।
तेषामुदेत्यघं काले रोगः पातकिनामिव ॥२७॥

santi hy asādhavo loke
durmaitrāś chadma-veśiṇaḥ
teṣām udety aghaṁ kāle
rogaḥ pātakinām iva

santi—are; *hi*—indeed; *asādhavaḥ*—dishonest persons; *loke*—within this world; *durmaitrāḥ*—cheating friends; *chadma-veśiṇaḥ*—wearing false garbs; *teṣām*—of all of them; *udeti*—arises; *agham*—the reaction of sinful life; *kāle*—in due course of time; *rogaḥ*—disease; *pātakinām*—of sinful men; *iva*—like.

TRANSLATION

In due course of time, various types of diseases are manifest in those who are sinful. Similarly, in this world there are many

deceptive friends in false garbs, but eventually, because of their false behavior, their actual enmity becomes manifest.

PURPORT

Being anxious about the education of his boy Prahlāda, Hiraṇyakaśipu was very much dissatisfied. When Prahlāda began teaching about devotional service, Hiraṇyakaśipu immediately regarded the teachers as his enemies in the garb of friends. In this verse the words *rogaḥ pātakinām iva* refer to disease, which is the most sinful and miserable of the conditions of material life (*janma-mṛtyu-jarā-vyādhi*). Disease is the symptom of the body of a sinful person. The *smṛti-śāstras* say,

brahma-hā kṣaya-rogī syāt
surāpaḥ śyāvadantakaḥ
svarṇa-hārī tu kunakhī
duścarmā guru-talpagaḥ

Murderers of *brāhmaṇas* are later afflicted by tuberculosis, drunkards become toothless, those who have stolen gold are afflicted by diseased nails, and sinful men who have sexual connections with the wife of a superior are afflicted by leprosy and similar skin diseases.

TEXT 28

श्रीगुरुपुत्र उवाच
न मत्प्रणीतं न परप्रणीतं
सुतो वदत्येष तवेन्द्रशत्रो ।
नैसर्गिकीयं मतिरस्य राजन्
नियच्छ मन्युं कद्दाः स्म मा नः ॥२८॥

śrī-guru-putra uvāca
na mat-praṇītaṁ na para-praṇītaṁ
suto vadaty eṣa tavendra-śatro
naisargikīyaṁ matir asya rājan
niyaccha manyuṁ kad adāḥ sma mā naḥ

śrī-guru-putraḥ uvāca—the son of Śukrācārya, Hiraṇyakaśipu's spiritual master, said; *na*—not; *mat-praṇītam*—educated by me; *na*—nor; *para-praṇītam*—educated by anyone else; *sutaḥ*—the son (Prahlāda); *vadati*—says; *eṣaḥ*—this; *tava*—your; *indra-śatro*—O enemy of King Indra; *naisargikī*—natural; *iyam*—this; *matiḥ*—inclination; *asya*—of him; *rājan*—O King; *niyaccha*—give up; *manyum*—your anger; *kad*—fault; *adāḥ*—attribute; *sma*—indeed; *mā*—do not; *naḥ*—unto us.

TRANSLATION

The son of Śukrācārya, Hiraṇyakaśipu's spiritual master, said: O enemy of King Indra, O King! Whatever your son Prahlāda has said was not taught to him by me or anyone else. His spontaneous devotional service has naturally developed in him. Therefore, please give up your anger and do not unnecessarily accuse us. It is not good to insult a brāhmaṇa in this way.

TEXT 29

श्रीनारद उवाच
गुरुणैवं प्रतिप्रोक्तो भूय आहासुरः सुतम् ।
न चेद्गुरुमुखीयं ते कुतोऽभद्रासती मतिः ॥२९॥

śrī-nārada uvāca
guruṇaivaṁ pratiprokto
bhūya āhāsuraḥ sutam
na ced guru-mukhīyaṁ te
kuto 'bhadrāsatī matiḥ

śrī-nāradaḥ uvāca—Nārada Muni said; *guruṇā*—by the teacher; *evam*—thus; *pratiproktaḥ*—being answered; *bhūyaḥ*—again; *āha*—said; *asuraḥ*—the great demon, Hiraṇyakaśipu; *sutam*—unto his son; *na*—not; *cet*—if; *guru-mukhī*—issued from the mouth of your teacher; *iyam*—this; *te*—your; *kutaḥ*—from where; *abhadra*—O inauspicious one; *asatī*—very bad; *matiḥ*—inclination.

TRANSLATION

Śrī Nārada Muni continued: When Hiraṇyakaśipu received this reply from the teacher, he again addressed his son Prahlāda. Hiraṇyakaśipu said: You rascal, most fallen of our family, if you have not received this education from your teachers, where have you gotten it?

PURPORT

Śrīla Viśvanātha Cakravartī Ṭhākura explains that devotional service is actually *bhadrā satī*, not *abhadra asatī*. In other words, knowledge of devotional service can be neither inauspicious nor contrary to etiquette. To learn devotional service is the duty of everyone. Therefore the spontaneous education of Prahlāda Mahārāja is supported as auspicious and perfect.

TEXT 30

श्रीप्रह्राद उवाच
मतिर्न कृष्णे परतः स्वतो वा
मिथोऽभिपद्येत गृहव्रतानाम् ।
अदान्तगोभिर्विशतां तमिस्रं
पुनः पुनश्चर्वितचर्वणानाम् ॥३०॥

śrī-prahrāda uvāca
matir na kṛṣṇe parataḥ svato vā
mitho 'bhipadyeta gṛha-vratānām
adānta-gobhir viśatāṁ tamisraṁ
punaḥ punaś carvita-carvaṇānām

śrī-prahrādaḥ uvāca—Prahlāda Mahārāja said; *matiḥ*—inclination; *na*—never; *kṛṣṇe*—unto Lord Kṛṣṇa; *parataḥ*—from the instructions of others; *svataḥ*—from their own understanding; *vā*—either; *mithaḥ*—from combined effort; *abhipadyeta*—is developed; *gṛha-vratānām*—of persons too addicted to the materialistic, bodily conception of life; *adānta*—uncontrolled; *gobhiḥ*—by the senses; *viśatām*—entering; *tamisram*—hellish life; *punaḥ*—again; *punaḥ*—again; *carvita*—things already chewed; *carvaṇānām*—who are chewing.

TRANSLATION

Prahlāda Mahārāja replied: Because of their uncontrolled senses, persons too addicted to materialistic life make progress toward hellish conditions and repeatedly chew that which has already been chewed. Their inclinations toward Kṛṣṇa are never aroused, either by the instructions of others, by their own efforts, or by a combination of both.

PURPORT

In this verse the words *matir na kṛṣṇe* refer to devotional service rendered to Kṛṣṇa. So-called politicians, erudite scholars and philosophers who read *Bhagavad-gītā* try to twist some meaning from it to suit their material purposes, but their misunderstandings of Kṛṣṇa will not yield them any profit. Because such politicians, philosophers and scholars are interested in using *Bhagavad-gītā* as a vehicle for adjusting things materially, for them constant thought of Kṛṣṇa, or Kṛṣṇa consciousness, is impossible (*matir na kṛṣṇe*). As stated in *Bhagavad-gītā* (18.55), *bhaktyā mām abhijānāti:* only through devotional service can one understand Kṛṣṇa as He is. The so-called politicians and scholars think of Kṛṣṇa as fictitious. The politician says that his Kṛṣṇa is different from the Kṛṣṇa depicted in *Bhagavad-gītā*. Even though he accepts Kṛṣṇa and Rāma as the Supreme he thinks of Rāma and Kṛṣṇa as impersonal because he has no idea of service to Kṛṣṇa. Thus his only business is *punaḥ punaś carvita-carvaṇānām*—chewing the chewed again and again. The aim of such politicians and academic scholars is to enjoy this material world with their bodily senses. Therefore it is clearly stated here that those who are *gṛha-vrata*, whose only aim is to live comfortably with the body in the material world, cannot understand Kṛṣṇa. The two expressions *gṛha-vrata* and *carvita-carvaṇānām* indicate that a materialistic person tries to enjoy sense gratification in different bodily forms, life after life, but is still unsatisfied. In the name of personalism, this ism or that ism, such persons always remain attached to the materialistic way of life. As stated in *Bhagavad-gītā* (2.44):

bhogaiśvarya-prasaktānāṁ
tayāpahṛta-cetasām

vyavasāyātmikā buddhiḥ
samādhau na vidhīyate

"In the minds of those who are too attached to sense enjoyment and material opulence, and who are bewildered by such things, the resolute determination for devotional service to the Supreme Lord does not take place." Those who are attached to material enjoyment cannot be fixed in devotional service to the Lord. They cannot understand Bhagavān, Kṛṣṇa, or His instruction, *Bhagavad-gītā. Adānta-gobhir viśatāṁ tamisram:* their path actually leads toward hellish life.

As confirmed by Ṛṣabhadeva, *mahat-sevāṁ dvāram āhur vimukteḥ:* one must try to understand Kṛṣṇa by serving a devotee. The word *mahat* refers to a devotee.

mahātmānas tu māṁ pārtha
daivīṁ prakṛtim āśritāḥ
bhajanty ananya-manaso
jñātvā bhūtādim avyayam

"O son of Pṛthā, those who are not deluded, the great souls, are under the protection of the divine nature. They are fully engaged in devotional service because they know Me as the Supreme Personality of Godhead, original and inexhaustible." (Bg. 9.13) A *mahātmā* is one who is constantly engaged in devotional service, twenty-four hours a day. As explained in the following verses, unless one adheres to such a great personality, one cannot understand Kṛṣṇa. Hiraṇyakaśipu wanted to know where Prahlāda had gotten this Kṛṣṇa consciousness. Who had taught him? Prahlāda sarcastically replied, "My dear father, persons like you never understand Kṛṣṇa. One can understand Kṛṣṇa only by serving a *mahat*, a great soul. Those who try to adjust material conditions are said to be chewing the chewed. No one has been able to adjust material conditions, but life after life, generation after generation, people try and repeatedly fail. Unless one is properly trained by a *mahat*—a *mahātmā*, or unalloyed devotee of the Lord—there is no possibility of one's understanding Kṛṣṇa and His devotional service."

TEXT 31

न ते विदुः स्वार्थगतिं हि विष्णुं
दुराशया ये बहिरर्थमानिनः ।
अन्धा यथान्धैरुपनीयमाना-
स्तेऽपीशतन्त्र्यामुरुदाम्नि बद्धाः ॥३१॥

na te viduḥ svārtha-gatiṁ hi viṣṇuṁ
durāśayā ye bahir-artha-māninaḥ
andhā yathāndhair upanīyamānās
te 'pīśa-tantryām uru-dāmni baddhāḥ

na—not; *te*—they; *viduḥ*—know; *sva-artha-gatim*—the ultimate goal of life, or their own real interest; *hi*—indeed; *viṣṇum*—Lord Viṣṇu and His abode; *durāśayāḥ*—being ambitious to enjoy this material world; *ye*—who; *bahiḥ*—external sense objects; *artha-māninaḥ*—considering as valuable; *andhāḥ*—persons who are blind; *yathā*—just as; *andhaiḥ*—by other blind men; *upanīyamānāḥ*—being led; *te*—they; *api*—although; *īśa-tantryām*—to the ropes (laws) of material nature; *uru*—having very strong; *dāmni*—cords; *baddhāḥ*—bound.

TRANSLATION

Persons who are strongly entrapped by the consciousness of enjoying material life, and who have therefore accepted as their leader or guru a similar blind man attached to external sense objects, cannot understand that the goal of life is to return home, back to Godhead, and engage in the service of Lord Viṣṇu. As blind men guided by another blind man miss the right path and fall into a ditch, materially attached men led by another materially attached man are bound by the ropes of fruitive labor, which are made of very strong cords, and they continue again and again in materialistic life, suffering the threefold miseries.

PURPORT

Since there must always be a difference of opinion between demons and devotees, Hiraṇyakaśipu, when criticized by his son Prahlāda

Mahārāja, should not have been surprised that Prahlāda Mahārāja differed from his way of life. Nonetheless, Hiraṇyakaśipu was extremely angry and wanted to rebuke his son for deriding his teacher or spiritual master, who had been born in the *brāhmaṇa* family of the great *ācārya* Śukrācārya. The word *śukra* means "semen," and *ācārya* refers to a teacher or *guru*. Hereditary *gurus*, or spiritual masters, have been accepted everywhere since time immemorial, but Prahlāda Mahārāja declined to accept such a seminal *guru* or take instruction from him. An actual *guru* is *śrotriya*, one who has heard or received perfect knowledge through *paramparā*, the disciplic succession. Therefore Prahlāda Mahārāja did not recognize a seminal spiritual master. Such spiritual masters are not at all interested in Viṣṇu. Indeed, they are hopeful of material success (*bahir-artha-māninaḥ*). The word *bahiḥ* means "external," *artha* means "interest," and *mānina* means "taking very seriously." Generally speaking, practically everyone is unaware of the spiritual world. The knowledge of the materialists is restricted within the four-billion-mile limit of this material world, which is in the dark portion of the creation; they do not know that beyond the material world is the spiritual world. Unless one is a devotee of the Lord, one cannot understand the existence of the spiritual world. *Gurus*, teachers, who are simply interested in this material world are described in this verse as *andha*, blind. Such blind men may lead many other blind followers without true knowledge of material conditions, but they are not accepted by devotees like Prahlāda Mahārāja. Such blind teachers, being interested in the external, material world, are always bound by the strong ropes of material nature.

TEXT 32

नैषां मतिस्तावदुरुक्रमाङ्घ्रिं
स्पृशत्यनर्थापगमो यदर्थः ।
महीयसां पादरजोऽभिषेकं
निष्किञ्चनानां न वृणीत यावत् ॥३२॥

naiṣāṁ matis tāvad urukramāṅghriṁ
spṛśaty anarthāpagamo yad-arthaḥ

mahīyasāṁ pāda-rajo-'bhiṣekaṁ
niṣkiñcanānāṁ na vṛṇīta yāvat

na—not; *eṣām*—of these; *matiḥ*—the consciousness; *tāvat*—that long; *urukrama-aṅghrim*—the lotus feet of the Supreme Personality of Godhead, who is famous for performing uncommon activities; *spṛśati*—does touch; *anartha*—of unwanted things; *apagamaḥ*—the disappearance; *yat*—of which; *arthaḥ*—the purpose; *mahīyasām*—of the great souls (the *mahātmās*, or devotees); *pāda-rajaḥ*—by the dust of the lotus feet; *abhiṣekam*—consecration; *niṣkiñcanānām*—of devotees who have nothing to do with this material world; *na*—not; *vṛṇīta*—may accept; *yāvat*—as long as.

TRANSLATION

Unless they smear upon their bodies the dust of the lotus feet of a Vaiṣṇava completely freed from material contamination, persons very much inclined toward materialistic life cannot be attached to the lotus feet of the Lord, who is glorified for His uncommon activities. Only by becoming Kṛṣṇa conscious and taking shelter at the lotus feet of the Lord in this way can one be freed from material contamination.

PURPORT

Becoming Kṛṣṇa conscious brings about *anartha-apagamaḥ*, the disappearance of all *anarthas*, the miserable conditions we have unnecessarily accepted. The material body is the basic principle of these unwanted miserable conditions. The entire Vedic civilization is meant to relieve one from these unwanted miseries, but persons bound by the laws of nature do not know the destination of life. As described in the previous verse, *īśa-tantryām uru-dāmni baddhāḥ:* they are conditioned by the three strong modes of material nature. The education that keeps the conditioned soul bound life after life is called materialistic education. Śrīla Bhaktivinoda Ṭhākura has explained that materialistic education expands the influence of *māyā*. Such an education induces the conditioned soul to be increasingly attracted to materialistic life and to stray further and further away from liberation from unwanted miseries.

One may ask why highly educated persons do not take to Kṛṣṇa consciousness. The reason is explained in this verse. Unless one takes shelter of a bona fide, fully Kṛṣṇa conscious spiritual master, there is no chance of understanding Kṛṣṇa. The educators, scholars and big political leaders worshiped by millions of people cannot understand the goal of life and take to Kṛṣṇa consciousness, for they have not accepted a bona fide spiritual master and the *Vedas*. Therefore in the *Muṇḍaka Upaniṣad* (3.2.3) it is said, *nāyam ātmā pravacanena labhyo na medhayā na bahunā śrutena:* one cannot become self-realized simply by having an academic education, by presenting lectures in an erudite way (*pravacanena labhyaḥ*), or by being an intelligent scientist who discovers many wonderful things. One cannot understand Kṛṣṇa unless one is graced by the Supreme Personality of Godhead. Only one who has surrendered to a pure devotee of Kṛṣṇa and taken the dust of his lotus feet can understand Kṛṣṇa. First one must understand how to get out of the clutches of *māyā*. The only means is to become Kṛṣṇa conscious. And to become Kṛṣṇa conscious very easily, one must take shelter of a realized soul—a *mahat*, or *mahātmā*—whose only interest is to engage in the service of the Supreme Lord. As the Lord says in *Bhagavad-gītā* (9.13):

mahātmānas tu māṁ pārtha
daivīṁ prakṛtim āśritāḥ
bhajanty ananya-manaso
jñātvā bhūtādim avyayam

"O son of Pṛthā, those who are not deluded, the great souls, are under the protection of the divine nature. They are fully engaged in devotional service because they know Me as the Supreme Personality of Godhead, original and inexhaustible." Therefore, to end the unwanted miseries of life, one must become a devotee.

yasyāsti bhaktir bhagavaty akiñcanā
sarvair guṇais tatra samāsate surāḥ

"One who has unflinching devotional faith in Kṛṣṇa consistently manifests all the good qualities of Kṛṣṇa and the demigods." (*Bhāg.* 5.18.12)

yasya deve parā bhaktir
yathā deve tathā gurau
tasyaite kathitā hy arthāḥ
prakāśante mahātmanaḥ

"Only unto those great souls who have implicit faith in both the Lord and the spiritual master are all the imports of Vedic knowledge automatically revealed." (*Śvetāśvatara Upaniṣad* 6.23)

yam evaiṣa vṛṇute tena labhyas
tasyaiṣa ātmā vivṛṇute tanūṁ svām

"The Lord is obtained only by one whom He Himself chooses. To such a person He manifests His own form." (*Muṇḍaka Upaniṣad* 3.2.3)

These are Vedic injunctions. One must take shelter of a self-realized spiritual master, not a materially educated scholar or politician. One must take shelter of a *niṣkiñcana*, a person engaged in devotional service and free from material contamination. That is the way to return home, back to Godhead.

TEXT 33

इत्युक्त्वोपरतं पुत्रं हिरण्यकशिपू रुषा ।
अन्धीकृतात्मा स्वोत्सङ्गान्निरस्यत महीतले ॥३३॥

ity uktvoparataṁ putraṁ
hiraṇyakaśipū ruṣā
andhīkṛtātmā svotsaṅgān
nirasyata mahī-tale

iti—thus; *uktvā*—speaking; *uparatam*—stopped; *putram*—the son; *hiraṇyakaśipuḥ*—Hiraṇyakaśipu; *ruṣā*—with great anger; *andhīkṛta-ātmā*—made blind to self-realization; *sva-utsaṅgāt*—from his lap; *nirasyata*—threw; *mahī-tale*—upon the ground.

TRANSLATION

After Prahlāda Mahārāja had spoken in this way and become silent, Hiraṇyakaśipu, blinded by anger, threw him off his lap and onto the ground.

TEXT 34

आहामर्षरुषाविष्टः कषायीभूतलोचनः ।
वध्यतामाश्वयं वध्यो निःसारयत नैर्ऋताः ॥३४॥

āhāmarṣa-ruṣāviṣṭaḥ
kaṣāyī-bhūta-locanaḥ
vadhyatām āśv ayaṁ vadhyo
niḥsārayata nairṛtāḥ

āha—he said; *amarṣa*—indignation; *ruṣā*—and by severe anger; *āviṣṭaḥ*—overpowered; *kaṣāyī-bhūta*—becoming exactly like red-hot copper; *locanaḥ*—whose eyes; *vadhyatām*—let him be killed; *āśu*—immediately; *ayam*—this; *vadhyaḥ*—who is to be killed; *niḥsārayata*—take away; *nairṛtāḥ*—O demons.

TRANSLATION

Indignant and angry, his reddish eyes like molten copper, Hiraṇyakaśipu said to his servants: O demons, take this boy away from me! He deserves to be killed. Kill him as soon as possible!

TEXT 35

अयं मे भ्रातृहा सोऽयं हित्वा स्वान् सुहृदोऽधमः।
पितृव्यहन्तुः पादौ यो विष्णोर्दासवदर्चति ॥३५॥

ayaṁ me bhrātṛ-hā so 'yaṁ
hitvā svān suhṛdo 'dhamaḥ
pitṛvya-hantuḥ pādau yo
viṣṇor dāsavad arcati

ayam—this; *me*—my; *bhrātṛ-hā*—killer of the brother; *saḥ*—he; *ayam*—this; *hitvā*—giving up; *svān*—own; *suhṛdaḥ*—well-wishers; *adhamaḥ*—very low; *pitṛvya-hantuḥ*—of He who killed his uncle

Hiraṇyākṣa; *pādau*—at the two feet; *yaḥ*—he who; *viṣṇoḥ*—of Lord Viṣṇu; *dāsa-vat*—like a servant; *arcati*—serves.

TRANSLATION

This boy Prahlāda is the killer of my brother, for he has given up his family to engage in the devotional service of the enemy, Lord Viṣṇu, like a menial servant.

PURPORT

Hiraṇyakaśipu considered his son Prahlāda Mahārāja to be the killer of his brother because Prahlāda Mahārāja was engaged in the devotional service of Lord Viṣṇu. In other words, Prahlāda Mahārāja would be elevated to *sārūpya* liberation, and in that sense he resembled Lord Viṣṇu. Therefore Prahlāda was to be killed by Hiraṇyakaśipu. Devotees, Vaiṣṇavas, attain the liberations of *sārūpya, sālokya, sārṣṭi* and *sāmīpya*, whereas the Māyāvādīs are supposed to attain the liberation known as *sāyujya. Sāyujya-mukti*, however, is not very secure, whereas *sārūpya-mukti, sālokya-mukti, sārṣṭi-mukti* and *sāmīpya-mukti* are most certain. Although the servants of Lord Viṣṇu, Nārāyaṇa, in the Vaikuṇṭha planets are equally situated with the Lord, the devotees there know very well that the Lord is the master whereas they are servants.

TEXT 36

विष्णोर्वा साध्वसौ किं नु करिष्यत्यसमञ्जसः ।
सौहृदं दुस्त्यजं पित्रोरहाद्यः पञ्चहायनः ॥३६॥

viṣṇor vā sādhv asau kiṁ nu
kariṣyaty asamañjasaḥ
sauhṛdaṁ dustyajaṁ pitror
ahād yaḥ pañca-hāyanaḥ

viṣṇoḥ—unto Viṣṇu; *vā*—either; *sādhu*—good; *asau*—this; *kim*—whether; *nu*—indeed; *kariṣyati*—will do; *asamañjasaḥ*—not trustworthy; *sauhṛdam*—affectionate relationship; *dustyajam*—difficult to relinquish; *pitroḥ*—of his father and mother; *ahāt*—gave up; *yaḥ*—he who; *pañca-hāyanaḥ*—only five years old.

TRANSLATION

Although Prahlāda is only five years old, even at this young age he has given up his affectionate relationship with his father and mother. Therefore, he is certainly untrustworthy. Indeed, it is not at all believable that he will behave well toward Viṣṇu.

TEXT 37

परोऽप्यपत्यं हितकृद्यथौषधं
स्वदेहजोऽप्यामयवत्सुतोऽहितः।
छिन्द्यात्तदङ्गं यदुतात्मनोऽहितं
शेषं सुखं जीवति यद्विवर्जनात् ॥३७॥

paro 'py apatyaṁ hita-kṛd yathauṣadhaṁ
sva-dehajo 'py āmayavat suto 'hitaḥ
chindyāt tad aṅgaṁ yad utātmano 'hitaṁ
śeṣaṁ sukhaṁ jīvati yad-vivarjanāt

paraḥ—not belonging to the same group or family; *api*—although; *apatyam*—a child; *hita-kṛt*—who is beneficial; *yathā*—just as; *auṣadham*—remedial herb; *sva-deha-jaḥ*—born of one's own body; *api*—although; *āmaya-vat*—like a disease; *sutaḥ*—a son; *ahitaḥ*—who is not a well-wisher; *chindyāt*—one should cut off; *tat*—that; *aṅgam*—part of the body; *yat*—which; *uta*—indeed; *ātmanaḥ*—for the body; *ahitam*—not beneficial; *śeṣam*—the balance; *sukham*—happily; *jīvati*—lives; *yat*—of which; *vivarjanāt*—by cutting off.

TRANSLATION

Although a medicinal herb, being born in the forest, does not belong to the same category as a man, if beneficial it is kept very carefully. Similarly, if someone outside one's family is favorable, he should be given protection like a son. On the other hand, if a limb of one's body is poisoned by disease, it must be amputated so

that the rest of the body may live happily. Similarly, even one's own son, if unfavorable, must be rejected, although born of one's own body.

PURPORT

Śrī Caitanya Mahāprabhu has instructed all devotees of the Lord to be humbler than the grass and more tolerant than trees; otherwise there will always be disturbances to their execution of devotional service. Here is a vivid example of how a devotee is disturbed by a nondevotee, even though the nondevotee is an affectionate father. The material world is such that a nondevotee father becomes an enemy of a devotee son. Having determined to kill even his son, Hiraṇyakaśipu gave the example of amputating a part of one's body that has become septic and therefore injurious to the rest of the body. The same example, of course, may also be applied to nondevotees. Cāṇakya Paṇḍita advises, *tyaja durjana-saṁsargaṁ bhaja sādhu-samāgamam.* Devotees actually serious about advancing in spiritual life should give up the company of nondevotees and always keep company with devotees. To be too attached to material existence is ignorance because material existence is temporary and miserable. Therefore devotees who are determined to perform *tapasya* (penances and austerities) to realize the self, and who are determined to become advanced in spiritual consciousness, must give up the company of atheistic nondevotees. Prahlāda Mahārāja maintained an attitude of noncooperation with the philosophy of his father, Hiraṇyakaśipu, yet he was tolerant and humble. Hiraṇyakaśipu, however, being a nondevotee, was so polluted that he was even prepared to kill his own son. He justified this by putting forward the logic of amputation.

TEXT 38

सर्वैरुपायैर्हन्तव्यः सम्भोजशयनासनैः ।
सुहृल्लिङ्गधरः शत्रुर्मुनेर्दुष्टमिवेन्द्रियम् ॥३८॥

sarvair upāyair hantavyaḥ
sambhoja-śayanāsanaiḥ
suhṛl-liṅga-dharaḥ śatrur
muner duṣṭam ivendriyam

sarvaiḥ—by all; *upāyaiḥ*—means; *hantavyaḥ*—must be killed; *sambhoja*—by eating; *śayana*—lying down; *āsanaiḥ*—by sitting; *suhṛt-liṅga-dharaḥ*—who has assumed the role of a friend; *śatruḥ*—an enemy; *muneḥ*—of a great sage; *duṣṭam*—uncontrollable; *iva*—like; *indriyam*—the senses.

TRANSLATION

Just as uncontrolled senses are the enemies of all yogīs engaged in advancing in spiritual life, this Prahlāda, who appears to be a friend, is an enemy because I cannot control him. Therefore this enemy, whether eating, sitting or sleeping, must be killed by all means.

PURPORT

Hiraṇyakaśipu planned a campaign to kill Prahlāda Mahārāja. He would kill his son by administering poison to him while he was eating, by making him sit in boiling oil, or by throwing him under the feet of an elephant while he was lying down. Thus Hiraṇyakaśipu decided to kill his innocent child, who was only five years old, simply because the boy had become a devotee of the Lord. This is the attitude of nondevotees toward devotees.

TEXTS 39–40

नैर्ऋतास्ते समादिष्टा भर्त्रा वै शूलपाणयः ।
तिग्मदंष्ट्रकरालास्यास्ताम्रश्मश्रुशिरोरुहाः ॥३९॥
नदन्तो भैरवं नादं छिन्धि भिन्धीति वादिनः।
आसीनं चाहनञ् शूलैः प्रह्रादं सर्वमर्मसु ॥४०॥

nairṛtās te samādiṣṭā
bhartrā vai śūla-pāṇayaḥ
tigma-daṁṣṭra-karālāsyās
tāmra-śmaśru-śiroruhāḥ

nadanto bhairavaṁ nādaṁ
chindhi bhindhīti vādinaḥ
āsīnaṁ cāhanañ śūlaiḥ
prahrādaṁ sarva-marmasu

nairṛtāḥ—the demons; *te*—they; *samādiṣṭāḥ*—being fully advised; *bhartrā*—by their master; *vai*—indeed; *śūla-pāṇayaḥ*—having tridents in their hands; *tigma*—very sharp; *daṁṣṭra*—teeth; *karāla*—and fearful; *āsyāḥ*—faces; *tāmra-śmaśru*—coppery mustaches; *śiroruhāḥ*—and hair on the head; *nadantaḥ*—vibrating; *bhairavam*—fearful; *nādam*—sound; *chindhi*—chop; *bhindhi*—divide into small parts; *iti*—thus; *vādinaḥ*—speaking; *āsīnam*—who was sitting silently; *ca*—and; *ahanan*—attacked; *śūlaiḥ*—with their tridents; *prahrādam*—Prahlāda Mahārāja; *sarva-marmasu*—on the tender parts of the body.

TRANSLATION

The demons [Rākṣasas], the servants of Hiraṇyakaśipu, thus began striking the tender parts of Prahlāda Mahārāja's body with their tridents. The demons all had fearful faces, sharp teeth and reddish, coppery beards and hair, and they appeared extremely threatening. Making a tumultuous sound, shouting, "Chop him up! Pierce him!" they began striking Prahlāda Mahārāja, who sat silently, meditating upon the Supreme Personality of Godhead.

TEXT 41

परे ब्रह्मण्यनिर्देश्ये भगवत्यखिलात्मनि ।
युक्तात्मन्यफला आसन्नपुण्यस्येव सत्क्रियाः ॥४१॥

pare brahmaṇy anirdeśye
bhagavaty akhilātmani
yuktātmany aphalā āsann
apuṇyasyeva sat-kriyāḥ

pare—in the supreme; *brahmaṇi*—absolute; *anirdeśye*—who is not perceivable by the senses; *bhagavati*—the Supreme Personality of Godhead; *akhila-ātmani*—the Supersoul of everyone; *yukta-ātmani*—on he whose mind was engaged (Prahlāda); *aphalāḥ*—without effect; *āsan*—were; *apuṇyasya*—of a person who has no assets in pious activities; *iva*—like; *sat-kriyāḥ*—good activities (like the performance of sacrifices or austerities).

TRANSLATION

Even though a person who has no assets in pious activities performs some good deed, it will have no result. Thus the weapons of the demons had no tangible effects upon Prahlāda Mahārāja because he was a devotee undisturbed by material conditions and fully engaged in meditating upon and serving the Supreme Personality of Godhead, who is unchangeable, who cannot be realized by the material senses, and who is the soul of the entire universe.

PURPORT

Prahlāda Mahārāja was constantly and fully engaged in thought of the Supreme Personality of Godhead. As it is said, *govinda-parirambhitaḥ*. Prahlāda Mahārāja engaged himself always in meditation, and thus he was protected by Govinda. Just as a small child on the lap of his father or mother is fully protected, a devotee, in all conditions, is protected by the Supreme Lord. Does this mean that when Prahlāda Mahārāja was attacked by the demons, the Rākṣasas, Govinda was also attacked by the demons? This is not possible. There have been many attempts by the demons to hurt or kill the Supreme Personality of Godhead, but He cannot be injured by any material means because He is always in transcendence. Therefore the words *pare brahmaṇi* are used here. The demons, the Rākṣasas, can neither see nor touch the Supreme Lord, although they may superficially think that they are striking the Lord's transcendental body with their material weapons. The Supreme Personality of Godhead is described in this verse as *anirdeśye*. We cannot understand Him to be in a particular place, for He is all-pervasive. Moreover, He is *akhilātmā*, the active principle of everything, even material weapons. Those who cannot understand the position of the Lord are unfortunate. They may think that they can kill the Supreme Personality of Godhead and His devotee, but all their attempts will be futile. The Lord knows how to deal with them.

TEXT 42

प्रयासेऽपहते तस्मिन् दैत्येन्द्रः परिशङ्कितः ।
चकार तद्वधोपायान्निर्बन्धेन युधिष्ठिर ॥४२॥

prayāse 'pahate tasmin
daityendraḥ pariśaṅkitaḥ
cakāra tad-vadhopāyān
nirbandhena yudhiṣṭhira

prayāse—when the endeavor; *apahate*—futile; *tasmin*—that; *daitya-indraḥ*—the King of the demons, Hiraṇyakaśipu; *pariśaṅkitaḥ*—very much afraid (considering how the boy was protected); *cakāra*—executed; *tat-vadha-upāyān*—various means for killing him; *nirbandhena*—with determination; *yudhiṣṭhira*—O King Yudhiṣṭhira.

TRANSLATION

My dear King Yudhiṣṭhira, when all the attempts of the demons to kill Prahlāda Mahārāja were futile, the King of the demons, Hiraṇyakaśipu, being most fearful, began contriving other means to kill him.

TEXTS 43–44

दिग्गजैर्दन्दशूकेन्द्रैरभिचारावपातनैः ।
मायाभिः संनिरोधैश्च गरदानैरभोजनैः ॥४३॥
हिमवाय्वग्निसलिलैः पर्वताक्रमणैरपि ।
न शशाक यदा हन्तुमपापमसुरः सुतम् ।
चिन्तां दीर्घतमां प्राप्तस्तत्कर्तुं नाभ्यपद्यत ॥४४॥

dig-gajair dandaśūkendrair
abhicārāvapātanaiḥ
māyābhiḥ sannirodhaiś ca
gara-dānair abhojanaiḥ

hima-vāyv-agni-salilaiḥ
parvatākramaṇair api
na śaśāka yadā hantum
apāpam asuraḥ sutam
cintāṁ dīrghatamāṁ prāptas
tat-kartuṁ nābhyapadyata

dik-gajaiḥ—by big elephants trained to smash anything under their feet; *danda-śūka-indraiḥ*—by the biting of the King's poisonous snakes; *abhicāra*—by destructive spells; *avapātanaiḥ*—by causing to fall from the top of a mountain; *māyābhiḥ*—by conjuring tricks; *sannirodhaiḥ*—by imprisonment; *ca*—as well as; *gara-dānaiḥ*—by administering poison; *abhojanaiḥ*—by starving; *hima*—by cold; *vāyu*—wind; *agni*—fire; *salilaiḥ*—and water; *parvata-ākramaṇaiḥ*—by crushing with big stones and hills; *api*—and also; *na śaśāka*—was not able; *yadā*—when; *hantum*—to kill; *apāpam*—who was not at all sinful; *asuraḥ*—the demon (Hiraṇyakaśipu); *sutam*—his son; *cintām*—anxiety; *dīrgha-tamām*—long-standing; *prāptaḥ*—obtained; *tat-kartum*—to do that; *na*—not; *abhyapadyata*—achieved.

TRANSLATION

Hiraṇyakaśipu could not kill his son by throwing him beneath the feet of big elephants, throwing him among huge, fearful snakes, employing destructive spells, hurling him from the top of a hill, conjuring up illusory tricks, administering poison, starving him, exposing him to severe cold, winds, fire and water, or throwing heavy stones to crush him. When Hiraṇyakaśipu found that he could not in any way harm Prahlāda, who was completely sinless, he was in great anxiety about what to do next.

TEXT 45

एष मे बह्वसाधूक्तो वधोपायाश्च निर्मिताः ।
तैस्तैर्द्रोहैरसद्धर्मैर्मुक्तः स्वेनैव तेजसा ॥४५॥

eṣa me bahv-asādhūkto
vadhopāyāś ca nirmitāḥ
tais tair drohair asad-dharmair
muktaḥ svenaiva tejasā

eṣaḥ—this; *me*—of me; *bahu*—many; *asādhu-uktaḥ*—ill names; *vadha-upāyāḥ*—many varieties of means to kill him; *ca*—and; *nirmitāḥ*—devised; *taiḥ*—by those; *taiḥ*—by those; *drohaiḥ*—treacheries; *asat-dharmaiḥ*—abominable actions; *muktaḥ*—released; *svena*—his own; *eva*—indeed; *tejasā*—by prowess.

TRANSLATION

Hiraṇyakaśipu thought: I have used many ill names in chastising this boy Prahlāda and have devised many means of killing him, but despite all my endeavors, he could not be killed. Indeed, he saved himself by his own powers, without being affected in the least by these treacheries and abominable actions.

TEXT 46

वर्तमानोऽविदूरे वै बालोऽप्यजडधीरयम् ।
न विस्मरति मेऽनार्यं शुनःशेप इव प्रभुः ॥४६॥

vartamāno 'vidūre vai
bālo 'py ajaḍa-dhīr ayam
na vismarati me 'nāryaṁ
śunaḥ śepa iva prabhuḥ

vartamānaḥ—being situated; *avidūre*—not very far away; *vai*—indeed; *bālaḥ*—a mere child; *api*—although; *ajaḍa-dhīḥ*—complete fearlessness; *ayam*—this; *na*—not; *vismarati*—forgets; *me*—my; *anāryam*—misbehavior; *śunaḥ śepaḥ*—the curved tail of a dog; *iva*—exactly like; *prabhuḥ*—being able or potent.

TRANSLATION

Although he is very near to me and is merely a child, he is situated in complete fearlessness. He resembles a dog's curved tail, which can never be straightened, because he never forgets my misbehavior and his connection with his master, Lord Viṣṇu.

PURPORT

The word *śunaḥ* means "of a dog," and *śepa* means "tail." The example is ordinary. However one may try to straighten a dog's tail, it is never straight but always curved. *Śunaḥ śepa* is also the name of the second son of Ajīgarta. He was sold to Hariścandra, but he later took shelter of Viśvāmitra, Hariścandra's enemy, and never left his side.

TEXT 47

अप्रमेयानुभावोऽयमकुतश्चिद्भयोऽमरः ।
नूनमेतद्विरोधेन मृत्युर्मे भविता न वा ॥४७॥

aprameyānubhāvo 'yam
akutaścid-bhayo 'maraḥ
nūnam etad-virodhena
mṛtyur me bhavitā na vā

aprameya—unlimited; *anubhāvaḥ*—glory; *ayam*—this; *akutaścit-bhayaḥ*—having no fear from any quarter; *amaraḥ*—immortal; *nūnam*—definitely; *etat-virodhena*—because of going against him; *mṛtyuḥ*—death; *me*—my; *bhavitā*—may be; *na*—not; *vā*—or.

TRANSLATION

I can see that this boy's strength is unlimited, for he has not feared any of my punishments. He appears immortal. Therefore, because of my enmity toward him, I shall die. Or maybe this will not take place.

TEXT 48

इति तच्चिन्तया किञ्चिन्म्लानश्रियमधोमुखम् ।
शण्डामर्कावौशनसौ विविक्त इति होचतुः ॥४८॥

iti tac-cintayā kiñcin
mlāna-śriyam adho-mukham
śaṇḍāmarkāv auśanasau
vivikta iti hocatuḥ

iti—thus; *tat-cintayā*—with full anxiety because of Prahlāda Mahārāja's position; *kiñcit*—somewhat; *mlāna*—lost; *śriyam*—bodily luster; *adhaḥ-mukham*—his face downward; *śaṇḍa-amarkau*—Ṣaṇḍa and Amarka; *auśanasau*—sons of Śukrācārya; *vivikte*—in a secret place; *iti*—thus; *ha*—indeed; *ūcatuḥ*—spoke.

TRANSLATION

Thinking in this way, the King of the Daityas, morose and bereft of bodily luster, remained silent with his face downward. Then Ṣaṇḍa and Amarka, the two sons of Śukrācārya, spoke to him in secret.

TEXT 49

जितं त्वयैकेन जगत्त्रयं भ्रुवो-
विजृम्भणत्रस्तसमस्तधिष्ण्यपम् ।
न तस्य चिन्त्यं तव नाथ चक्ष्वहे
न वै शिशूनां गुणदोषयोः पदम् ॥४९॥

jitaṁ tvayaikena jagat-trayaṁ bhruvor
vijṛmbhaṇa-trasta-samasta-dhiṣṇyapam
na tasya cintyaṁ tava nātha cakṣvahe
na vai śiśūnāṁ guṇa-doṣayoḥ padam

jitam—conquered; *tvayā*—by you; *ekena*—alone; *jagat-trayam*—the three worlds; *bhruvoḥ*—of the eyebrows; *vijṛmbhaṇa*—by the expanding; *trasta*—become afraid; *samasta*—all; *dhiṣṇyapam*—the chief persons in every planet; *na*—not; *tasya*—from him; *cintyam*—to be anxious; *tava*—of you; *nātha*—O master; *cakṣvahe*—we find; *na*—nor; *vai*—indeed; *śiśūnām*—of children; *guṇa-doṣayoḥ*—of a good quality or fault; *padam*—the subject matter.

TRANSLATION

O lord, we know that when you simply move your eyebrows, all the commanders of the various planets are most afraid. Without the help of any assistant, you have conquered all the three worlds. Therefore, we do not find any reason for you to be morose and full of anxiety. As for Prahlāda, he is nothing but a child and cannot be a cause of anxiety. After all, his bad or good qualities have no value.

TEXT 50

इमं तु पाशैर्वरुणस्य बद्ध्वा
निधेहि भीतो न पलायते यथा ।
बुद्धिश्च पुंसो वयसार्यसेवया
यावद् गुरुर्भार्गव आगमिष्यति ॥५०॥

imaṁ tu pāśair varuṇasya baddhvā
nidhehi bhīto na palāyate yathā
buddhiś ca puṁso vayasārya-sevayā
yāvad gurur bhārgava āgamiṣyati

imam—this; *tu*—but; *pāśaiḥ*—by the ropes; *varuṇasya*—of the demigod known as Varuṇa; *baddhvā*—binding; *nidhehi*—keep (him); *bhītaḥ*—being afraid; *na*—not; *palāyate*—runs away; *yathā*—so that; *buddhiḥ*—the intelligence; *ca*—also; *puṁsaḥ*—of a man; *vayasā*—by increase of age; *ārya*—of experienced, advanced persons; *sevayā*—by the service; *yāvat*—until; *guruḥ*—our spiritual master; *bhārgavaḥ*—Śukrācārya; *āgamiṣyati*—will come.

TRANSLATION

Until the return of our spiritual master, Śukrācārya, arrest this child with the ropes of Varuṇa so that he will not flee in fear. In any case, by the time he is somewhat grown up and has assimilated our instructions or served our spiritual master, he will change in his intelligence. Thus there need be no cause for anxiety.

TEXT 51

तथेति गुरुपुत्रोक्तमनुज्ञायेदमब्रवीत् ।
धर्मो ह्यस्योपदेष्टव्यो राज्ञां यो गृहमेधिनाम् ॥५१॥

tatheti guru-putroktam
anujñāyedam abravīt
dharmo hy asyopadeṣṭavyo
rājñāṁ yo gṛha-medhinām

tathā—in this way; *iti*—thus; *guru-putra-uktam*—advised by Ṣaṇḍa and Amarka, the sons of Śukrācārya; *anujñāya*—accepting; *idam*—this; *abravīt*—said; *dharmaḥ*—the duty; *hi*—indeed; *asya*—unto Prahlāda; *upadeṣṭavyaḥ*—to be instructed; *rājñām*—of the kings; *yaḥ*—which; *gṛha-medhinām*—who are interested in householder life.

TRANSLATION

After hearing these instructions of Ṣaṇḍa and Amarka, the sons of his spiritual master, Hiraṇyakaśipu agreed and requested them to instruct Prahlāda in that system of occupational duty which is followed by royal householder families.

PURPORT

Hiraṇyakaśipu wanted Prahlāda Mahārāja to be trained as a diplomatic king in ruling the kingdom, the country or the world, but not to be advised about renunciation or the renounced order of life. The word *dharma* here does not refer to some religious faith. As clearly stated, *dharmo hy asyopadeṣṭavyo rājñāṁ yo gṛha-medhinām.* There are two kinds of royal families—one whose members are simply attached to household life and the other consisting of *rājarṣis*, kings who govern with ruling power but are as good as great saints. Prahlāda Mahārāja wanted to become a *rājarṣi*, whereas Hiraṇyakśipu wanted him to become a king attached to sense enjoyment (*gṛha-medhinām*). Therefore in the Āryan system there is *varṇāśrama-dharma*, by which everyone should be educated according to his position in society's division of *varṇa* (*brāhmaṇa, kṣatriya, vaiśya* and *śūdra*) and *āśrama* (*brahmacarya, gṛhastha, vānaprastha* and *sannyāsa*).

A devotee purified by devotional service is always in the transcendental position above the mundane qualities. Thus the difference between Prahlāda Mahārāja and Hiraṇyakaśipu was that Hiraṇyakaśipu wanted to keep Prahlāda in mundane attachment whereas Prahlāda was above the modes of material nature. As long as one is under the control of material nature, his occupational duty is different from that of a person not under such control. One's real *dharma*, or occupational duty, is described in *Śrīmad-Bhāgavatam* (*dharmaṁ tu sākṣād bhagavat-praṇītam*). As described to his order carriers by Dharmarāja, or Yamarāja, a living being is a spiritual identity, and therefore his occupational duty is also spiritual. The real *dharma* is that which is advised in *Bhagavad-gītā: sarva-dharmān parityajya mām ekaṁ śaraṇaṁ vraja.* One must give up one's material occupational duties, just as one must give up his material body. Whatever one's occupational duty, even according to the *varṇāśrama* system, one must give it up and engage in one's spiritual function. One's real *dharma,* or occupational duty, is explained by Śrī Caitanya Mahāprabhu. *Jīvera 'svarūpa' haya—kṛṣṇera 'nitya-dāsa':* every living being is an eternal servant of Kṛṣṇa. That is one's real occupational duty.

TEXT 52

धर्ममर्थं च कामं च नितरां चानुपूर्वशः ।
प्रह्रादायोचतू राजन् प्रश्रितावनताय च ॥५२॥

dharmam arthaṁ ca kāmaṁ ca
nitarāṁ cānupūrvaśaḥ
prahrādāyocatū rājan
praśritāvanatāya ca

dharmam—mundane occupational duty; *artham*—economic development; *ca*—and; *kāmam*—sense gratification; *ca*—and; *nitarām*—always; *ca*—and; *anupūrvaśaḥ*—according to order, or from the beginning to the end; *prahrādāya*—unto Prahlāda Mahārāja; *ūcatuḥ*—they spoke; *rājan*—O King; *praśrita*—who was humble; *avanatāya*—and submissive; *ca*—also.

TRANSLATION

Thereafter, Ṣaṇḍa and Amarka systematically and unceasingly taught Prahlāda Mahārāja, who was very submissive and humble, about mundane religion, economic development and sense gratification.

PURPORT

There are four processes for human society—*dharma, artha, kāma* and *mokṣa*—and they culminate in liberation. Human society must follow a process of religion to advance, and on the basis of religion one should try to develop his economic condition so that he can fulfill his needs for sense gratification according to the religious rules and regulations. Then liberation from material bondage will be easier to attain. That is the Vedic process. When one is above the stages of *dharma, artha, kāma* and *mokṣa*, one becomes a devotee. He is then on the platform from which he is guaranteed not to fall again to material existence (*yad gatvā na nivartante*). As advised in *Bhagavad-gītā* if one transcends these four processes and is actually liberated, one engages in devotional service. Then he is guaranteed not to fall to material existence again.

TEXT 53

यथा त्रिवर्गं गुरुभिरात्मने उपशिक्षितम् ।
न साधु मेने तच्छिक्षां द्वन्द्वारामोपवर्णिताम् ॥५३॥

yathā tri-vargaṁ gurubhir
ātmane upaśikṣitam
na sādhu mene tac-chikṣāṁ
dvandvārāmopavarṇitām

yathā—as; *tri-vargam*—the three processes (religion, economic development and sense gratification); *gurubhiḥ*—by the teachers; *ātmane*—unto himself (Prahlāda Mahārāja); *upaśikṣitam*—instructed; *na*—not; *sādhu*—really good; *mene*—he considered; *tat-śikṣām*—the education in that; *dvandva-ārāma*—by persons taking pleasure in duality (in material enmity and friendship); *upavarṇitām*—which is prescribed.

TRANSLATION

The teachers Ṣaṇḍa and Amarka instructed Prahlāda Mahārāja in the three kinds of material advancement called religion, economic development and sense gratification. Prahlāda, however, being situated above such instructions, did not like them, for such instructions are based on the duality of worldly affairs, which involve one in a materialistic way of life marked by birth, death, old age and disease.

PURPORT

The entire world is interested in the materialistic way of life. Indeed, practically 99.9 percent of the people in the three worlds are uninterested in liberation or spiritual education. Only the devotees of the Lord, headed by such great personalities as Prahlāda Mahārāja and Nārada Muni, are interested in the real education of spiritual life. One cannot understand the principles of religion while staying on the material platform. Therefore one must follow these great personalities. As stated in *Śrīmad-Bhāgavatam* (6.3.20):

svayambhūr nāradaḥ śambhuḥ
kumāraḥ kapilo manuḥ
prahlādo janako bhīṣmo
balir vaiyāsakir vayam

One must follow in the footsteps of such great personalities as Lord Brahmā, Nārada, Lord Śiva, Kapila, Manu, the Kumāras, Prahlāda Mahārāja, Bhīṣma, Janaka, Bali Mahārāja, Śukadeva Gosvāmī and Yamarāja. Those interested in spiritual life should follow Prahlāda Mahārāja in rejecting the education of religion, economic development and sense gratification. One should be interested in spiritual education. Therefore the Kṛṣṇa consciousness movement is spreading all over the world, following in the footsteps of Prahlāda Mahārāja, who did not like any of the materialistic education he received from his teachers.

TEXT 54

यदाचार्यः परावृत्तो गृहमेधीयकर्मसु ।
वयस्यैर्बालकैस्तत्र सोपहूतः कृतक्षणैः ॥५४॥

yadācāryaḥ parāvṛtto
gṛhamedhīya-karmasu
vayasyair bālakais tatra
sopahūtaḥ kṛta-kṣaṇaiḥ

yadā—when; *ācāryaḥ*—the teachers; *parāvṛttaḥ*—became engaged; *gṛha-medhīya*—of household life; *karmasu*—in duties; *vayasyaiḥ*—by his friends of the same age; *bālakaiḥ*—boys; *tatra*—there; *saḥ*—he (Prahlāda Mahārāja); *apahūtaḥ*—called; *kṛta-kṣaṇaiḥ*—obtaining an opportune moment.

TRANSLATION

When the teachers went home to attend to their household affairs, the students of the same age as Prahlāda Mahārāja would call him to take the opportunity of leisure hours for play.

PURPORT

In tiffin hours, the hours when the teachers were absent from the classroom, the students called Prahlāda Mahārāja, wanting to play with him. As will be seen from the following verses, however, Prahlāda Mahārāja was not very much interested in playing. Instead, he wanted to utilize every moment for advancing in Kṛṣṇa consciousness. Therefore, as indicated in this verse by the word *kṛta-kṣaṇaiḥ*, at the opportune moment when it was possible to preach about Kṛṣṇa consciousness, Prahlāda Mahārāja used the time as follows.

TEXT 55

अथ ताञ् श्लक्ष्णया वाचा प्रत्याहूय महाबुधः ।
उवाच विद्वांस्तन्निष्ठां कृपया प्रहसन्निव ॥५५॥

atha tāñ ślakṣṇayā vācā
pratyāhūya mahā-budhaḥ
uvāca vidvāṁs tan-niṣṭhāṁ
kṛpayā prahasann iva

atha—then; *tān*—the class friends; *ślakṣṇayā*—with very pleasing; *vācā*—speech; *pratyāhūya*—addressing; *mahā-budhaḥ*—Prahlāda Mahārāja, who was highly learned and advanced in spiritual consciousness (*mahā* means "great," and *budha* means "learned"); *uvāca*—said; *vidvān*—very learned; *tat-niṣṭhām*—the path of God realization; *kṛpayā*—being merciful; *prahasan*—smiling; *iva*—like.

TRANSLATION

Prahlāda Mahārāja, who was truly the supreme learned person, then addressed his class friends in very sweet language. Smiling,

he began to teach them about the uselessness of the materialistic way of life. Being very kind to them, he instructed them as follows.

PURPORT

Prahlāda Mahārāja's smiling is very significant. The other students were very much advanced in enjoying materialistic life through religion, economic development and sense gratification, but Prahlāda Mahārāja laughed at them, knowing that this was not actual happiness, for real happiness is advancement in Kṛṣṇa consciousness. The duty of those who follow in the footsteps of Prahlāda Mahārāja is to teach the entire world how to be Kṛṣṇa conscious and thus be really happy. Materialistic persons take to so-called religion to get some blessings so that they can improve their economic position and enjoy the material world through sense gratification. But devotees like Prahlāda Mahārāja laugh at how foolish they are to be busy in a temporary life without knowledge of the soul's transmigration from one body to another. Materialistic persons are engaged in striving for temporary benefits, whereas persons advanced in spiritual knowledge, such as Prahlāda Mahārāja, are not interested in the materialistic way of life. Instead, they want to be elevated to an eternal life of knowlege and bliss. Therefore, as Kṛṣṇa is always compassionate to the fallen souls, His servants, the devotees of Lord Kṛṣṇa, are also interested in educating the entire populace in Kṛṣṇa consciousness. The mistake of materialistic life is understood by devotees, and therefore they smile upon it, considering it insignificant. Out of compassion, however, such devotees preach the gospel of *Bhagavad-gītā* all over the world.

TEXTS 56–57

ते तु तद्गौरवात्सर्वे त्यक्तक्रीडापरिच्छदाः ।
बाला अदूषितधियो द्वन्द्वारामेरितेहितैः ॥५६॥
पर्युपासत राजेन्द्र तन्न्यस्तहृदयेक्षणाः ।
तानाह करुणो मैत्रो महाभागवतोऽसुरः ॥५७॥

te tu tad-gauravāt sarve
tyakta-krīḍā-paricchadāḥ

bālā adūṣita-dhiyo
dvandvārāmeritehitaiḥ

paryupāsata rājendra
tan-nyasta-hṛdayekṣaṇāḥ
tān āha karuṇo maitro
mahā-bhāgavato 'suraḥ

te—they; *tu*—indeed; *tat-gauravāt*—from great respect for the words of Prahlāda Mahārāja (due to his being a devotee); *sarve*—all of them; *tyakta*—having given up; *krīḍā-paricchadāḥ*—toys for playing; *bālāḥ*—the boys; *adūṣita-dhiyaḥ*—whose intelligence was not as polluted (as that of their fathers); *dvandva*—in duality; *ārāma*—of those taking pleasure (the instructors, namely Ṣaṇḍa and Amarka); *īrita*—by the instructions; *īhitaiḥ*—and actions; *paryupāsata*—sat down around; *rāja-indra*—O King Yudhiṣṭhira; *tat*—unto him; *nyasta*—having given up; *hṛdaya-īkṣaṇāḥ*—their hearts and eyes; *tān*—unto them; *āha*—spoke; *karuṇaḥ*—very merciful; *maitraḥ*—a real friend; *mahā-bhāgavataḥ*—a most exalted devotee; *asuraḥ*—Prahlāda Mahārāja, although born of an *asura* father.

TRANSLATION

My dear King Yudhiṣṭhira, all the children were very much affectionate and respectful to Prahlāda Mahārāja, and because of their tender age they were not so polluted by the instructions and actions of their teachers, who were attached to condemned duality and bodily comfort. Thus the boys surrounded Prahlāda Mahārāja, giving up their playthings, and sat down to hear him. Their hearts and eyes being fixed upon him, they looked at him with great earnestness. Prahlāda Mahārāja, although born in a demon family, was an exalted devotee, and he desired their welfare. Thus he began instructing them about the futility of materialistic life.

PURPORT

The words *bālā adūṣita-dhiyaḥ* indicate that the children, being of a tender age, were not as polluted by materialistic life as their fathers.

Prahlāda Mahārāja, therefore, taking advantage of the innocence of his class friends, began teaching them about the importance of spiritual life and the insignificance of materialistic life. Although the teachers Ṣaṇḍa and Amarka were instructing all the boys in the materialistic life of religion, economic development and sense gratification, the boys were not much polluted. Therefore, with great attention they wanted to hear from Prahlāda Mahārāja about Kṛṣṇa consciousness. In our Kṛṣṇa consciousness movement, the *guru-kula* plays an extremely important part in our activities because right from childhood the boys at the *guru-kula* are instructed about Kṛṣṇa consciousness. Thus they become steady within the cores of their hearts, and there is very little possibility that they will be conquered by the modes of material nature when they are older.

Thus end the Bhaktivedanta purports of the Seventh Canto, Fifth Chapter, of the Śrīmad-Bhāgavatam, *entitled "Prahlāda Mahārāja, the Saintly Son of Hiraṇyakaśipu."*

Appendixes

The Author

His Divine Grace A. C. Bhaktivedanta Swami Prabhupāda appeared in this world in 1896 in Calcutta, India. He first met his spiritual master, Śrīla Bhaktisiddhānta Sarasvatī Gosvāmī, in Calcutta in 1922. Bhaktisiddhānta Sarasvatī, a prominent devotional scholar and the founder of sixty-four Gauḍīya Maṭhas (Vedic institutes), liked this educated young man and convinced him to dedicate his life to teaching Vedic knowledge. Śrīla Prabhupāda became his student, and eleven years later (1933) at Allahabad he became his formally initiated disciple.

At their first meeting, in 1922, Śrīla Bhaktisiddhānta Sarasvatī Ṭhākura requested Śrīla Prabhupāda to broadcast Vedic knowledge through the English language. In the years that followed, Śrīla Prabhupāda wrote a commentary on the *Bhagavad-gītā*, assisted the Gauḍīya Maṭha in its work and, in 1944, without assistance, started an English fortnightly magazine, edited it, typed the manuscripts and checked the galley proofs. He even distributed the individual copies freely and struggled to maintain the publication. Once begun, the magazine never stopped; it is now being continued by his disciples in the West.

Recognizing Śrīla Prabhupāda's philosophical learning and devotion, the Gauḍīya Vaiṣṇava Society honored him in 1947 with the title "Bhaktivedanta." In 1950, at the age of fifty-four, Śrīla Prabhupāda retired from married life, and four years later he adopted the *vānaprastha* (retired) order to devote more time to his studies and writing. Śrīla Prabhupāda traveled to the holy city of Vṛndāvana, where he lived in very humble circumstances in the historic medieval temple of Rādhā-Dāmodara. There he engaged for several years in deep study and writing. He accepted the renounced order of life (*sannyāsa*) in 1959. At Rādhā-Dāmodara, Śrīla Prabhupāda began work on his life's masterpiece: a multivolume translation and commentary on the eighteen thousand verse *Śrīmad-Bhāgavatam* (*Bhāgavata Purāṇa*). He also wrote *Easy Journey to Other Planets.*

After publishing three volumes of *Bhāgavatam*, Śrīla Prabhupāda came to the United States, in 1965, to fulfill the mission of his spiritual master. Since that time, His Divine Grace has written over forty volumes of authoritative translations, commentaries and summary studies of the philosophical and religious classics of India.

In 1965, when he first arrived by freighter in New York City, Śrīla Prabhupāda was practically penniless. It was after almost a year of great difficulty that he established the International Society for Krishna Consciousness in July of 1966. Under his careful guidance, the Society has grown within a decade to a worldwide confederation of almost one hundred *āśramas*, schools, temples, institutes and farm communities.

In 1968, Śrīla Prabhupāda created New Vṛndāvana, an experimental Vedic community in the hills of West Virginia. Inspired by the success of New Vṛndāvana, now a thriving farm community of more than one thousand acres, his students have since founded several similar communities in the United States and abroad.

In 1972, His Divine Grace introduced the Vedic system of primary and secondary education in the West by founding the Gurukula school in Dallas, Texas. The school began with 3 children in 1972, and by the beginning of 1975 the enrollment had grown to 150.

Śrīla Prabhupāda has also inspired the construction of a large international center at Śrīdhāma Māyāpur in West Bengal, India, which is also the site for a planned Institute of Vedic Studies. A similar project is the magnificent Kṛṣṇa-Balarāma Temple and International Guest House in Vṛndāvana, India. These are centers where Westerners can live to gain firsthand experience of Vedic culture.

Śrīla Prabhupāda's most significant contribution, however, is his books. Highly respected by the academic community for their authoritativeness, depth and clarity, they are used as standard textbooks in numerous college courses. His writings have been translated into eleven languages. The Bhaktivedanta Book Trust, established in 1972 exclusively to publish the works of His Divine Grace, has thus become the world's largest publisher of books in the field of Indian religion and philosophy. Its latest project is the publishing of Śrīla Prabhupāda's most recent work: a seventeen-volume translation and commentary—completed by Śrīla Prabhupāda in only eighteen months—on the Bengali religious classic *Śrī Caitanya-caritāmṛta*.

In the past ten years, in spite of his advanced age, Śrīla Prabhupāda has circled the globe twelve times on lecture tours that have taken him to six continents. In spite of such a vigorous schedule, Śrīla Prabhupāda continues to write prolifically. His writings constitute a veritable library of Vedic philosophy, religion, literature and culture.

References

The purports of *Śrīmad-Bhāgavatam* are all confirmed by standard Vedic authorities. The following authentic scriptures are specifically cited in this volume.

Ādi-varāha Purāṇa, 259

Agastya-saṁhitā, 261

Bhagavad-gītā, 2, 4, 5, 8, 11–12, 13, 15, 17, 18, 19, 20, **25**–26, 29, 32, 34–36, 39, 40, 46, 64, 65, 66, 68, 69, 76, 78, 81, 83, 97, 98, 100, 106, 108, 109, 110–111, 112, 113, 119, 122, 127, 136, 140, 141, 151, 158, 159, 186, 191, 197, 202, 211, 219, 220, 224, 229, 232, 233–234, 236–237, 248, 267–268, 272, 288

Bhāgavata-sandarbha, 10–11

Bhakti-viveka, 261–262

Brahmāṇḍa Purāṇa, 72–73, 259

Brahma-saṁhitā, 19, 161, 203

Brahma-tarka, 153

Brahma-vaivarta Purāṇa, 125, 260

Caitanya-caritāmṛta, 37, 43, 157, 203

Gautamīya Tantra, 259–260

Gopāla-tāpanī Upaniṣad, 249

Glossary

A

Ācārya—a spiritual master who teaches by example.

Acintya-bhedābheda-tattva—the Supreme Lord is inconceivably, simultaneously one with His material and spiritual energies and different from them.

Aṇimā—yogic power to become as small as an atom.

Antaryāmī—the expansion of the Supreme Lord situated in everyone's heart (Supersoul).

Ārati—a ceremony for greeting the Lord with offerings of food, lamps, fans, flowers and incense.

Arcanā—the devotional practice of Deity worship.

Āśrama—a spiritual order of life.

Asuras—atheistic demons.

Ātmārāma—one who is self-satisfied, free from external material desires.

Avatāra—a descent of the Supreme Lord.

B

Bhagavad-gītā—the basic directions for spiritual life spoken by the Lord Himself.

Bhakta—a devotee.

Bhakti-yoga—linking with the Supreme Lord in ecstatic devotional service.

Bhāva—the preliminary stage of ecstatic love of God.

Bhūti—opulence.

Brahmacarya—celibate student life; the first order of Vedic spiritual life.

Brahman—the Absolute Truth; especially, the impersonal aspect of the Absolute.

Brāhmaṇa—a person in the mode of goodness; first Vedic social order.

D

Dāsya-rasa—the servitor relationship with the Lord.

Dhāma—abode, place of residence; usually referring to the Lord's abodes.

Dharma—eternal occupational duty; religious principles.

Duṣkṛtīs—miscreants.

E

Ekādaśī—a special fast day for increased remembrance of Kṛṣṇa, which comes on the eleventh day of both the waxing and waning moon.

G

Goloka (Kṛṣṇaloka)—the highest spiritual planet, containing Kṛṣṇa's personal abodes, Dvārakā, Mathurā and Vṛndāvana.

Gopīs—Kṛṣṇa's cowherd girl friends, His most confidential servitors.

Gṛhastha—regulated householder life; the second order of Vedic spiritual life.

Guru—a spiritual master or superior person.

Guru-kula—school of Vedic learning; boys begin at the age of five and live as celibate students, guided by a spiritual master.

H

Hare Kṛṣṇa mantra—*See: Mahā-mantra*

J

Jīvātmā—the minute living entity, part and parcel of the Supreme Lord.

Jīva-tattva—the living entities, who are small parts of the Lord.

K

Kali-yuga (Age of Kali)—the present age, which is characterized by quarrel. It is last in the cycle of four, and began five thousand years ago.

Karatālas—hand cymbals used in *kīrtana.*

Karma—fruitive action, for which there is always reaction, good or bad.

Karma-kāṇḍa—the section of the *Vedas* describing fruitive activities for elevation to a higher material position.

Karmī—one who is satisfied with working hard for flickering sense gratification.

Kīrtana—chanting the glories of the Supreme Lord.

Kṛṣṇaloka—*See:* Goloka

Kṣatriyas—a warrior or administrator; the second Vedic social order.

L

Laghimā—the yogic power to become as light as a feather.

M

Mādhurya-rasa—conjugal love relationship with the Lord.
Mahā-bhāgavata—a pure devotee of the Lord.
Mahā-mantra—the great chanting for deliverance: Hare Kṛṣṇa, Hare Kṛṣṇa, Kṛṣṇa Kṛṣṇa, Hare Hare/ Hare Rāma, Hare Rāma, Rāma Rāma, Hare Hare.
Mahāmāyā—the illusory material energy of the Lord.
Mantra—a sound vibration that can deliver the mind from illusion.
Mathurā—Lord Kṛṣṇa's abode, surrounding Vṛndāvana, where He took birth and later returned to after performing His Vṛndāvana pastimes.
Mauṣala-līlā—pastime of the Yadu dynasty's departure from the earth.
Māyā—(mā—not; *yā*—this), illusion; forgetfulness of one's relationship with Kṛṣṇa.
Māyāvādīs—impersonal philosophers who say that the Lord cannot have a transcendental body.
Mṛdaṅga—a clay drum used for congregational chanting.

P

Pañca-mahāyajña—the five daily sacrifices performed by householders to become free from unintentionally committed sins.
Parakīya-rasa—the relationship between a married woman and her paramour, particularly the relationship between Kṛṣṇa and the damsels of Vṛndāvana.
Paramparā—the chain of spiritual masters in disciplic succession.
Prakṛti—the energy of the Supreme Lord.
Prasāda—food spiritualized by being offered to the Lord.
Purāṇas—Vedic histories of the universe in relation to the Supreme Lord and His devotees.

R

Rāga-mārga—the path of spontaneous love of Godhead.
Rākṣasas—man-eating demons.

S

Sac-cid-ānanda-vigraha—the Lord's transcendental form, which is eternal, full of knowledge and bliss.

Sādhu—a saintly man.

Sakhya-rasa—friend relationship with the Lord.

Sālokya-mukti—the liberation of residing on the same planet as the Lord.

Samādhi—trance; mind fixed on the Supreme.

Sāmīpya-mukti—the liberation of becoming a personal associate of the Lord.

Saṁsāra—the cycle of repeated birth and death.

Saṅkīrtana—public chanting of the names of God, the approved *yoga* process for this age.

Sannyāsa—renounced life; the fourth order of Vedic spiritual life.

Sārṣṭi-mukti—the liberation of having the same opulences as the Lord.

Sārūpya-mukti—the liberation of getting a form similar to the Lord's.

Śāstras—revealed scriptures.

Sāyujya-mukti—the liberation of merging into the existence of the Lord.

Śravaṇaṁ kīrtanaṁ viṣṇoḥ—the devotional processes of hearing and chanting about Lord Viṣṇu.

Śūdra—a laborer; the fourth of the Vedic social orders.

Svāmī—one who controls his mind and senses; title of one in the renounced order of life.

T

Tapasya—austerity; accepting some voluntary inconvenience for a higher purpose.

Tilaka—auspicious clay marks that sanctify a devotee's body as a temple of the Lord.

V

Vaikuṇṭha—the spiritual world, where there is no anxiety.

Vaiṣṇava—a devotee of Lord Viṣṇu, Kṛṣṇa.

Vaiśyas—farmers and merchants; the third Vedic social order.

Vānaprastha—one who has retired from family life; the third order of Vedic spiritual life.

Varṇāśrama—the Vedic social system of four social and four spiritual orders.

Vātsalya-rasa—parental relationship with the Lord.

Vedas—the original revealed scriptures, first spoken by the Lord Himself.

Vibhūti—the opulence and power of the Supreme Lord.

Viṣṇu, Lord—Kṛṣṇa's first expansion for the creation and maintenance of the material universes.

Viṣṇuloka—the abode of Lord Viṣṇu, the Supreme Personality of Godhead.

Vṛndāvana—Kṛṣṇa's personal abode, where He fully manifests His quality of sweetness.

Vyāsadeva—Kṛṣṇa's incarnation, at the end of Dvāpara-yuga, for compiling the *Vedas*.

Y

Yajña—sacrifice, work done for the satisfaction of Lord Viṣṇu.

Yogamāyā—the internal spiritual energy of the Lord.

Yogī—a transcendentalist who, in one way or another, is striving for union with the Supreme.

Yugas—ages in the life of a universe, occurring in a repeated cycle of four.

Sanskrit Pronunciation Guide

Vowels

अ a आ ā इ i ई ī उ u ऊ ū ऋ ṛ ॠ ṝ
ऌ ḷ ए e ऐ ai ओ o औ au

ं ṁ *(anusvāra)* ः ḥ *(visarga)*

Consonants

Gutturals:	क ka	ख kha	ग ga	घ gha	ङ ṅa
Palatals:	च ca	छ cha	ज ja	झ jha	ञ ña
Cerebrals:	ट ṭa	ठ ṭha	ड ḍa	ढ ḍha	ण ṇa
Dentals:	त ta	थ tha	द da	ध dha	न na
Labials:	प pa	फ pha	ब ba	भ bha	म ma
Semivowels:	य ya	र ra	ल la	व va	
Sibilants:	श śa	ष ṣa	स sa		
Aspirate:	ह ha	ऽ ' *(avagraha)* – the apostrophe			

The vowels above should be pronounced as follows:

a – like the *a* in org*a*n or the *u* in b*u*t.
ā – like the *a* in f*a*r but held twice as long as short *a*.
i – like the *i* in p*i*n.
ī – like the *i* in p*i*que but held twice as long as short *i*.
u – like the *u* in p*u*sh.
ū – like the *u* in r*u*le but held twice as long as short *u*.

ṛ – like the *ri* in *ri*m.
ṝ – like *ree* in *ree*d.
ḷ – like *l* followed by *ṛ* (*lṛ*).
e – like the *e* in th*ey*.
ai – like the *ai* in *ai*sle.
o – like the *o* in g*o*.
au – like the *ow* in h*ow*.
ṁ (*anusvāra*) – a resonant nasal like the *n* in the French word *bon*.
ḥ (*visarga*) – a final *h*-sound: *aḥ* is pronounced like *aha; iḥ* like *ihi*.

The consonants are pronounced as follows:

k – as in *k*ite
kh – as in Ec*kh*art
g – as in *g*ive
gh – as in di*g-h*ard
ṅ – as in si*ng*
c – as in *ch*air
ch – as in staun*ch-h*eart
j – as in *j*oy
jh – as in he*dgeh*og
ñ – as in ca*ny*on
ṭ – as in *t*ub
ṭh – as in ligh*t-h*eart
ḍ – as in *d*ove
ḍha- as in re*d-h*ot
ṇ – as r*na* (prepare to say the *r* and say *na*).

Cerebrals are pronounced with tongue to roof of mouth, but the following dentals are pronounced with tongue against teeth:

t – as in *t*ub but with tongue against teeth.
th – as in ligh*t-h*eart but with tongue against teeth.
d – as in *d*ove but with tongue against teeth.
dh – as in re*d-h*ot but with tongue against teeth.
n – as in *n*ut but with tongue between teeth.
p – as in *p*ine
ph – as in u*ph*ill (not *f*)
b – as in *b*ird
bh – as in ru*b-h*ard
m – as in *m*other
y – as in *y*es
r – as in *r*un
l – as in *l*ight
v – as in *v*ine
ś (palatal) – as in the *s* in the German word *sprechen*
ṣ (cerebral) – as the *sh* in *sh*ine
s – as in *s*un
h – as in *h*ome

There is no strong accentuation of syllables in Sanskrit, only a flowing of short and long (twice as long as the short) syllables.

Index of Sanskrit Verses

This index constitutes a complete listing of the first and third lines of each of the Sanskrit poetry verses and the first line of each Sanskrit prose verse of this volume of *Śrīmad-Bhāgavatam*, arranged in English alphabetical order. In the first column the Sanskrit transliteration is given, and in the second and third columns respectively the chapter-verse reference and page number for each verse are to be found.

T

U

General Index

Numerals in boldface type indicate references to translations of the verses of *Śrīmad-Bhāgavatam*.

E

F

G

N

O

P

T

U

V

W